"Insightful and entertaining look at how comic book heroes would be affected by real-life laws . . . Fortunately, Daily and Davidson are neither smart alecks nor ironic, and they take their work as seriously as Batman taking on his arch-villain Bane (although they can be as witty and sly as Catwoman at her best)." —*Publishers Weekly*

"Attorneys James Daily and Ryan Davidson have pulled it off so flawlessly in the educational and fun *The Law of Superheroes* . . . people who aren't lawyers or law-geeks will learn something about the law, and lawyers and law-geeks will be thoroughly entertained at the application of familiar principles to comic extravaganzas." —*Popehat*

"Superpowered geekery of epically entertaining proportions . . . A must-read for a dose of good geeky fun." —*Shelf Awareness*

"A pair of lawyers from the Midwest have decided to ask these questions in this engaging book. Legal tomes are not known for being readable and accessible, but this one manages to be." —*Book Guys*

"Their website has spawned a book, *The Law of Superheroes*, which has to be one of the most subversive and nefarious books of the year. I came away from it feeling like I'd actually learned something about the history of American jurisprudence and how our laws actually work." —*Unleash the Fanboy*

"An interesting mash-up of law and pop culture that draws hypotheticals from the world of superheroes to the end of better explaining complex legal doctrine . . . this book offers a clear and creative description of basic legal concepts, disrupting the often much too self-serious tone of academic legal discourse while demystifying complex ideas that are often thought to be better left to legal experts." —*Law and Politics Book Review*

James Daily, J.D., *(left)* is an attorney and creator and coauthor of LawandtheMultiverse.com. He is licensed to practice in Missouri and is also registered to practice before the United States Patent and Trademark Office. By day he works for the Stanford University Hoover Institution's Project on Commercializing Innovation and also represents clients in a variety of intellectual property matters. He has been reading comics since he was ten, and some of his earliest and fondest childhood memories are of the Batman television series starring Adam West.

Ryan Davidson, J.D., *(right)* is an attorney living in Hershey, Pennsylvania, and coauthor of LawandtheMultiverse.com. He is licensed to practice in Indiana and Pennsylvania. He obtained his law degree from Notre Dame Law School in 2009. Mr. Davidson cut his teeth on speculative fiction in the first grade and has been reading graphic novels since college.

THE
LAW OF
SUPERHEROES

JAMES E. DAILY, *J.D.,*

AND

RYAN M. DAVIDSON, *J.D.*

GOTHAM BOOKS

GOTHAM BOOKS
Published by the Penguin Group
Penguin Group (USA) Inc., 375 Hudson Street,
New York, New York 10014, USA

USA | Canada | UK | Ireland | Australia | New Zealand | India | South Africa | China

Penguin Books Ltd, Registered Offices: 80 Strand, London WC2R 0RL, England
For more information about the Penguin Group visit penguin.com.

Published by Gotham Books, a member of Penguin Group (USA) Inc.

Previously published as a Gotham Books hardcover

Gotham Books and the skyscraper logo are trademarks of Penguin Group (USA) Inc.

The Library of Congress has catalogued the hardcover edition as follows:
Daily, James. The law of superheroes / James Daily and Ryan Davidson.
p. cm.
ISBN 978-1-59240-726-2 1 (HC)   978-1-59240-839-9 (PBK)
Superheroes in literature. 2. Law and literature—United States. 3. Law—United
States—Popular works.
I. Davidson, Ryan. II. Title.
PN6714.D26 2012
741.5'3554—dc23 201201437

Set in Trump Mediaeval Office
Designed by Elke Sigal

While the author has made every effort to provide accurate telephone numbers and
Internet addresses at the time of publication, neither the publisher nor the author assumes any responsibility for errors, or for changes that occur after publication. Further, the publisher does not have any control over and does not assume any
responsibility for author or third-party Web sites or their content.

147204767

To Jennifer and Liesel

CONTENTS

Does Superman violate privacy laws when he uses his X-ray vision? Does the Second Amendment protect Iron Man's suit? Is the Joker really legally insane? If you've ever wondered about any of these questions—or if they just sound awesome—then this is the book for you.

The Law of Superheroes grew out of the blog Law and the Multiverse, which applies real-world law and legal principles to comic book stories and characters. We, your coauthors, are both lawyers and comic book nerds, and this book blends those interests.

So why comic books? Well, for one thing, they're both interesting and popular. The main problem with a lot of legal educational materials is that they are boring. Examples include such thrilling stories as "A sells Blackacre to B, who then gives a life estate to C," and right there, before we even get to the law, the audience is asleep. But who doesn't like Batman? More to the point, who doesn't know who Batman is? Even someone who hasn't read any comic books—and you needn't have to in order to enjoy this book—will probably know that Batman's alter ego is Bruce Wayne, billionaire industrialist. So rather than making up people who may not even have names, or using cases involving people you've never heard of, The Law of Superheroes uses characters you already know and love.

Second, comic book authors have been creating new stories for decades, which gives us an enormous supply of material. Action Comics, home of Superman, hit issue #904 in October 2011, part of an almost uninterrupted run since 1938. While this is the longest-running comic in history, there are plenty of others with hundreds and hundreds of issues. Comic book authors have created incredibly detailed worlds with their own histories, so detailed that the authors have felt the need to simplify things on a number of occasions. But continuity snarls aside, this means that comic book stories are ideal for this kind of analysis, because their longevity has given them the opportunity to cover a variety of legal situations that most other works simply don't reach. As a matter of fact, these situations often hold up remarkably well under legal scrutiny, which is a testament to the ingenuity of their authors, who have created such enormous yet cohesive and consistent worlds.

But most important, comic books are fun and invite good-natured overthinking. Like all comic book fans, we love wondering about how these richly detailed worlds would work in all sorts of ways, whether it be the physics of Superman's flight or his immigration status. We've certainly had fun doing the research for this book—tax-deductible comic books!—and we hope to share that with you.

—James E. Daily, J.D., and Ryan M. Davidson, J.D.

DISCLAIMER

This book discusses the hypothetical legal implications of fictional characters and situations and should not be relied upon in real-world legal situations. Nothing in this book constitutes legal advice or implies the existence of an attorney-client relationship with the authors. If you need legal advice or representation, consult a competent attorney in your jurisdiction.

The copyrighted DC Comics, Marvel, and Dark Horse illustrations in this book are reproduced for commentary, critical, and scholarly purposes. The copyright dates adjacent to the illustrations are the dates printed in the comics in which the illustrations were first published.

The terms "superhero" and "supervillain" are trademarks co-owned by Marvel Characters, Inc. and DC Comics, Inc. These terms are used throughout this book solely to refer descriptively to Marvel and DC characters. The copyright and trademark rights for the comic book characters and related logos and indicia mentioned throughout this book are the property of their respective owners.

LEGAL SOURCES AND CITATIONS

Throughout this book you will see references and citations to legal sources such as statutes and cases. Many of these primary sources are available for free online, and we encourage interested readers to seek them out. In order to assist the reader, we present an overview of the citation format used in this book and in most legal writing, the *Bluebook*.[1] Unfortunately, this overview is necessarily incomplete because the *Bluebook* format is rather complicated and resists summarization.[2] Fortunately, there are free resources available online that explain the format in more detail.[3]

Cases are generally cited in this form: [Case Name], [Volume Number] [Reporter] [Page Number] ([Court] [Year]). For example, United States v. Carroll Towing Co., 159 F.2d 169 (2d Cir. 1947) shows that the name of the case was *United States v. Carroll Towing Co.* and it was published in the 159th volume of the 2nd edition of

---

1. THE BLUEBOOK: A UNIFORM SYSTEM OF CITATION (Columbia Law Review Ass'n et al. eds., 19th ed. 2010).

2. The current edition of the *Bluebook*, the nineteenth, is 511 pages long. As well-known federal circuit judge Richard Posner has said, the *Bluebook* "is a monstrous growth, remote from the functional need for legal citation forms, that serves obscure needs of the legal culture and its student subculture. . . . I am put in mind of Mr. Kurtz's dying words in *Heart of Darkness*—'The horror! The horror!'" Richard A. Posner, *The Bluebook Blues*, 120 YALE L.J. 850, 851–52 (2011) reviewing THE BLUEBOOK: A UNIFORM SYSTEM OF CITATION [Columbia Law Review Ass'n et al. eds., 19th ed. 2010]).

3. *See, e.g.*, Peter W. Martin, *Introduction to Basic Legal Citation*, http://www.law.cornell.edu/citation/.

the *Federal Reporter* beginning on page 169. We can also see that it was a decision of the Second Circuit Court of Appeals made in 1947.

When a particular portion of the opinion is cited, the specific page numbers will follow the first page number. For example, United States v. Carroll Towing Co., 159 F.2d 169, 170–71 (2d Cir. 1947). Sometimes the court may be inferred from the reporter, as in United States Supreme Court cases, which are published in the *United States Reports*, abbreviated "U.S." For example, Miranda v. Arizona, 384 U.S. 436 (1966). Many state supreme courts (e.g., California and New York) have similar official reports.

Unfortunately, citations to statutes (particularly state statutes) are less regular, but most of the statutory citations in this book are to the United States Code. The general form is [Title] [Statutory Code] [Section]. For example, 18 U.S.C. § 1111 is Title 18 of the United States Code, Section 1111.

Most of the cases cited in this book may be found online via Google Scholar.[4] Federal statutes can be found online from multiple sources.[5] State statutes are typically available on the website of the state legislature in question. For other kinds of citations and sources, see Professor Peter Martin's guide, discussed in footnote 3 or the *Bluebook* itself. Readers with a further interest should contact their local law library or an attorney.

The *Bluebook* does not provide a citation format for comic books, so we have followed the citation format created by Britton Payne for the Fordham Intellectual Property, Media, and Entertainment Law Journal.[6] This format has been used in other pub-

---

4. http://scholar.google.com (select "Legal opinions and journals" and enter the case citation).

5. http://www.gpoaccess.gov/uscode/index.html and http://www.law.cornell.edu/us code/text are two useful sources.

6. Britton Payne, *Comic Book Legal Citation Format*, 16 FORDHAM INTELL. PROP. MEDIA & ENT. L.J. 1017 (2005-06), *available at* http://ir.lawnet.fordham.edu/cgi/viewcontent. cgi?article=1358&context=iplj

lished works[7] and we think it captures all of the important information about a particular comic book. The general form of the citation is: Creative Contributors, *Story Title*, COMIC BOOK TITLE (VOLUME NUMBER) [Issue Number] (Publisher Cover Date Month and Year). For brevity we typically only list the writer rather than the full panoply of creative contributors.

Consecutive citations to the same source are typically abbreviated as "*Id.*" This is Latin for *idem*, which means "the same." To find the source referred to, just go back a few footnotes until you find a regular citation.

---

7. *See, e.g.*, William A. Hilyerd, *Hi Superman, I'm a Lawyer: A Guide to Attorneys (& Other Legal Professionals) Portrayed in American Comic Books: 1910-2007*, 15 WIDENER L. REV. 159 (2009).

CHAPTER 1

Constitutional Law

The prosecution has made its case: Batman responded to the Bat Signal, apprehended the crooks, and left them for the authorities. The police showed up, rounded up the incapacitated—but not dead!—criminals, made arrests, and gathered the evidence on the scene. The district attorney took the case, filed charges, and hauled the perps, who are guilty as sin and caught red-handed, in front of the judge for their arraignment . . . and the judge tosses out the case as a violation of the defendants' constitutional rights.

Huh?

Turns out that Batman and Gotham City's finest just ran afoul of the "state actor" doctrine, one of the cornerstones of American constitutional law, and it cost them their conviction on this one. But that's just the tip of the iceberg. Constitutional law is a broad topic, so broad, in fact, that it is usually divided into multiple law school courses. While some constitutional law issues are not important to superheroes and supervillains,[1] comic book plots raise a surprising

---

1. For example, the intricacies of federal court jurisdiction rarely come up in comic books.

number of constitutional issues either explicitly or implicitly. These run the gamut from wearing a costume in court, to regulating superhero abilities, to banning superheroics outright.

State Action

Before we can get into the details of constitutional law we first have to talk about what the Constitution regulates. The United States Constitution is primarily a limitation on what the *government* can and can't do, not what *individuals* can and can't do. In fact, the Thirteenth Amendment, which prohibits slavery, is the only constitutional provision that directly regulates conduct by private individuals. When we talk about constitutional law, then, we are talking about the exercise of *government* power, which is called "state action." Anyone who is acting with government authority or at the behest of a government agent is called a "state actor." Government employees and officials are obviously state actors when they're on the clock, but most private individuals, including most superheroes, are not bound by the limitations imposed by the Constitution.

Superheroes that have some relationship with the government, such as agents of S.H.I.E.L.D. or the Fifty State Initiative, are state actors. But what about superheroes who work *with* the government but not *for* the government? A good example here is Batman, who sometimes works in very close cooperation with the Gotham City Police Department (GCPD), which often calls on his services via the Bat Signal or even, as in the Adam West TV series, maintains a private hotline between the Bat Cave and the police commissioner's office. Could Batman be considered a state actor?

The Supreme Court has held that private individuals can be considered state actors under certain circumstances. The reason this is an issue is so the cops can't get around constitutional protections by having private individuals do their dirty work for them. The basic rule of thumb is that if the cops can't do something on their own, they can't have someone else do it for them either. There are a few different tests,[2] but we will focus on the *Lugar* test: first, whether the action results from an exercise of a right or privilege having its source in state authority, and second, whether the private party can be described in all fairness as a state actor?[3]

As to the first part of the test, Batman sometimes acts on the suggestion of the GCPD, though he is rarely (if ever) actually ordered to do something. The Supreme Court has held that "mere approval of or acquiescence in the initiatives of a private party is not sufficient," but state action may be found when the State "has provided such significant encouragement, either overt or covert, that the choice must in law be deemed to be that of the State."[4] In many cases it seems that Batman does what he does because he has the approval of the police. And in the other direction, it seems that the police often make decisions based on Batman's plans (e.g., the police may wait for Batman to act before attempting an arrest).

The Supreme Court has elaborated on the second part of the test. Two relevant factors that the Court has described are (1) the extent to which the actor relies on governmental assistance and benefits and (2) whether the actor is performing a traditional governmental function.[5] Batman usually relies on the GCPD to formally arrest the villains after he has caught them implicating the first factor. The second factor, whether the actor is performing a traditional government function, also argues in favor of considering Batman to be a state actor. Policing and investigation are traditional governmental

---

2. For example, the "entwinement" test set out in Brentwood Academy v. Tennessee Secondary School Athletic Ass'n, 531 U.S. 288 (2001).

3. Edmonson v. Leesville Concrete Co., Inc., 500 U.S. 614, 620 (1991). The *Lugar* state action test was first set forth in Lugar v. Edmonson Oil Co., 457 U.S. 922 (1982).

4. Blum v. Yaretsky, 457 U.S. 991, 1004 (1982).

5. *Leesville Concrete*, 500 U.S. at 621.

functions, so by engaging in the same kind of work that the GCPD does with their cooperation and approval, Batman may be fairly described as a state actor.

Overall, the more closely Batman and other superheroes work with the police, the more likely they are to be described as state actors, which makes a certain amount of intuitive sense. There wouldn't be much value to the Constitution if the government could do an end run around it by having private parties break the law on its behalf.

But law in the real world aside, it's clear that Batman is *not* actually considered to be a state actor in the DC Universe, because if he was, then the GCPD would likely be sued into the ground by villains alleging violations of their civil rights. So why the discrepancy? As Justice Sandra Day O'Connor once said, the state action cases "have not been a model of consistency."[6] These are highly fact-specific cases, and reasonable minds can disagree on the right outcome. It's also possible that the courts in the DC Universe have weakened the state actor doctrine somewhat to give superheroes like Batman a free hand to address the threats that the regular police can't handle.

The reason all of this is important is because the Constitution imposes important limits on the government's law enforcement activities, but these limitations apply only to state actors. There are plenty of things that the government can't do that private individuals can, but as soon as those individuals—superheroes, say—start getting involved in things like fighting crime, we need to start asking ourselves whether they might not be subject to some of these limitations just like traditional government employees. For example, there's no constitutional problem with superheroes wearing costumes as they go about their daily activities, but as soon as a prosecutor wants to have a masked hero testify in court, we run into Sixth Amendment problems. The Constitution *does* limit the state's ability to use anonymous witnesses. Similarly, there's no constitutional problem with a telepath reading someone's mind for private purposes,

---

6. *Leesville Concrete* at 632 (O'Conner, J., dissenting).

Hawkman takes the stand in an identity-concealing costume. Frankly, we're surprised the judge didn't threaten him with contempt for showing up shirtless. Marc Andreyko et al., *Trial by Fire, Part 2: Witness for the Prosecution*, in MANHUNTER (VOL. 3) 7 (DC Comics April 2005).

but the Fifth Amendment creates problems for using mind reading as a source of evidence in criminal trials. The rest of the chapter is going to be devoted to issues of constitutional law that are of particular interest to superheroes and supervillains, but keep in mind that these issues are only relevant where there is a state actor involved.

With that introduction in mind, let's delve into some issues of constitutional law that are of particular interest to superheroes and supervillains.

Testifying in Costume and the Confrontation Clause

Superheroes must often testify in court in order to ensure the conviction of villains. Superheroes who wear identity-concealing costumes must be able to testify in costume or else risk exposing their secret identity. And here we have a constitutional problem, specifically the Confrontation Clause of the Sixth Amendment, which states that "in all criminal prosecutions, the accused shall enjoy the right . . . to be confronted with the witnesses against him."[7]

The DC Universe has neatly solved this problem with its fictional version of the Twelfth Amendment.[8] The DC version allows members of the Federal Authority of Registered Meta-Humans to decline to answer questions about their secret identities.[9] The comics suggest that this operates similar to the Fifth Amendment protection against self-incrimination. In the Marvel Universe, a colleague of She-Hulk once sidestepped the issue by introducing a

---

7. U.S. CONST. amend. VI.

8. The real Twelfth Amendment revised the process by which the President and Vice-President are elected. Which is *way* less interesting.

9. *The Flash* v. 2 #135 (March 1998).

device purported to be able to establish that the person wearing Spider-Man's costume is the "real" Spider-Man without revealing that Spider-Man is actually Peter Parker. The judge permits this, and Spider-Man takes the stand.[10]

The reason that particular stunt is unlikely to work is that it doesn't address the contemporary justifications for the right to confront witnesses, primarily cross-examination and credibility judgment. Cross-examination is an essential part of the adversarial system, and requiring witnesses to be present allows the fact finder (usually the jury) to better judge the witnesses' credibility. Further, most judges view the ability of the jury to see the witness's face as an absolutely critical part of this process, and most would not permit *any* witness to testify while concealed, whether by being in a different room or wearing a mask. Because of the fundamental importance of cross-examination, the long history of the right to confront one's accusers, and its value to criminal defendants, the Confrontation Clause enjoys strong support from both conservative and liberal judges—although that support is not universal.

The general rule of the Confrontation Clause is that "[a] witness's testimony against a defendant is . . . inadmissible unless the witness appears at trial or, if the witness is unavailable, the defendant had a prior opportunity for cross-examination."[11] It is an important technical point that the clause only covers testimonial statements, but for now let's focus on actual in-court testimony in criminal cases, to which the clause definitely applies.

But what about that "unavailability" exception? One of the main exceptions to the cross-examination requirement is if the witness is somehow "unavailable," either because they're *dead* or otherwise can't be present for trial. Does that provide an out for superheroes?

---

10. *She-Hulk* v. 1 #4 (August 2004).

11. Melendez-Diaz v. Massachusetts, 129 S. Ct. 2527, 2531 (2009). This "prior opportunity" is generally at the witness's deposition.

What if, for example, Spider-Man prepares a description of a villain's activities and pins it to the villain, whom he has left hanging in a web for the police to find? Spider-Man is presumably unavailable unless he voluntarily shows up in court (and good luck serving him with a subpoena!), so could the document still be entered into evidence? The answer hinges on whether the document was "made under circumstances which would lead an objective witness reasonably to believe that the statement would be available for use at a later trial."[12] In this case, it would seem objectively reasonable to believe that Spider-Man's description was intended for use at the villain's trial. But note that non-testimonial evidence, such as photographs, weapons, and other physical or forensic evidence, would not run afoul of the Confrontation Clause. If superheroes stick to that kind of evidence, they can avoid a lot of headaches and tedious court appearances.

But let's suppose that non-testimonial evidence is unavailable and the only way to put away, say, Kingpin is for Spider-Man to show up in court and testify against him (and let's also presume this is pre–*Civil War* or post–*Brand New Day* Spider-Man and that his identity is still secret). Could Spider-Man wear his mask? And could he somehow dodge questions about his identity?

Shielding Witnesses from Defendants

Although costumed vigilantes rarely make court appearances in the real world, the scope of the Confrontation Clause has been considered in other contexts, particularly shielding child witnesses against accused abusers from face-to-face confrontation. The Supreme Court has only rarely made exceptions to a criminal defendant's right to confront the witnesses against him. Although the Court has "never held . . . that the Confrontation Clause guarantees criminal defendants the absolute right to a face-to-face meeting with witnesses

---

12. Crawford v. Washington, 541 U.S. 36, 52 (2004).

against them at trial. . . . [A]ny exception to the right would surely be allowed only when necessary to further an important public policy."[13] In another case the Court held that "[s]o long as a trial court makes such a case-specific finding of necessity, the Confrontation Clause does not prohibit a State from using a one-way closed circuit television procedure for the receipt of testimony by a child witness in a child abuse case."[14] But on the other hand, it has also held that a screen that obscured a child witness from the view of the defendant violated the Confrontation Clause.[15]

But it's important to recognize that the main tool that courts typically use to deal with these sorts of issues isn't necessarily going to help in the case of a superhero trying to keep his identity secret. When a party wants to shield a witness for whatever reason, the judge usually conducts what's called an "in camera review," i.e., he brings the lawyers and the witness into his chambers and lets the party that wants the protection explain what's going on. If we were talking about a child witness whose identity was already known, this would serve to protect the child from the defendant while still permitting the judge to be appraised of all the relevant information. But with a masked superhero, the goal is to prevent *anyone* from knowing the hero's secret identity, including the judge. This amounts to asking the judge to accept the superhero's reasoning at face value without any opportunity to investigate whether the concerns are valid. So, for example, while *we* know that Spider-Man has compelling reasons for wanting to keep his identity secret, a judge faced with the request wouldn't have any actual evidence beyond Spider-Man's assertion that he even had family at all. This is going to be a really tough sell.

---

13. Maryland v. Craig, 497 U.S. 836, 844–45 (1990) (quoting Coy v. Iowa, 487 U.S. 1012, 1021 (1988)).

14. *Craig*, 497 U.S. at 860.

15. Coy v. Iowa, 487 U.S. 1012, 1021 (1988).

An identity-concealing costume seems much closer to a screen than one-way closed-circuit television, so it may be quite difficult to argue that a superhero should be allowed to testify in costume. However, a court could make a strong case-specific finding of necessity in instances in which the superhero's friends or family were particularly likely to be targeted for reprisal and in which the defendant had a history of retaliating against accusers. Think of how much danger Aunt May would be in if all of New York's supervillains knew that Peter Parker was her nephew. It is also possible that allowing superheroes to do their work and present testimony in court could be considered an important public policy. It may also depend on the costume. A full mask is much closer to a screen than a mask that only covers part of the face. But the further one gets from these ideal facts the harder it will be to overcome the defendant's strong rights under the Confrontation Clause.

Questioning a Superhero's Identity

Regardless, winning the right to wear a mask in court may be moot if the first question on cross-examination is "What is your real name?" And indeed this also applies to a non-masked superhero whose real identity is nonetheless unknown (e.g., Superman, though he has the "Twelfth Amendment" to rely on). Here the only option may be for the superhero to plead the Fifth Amendment, i.e., refuse to answer the question on the grounds that doing so may incriminate him or her.[16] This can work for non-superhero witnesses too. Take, for example, accomplices in a bank robbery. They obviously can't be forced to testify against themselves, but they can't really be

---

16. Normally, requiring someone to identify him- or herself by giving a name does not trigger the Fifth Amendment. Hiibel v. Sixth Judicial Dist. Ct. of Nev., Humboldt Cty., 542 U.S. 177 (2004). ("Answering a request to disclose a name is likely to be so insignificant in the scheme of things as to be incriminating *only in unusual circumstances.*") (emphasis added).

forced to testify against their partners either, because doing so would inherently expose them to criminal prosecution given the fact that they were involved in the crime.

This could easily be a problem for superheroes too. Batman may be able to testify that a perpetrator committed a certain crime, but by doing so he may be forced to admit that he himself was trespassing or committing various other crimes. One might understand why he might be reluctant to take the stand, and the Fifth Amendment would probably permit him to refuse to do so.

The Fifth Amendment does not require that answering a question actually directly implicate the witness in a crime, only that one could reasonably believe that it could. "[T]he privilege's protection extends only to witnesses who have reasonable cause to apprehend danger from a direct answer. . . . Truthful responses of an innocent witness, as well as those of a wrongdoer, may provide the government with incriminating evidence from the speaker's own mouth."[17] As long as the judge is satisfied that the danger of self-incrimination is not of an "imaginary and unsubstantial character," then the superhero may decline to answer questions about his or her secret identity.[18]

Of course, it's always possible for the prosecution to force immunity upon a witness, which removes the Fifth Amendment protection against self-incrimination. This would involve the district attorney's signing an affidavit to the effect that no prosecutions would result from anything the superhero said in a given deposition or court case. Immunity cannot be refused, and once someone is immune from prosecution, the Fifth Amendment no longer applies.[19] Superheroes are generally witnesses for the prosecution, so the prosecutor would have no reason to pry into the superhero's secret identity and thus no reason to worry about imposing immunity.

---

17. Ohio v. Reiner, 532 U.S. 17, 21 (2001).

18. *Id.*

19. Kastigar v. United States, 406 U.S. 441 (1972).

It's tempting to argue that the Fifth Amendment provides a solution to the Confrontation Clause problem. Why can't a superhero simply assert that requiring him to reveal his identity would incriminate him, thus violating his Fifth Amendment rights? Unfortunately, the Fifth Amendment only protects a person from making self-incriminating *statements*, and wearing (or rather not wearing) a mask is probably not a statement for Fifth Amendment purposes. It might, however, be a form of speech for First Amendment purposes, which we discuss later in this chapter.

Psychic Powers and the Fifth Amendment

As we discuss in chapter 3 on evidence, using psychics (such as Professor X, the telepathic leader of the X-Men) to verify that a witness is being truthful is a complicated legal issue. In addition to the law of evidence, however, constitutional law is also relevant here, specifically the Fifth Amendment rights to be silent and not to incriminate oneself. Could the government use a psychic to extract evidence from a witness who pleads the Fifth? In order to answer that question we must first ask what the Fifth Amendment actually protects.

The Supreme Court has held that "the privilege protects a person only against being incriminated by his own compelled *testimonial* communications."[20] So what is a testimonial communication? The Court explained in a later case that "in order to be testimonial, an accused's communication must itself, explicitly or implicitly, relate a factual assertion or disclose information."[21] There are many kinds of evidence that are non-testimonial and may be demanded without running afoul of the Fifth Amendment, including blood, handwriting, and even voice samples.[22] Perhaps the best example of the dis-

---

20. Fisher v. United States, 425 U.S. 391, 409 (1976) (emphasis added).

21. Doe v. United States, 487 U.S. 201, 210 (1988).

22. *Id.* at 210.

tinction between testimonial and non-testimonial communication is that requiring a witness to turn over a key to a lockbox is non-testimonial, while requiring a witness to divulge the combination to a safe is testimonial.[23]

We need not wonder whether reading someone's thoughts counts as testimonial communication, however. As the Court explained, "The expression of the contents of an individual's mind is testimonial communication for purposes of the Fifth Amendment."[24]

One might be tempted to argue that the Fifth Amendment shouldn't apply because the testimony is the psychic's rather than the witness's (i.e., the difference between the witness's saying "I saw Magneto kill Jean Grey," and the psychic's saying "The witness remembers seeing Magneto kill Jean Grey"). However, the Supreme Court actually addressed this issue in *Estelle v. Smith*.[25] In that case, a defendant was subjected to a psychiatric evaluation, and the psychiatrist's expert testimony was offered against the defendant. The Court held that the expert testimony violated the right against self-incrimination because the expert testimony was based in part on the defendant's own statements (and omissions). Thus, using an intermediary expert witness to interpret a witness's statements will not evade the Fifth Amendment.

So psychic powers could likely not be used to produce evidence from a witness who invoked the Fifth Amendment. And, believe it or not, this issue actually has contemporary resonance. Although a far cry from the kind of psychic powers that Professor X is capable of, technologies like functional MRI (fMRI) may someday see regular

---

23. *Id.* This distinction is of vital importance in the era of password-based encryption, and it is not entirely clear whether the Fifth Amendment protects passwords. One court decided the issue by holding that the defendant need not give up the password but rather only produce the contents of the encrypted drive. *In re* Boucher, No. 2:06-mj-91, 2009 WL 424718 (D. Vt. Feb. 19, 2009). Thus, the protected evidence (the contents of the defendant's mind) remained secret while the unprotected evidence (the contents of the drive) were discovered.

24. *Doe*, 487 U.S. at 210 n. 9.

25. 451 U.S. 454 (1981).

use in criminal investigation. However, scholars and commentators are divided on whether fMRI-like tests fall under the scope of the Fifth Amendment (i.e., is it more like a blood sample or like speech?).[26] Time will tell whether the Fifth Amendment protects people from unwanted mind reading or not.

The Keene Act, Federalism, and the First Amendment

The Keene Act was the fictional federal law passed in the *Watchmen* Universe[27] that prohibited "costumed adventuring" (i.e., being a superhero), with a few exceptions for superheroes that worked for the government. Would such a law be constitutional in the real-world United States? A similar analysis could be applied to similar fictional laws such as the Marvel Universe's Superhuman Registration Act (more on that law later).

Unlike state governments, the United States Congress does not have what is called a "general police power." Instead, its powers are specified in the Constitution,[28] and anything not specifically listed is reserved to the states and the people by the Tenth Amendment. This allocation of power between the federal and state governments is called "federalism." The basic idea here is that while state govern-

---

26. *See, e.g.,* Benjamin Holley, *It's All in Your Head: Neurotechnological Lie Detection and the Fourth and Fifth Amendments,* 28 DEV. MENTAL HEALTH L. 1 (2009); Matthew Baptiste Holloway, *One Image, One Thousand Incriminating Words: Images of Brain Activity and the Privilege Against Self-incrimination,* 27 TEMP. J. SCI. TECH. & ENVTL. L. 141 (2008); Dov Fox, *The Right to Silence as Protecting Mental Control,* 42 AKRON L. REV. 763 (2009).

27. Although *Watchmen* was published by DC Comics, it is unrelated to the mainstream DC continuity. This is important because it means that the DC Universe's legal protections for superheroes (like the "Twelfth Amendment" discussed earlier) do not apply.

28. U.S. CONST. art. 1 § 8.

The Keene Act outlawed vigilantes known as "costumed adventurers" in the
Watchmen universe. Like many emergency laws, it was of questionable effectiveness. Alan Moore et al., WATCHMEN 4 (DC Comics December 1986).

ments can do anything the Constitution doesn't specifically say they
can't, Congress can only do things the Constitution specifically says
it can. For the Keene Act to be constitutional, there must be some
justification for it in the Constitution. First, let's consider two powers
that might seem appealing but don't quite make the cut.

Congress's spending power,[29] which is very broad,[30] can be used
to force states to pass laws that the federal government couldn't pass

29. U.S. CONST., art. 1, § 8, cl. 1. The spending power is derived from the power to tax.
After all, what's the point of taxing if you can't spend it?

30. "The power of Congress to authorize expenditure of public moneys for public purposes is not limited by the direct grants of legislative power found in the Constitution.
Thus, objectives not thought to be within Article I's enumerated legislative fields may
nevertheless be attained through the use of the spending power and the conditional
grant of federal funds." South Dakota v. Dole, 483 U.S. 203, 207 (1987).

itself by threatening to withhold federal funding.[31] For example, the federal government does not generally have the authority to set speed limits on nonfederal highways or set the drinking age—the Twenty-First Amendment is explicit about that last one—but it *can* tie federal highway funding to states setting speed limits in compliance with federal guidelines.[32] The spending power is general enough that it could address this issue, but the Keene Act seems to be a self-contained piece of federal legislation, not a coercive act designed to prompt action by the states. So while Congress could use the spending power to require the passage of state-level costumed adventuring bans (by, for example, threatening to withhold law enforcement funding), that doesn't seem to be the approach used in the Watchmen Universe.

Another route to making something a federal crime is to limit it to cases in which the federal government has jurisdiction, e.g., cases involving federal land, property, or employees. But the Keene Act applied to everything, not just costumed adventuring in federal parks and the like. No, we must go big, and that means the Commerce Clause.

The Commerce Clause allows the federal government to "regulate Commerce with foreign Nations, and among the several States, and with the Indian Tribes,"[33] and it is the mainstay of modern congressional authority. Although it does have some limits,[34] the scope of the Commerce Clause has expanded greatly over the past century, beginning with the New Deal and continuing on through the Civil Rights era and modern federal regulations. Social Security, Medicare, most of the federal regulatory agencies, federal trademark law, and many federal civil rights and antidiscrimination laws are all

---

31. *Id.* at 206–07.

32. *Id.*

33. U.S. Const. art. 1, § 8, cl. 3.

34. *See, e.g.*, United States v. Morrison, 529 US 598 (2000); United States v. Lopez, 514 U.S. 549 (1995).

founded on the Commerce Power. If anything could form the basis of the Keene Act, it's the Commerce Clause.

In this case we're concerned with regulation of interstate commerce (meaning, commerce "among the several States"). The Commerce Clause allows the federal government to regulate the channels of interstate commerce, the instrumentalities of interstate commerce, persons, or things in interstate commerce, and activities that substantially affect interstate commerce.[35] Of these, the third is the best bet for supporting the Keene Act.

Specifically, there is an interstate market for crime prevention and investigation services (e.g., private security firms, private investigators, bounty hunters). Firms and individuals involved in this market routinely work across state lines. The Keene Act could require, for example, that anyone working in such a market do so under his or her real identity. The legitimate government interest would be the safety of consumers of such services; it is important for consumers of such services to know whom they are dealing with.

The fact that costumed adventurers sometimes provide their service for free and often without contracting with clients is of no account, as is the fact that they may work only within one state. The Commerce Clause extends to noncommercial transactions and even intrastate activities as long as doing so is necessary to make the interstate regulation effective.[36] If the local or noncommercial activity affects the interstate market, the Commerce Clause can reach it.[37] The existence of costumed adventurers who work for free no doubt affects the market for regular security firms, private investigators, and bounty hunters. If the aggregate impact on the market is substantial or significant, then that is enough.[38] So invoking the Commerce Clause may work.

---

35. Gonzales v. Raich, 545 U.S. 1, 16–17 (2005).

36. *Raich. See also* Wickard v. Filburn, 317 U.S. 111 (1942).

37. *Raich* at 19. 545 U.S.

38. *Id.* at 19–20.

But federalism isn't the Keene Act's only hurdle. By prohibiting certain kinds of clothing in certain situations, the Keene Act implicates the First Amendment, which, among other things, grants the right to freedom of speech. Specifically, wearing expressive clothing has been held to be a form of speech protected by the First Amendment.[39] Speech can be found where "[a]n intent to convey a particularized message was present, and the likelihood was great that the message would be understood by those who viewed it."[40] A superhero's costume conveys the message of the identity of the wearer. There is also a First Amendment right to anonymous speech, which may protect the wearing of identity-concealing costumes, at least under certain circumstances.[41]

The government can regulate speech, although only under narrow circumstances. There are two major kinds of speech regulation: content-based and content-neutral. Content-based restrictions (e.g., "you can't say that") must be narrowly tailored to serve a compelling state interest.[42] In practice, content-based restrictions are rarely upheld by federal courts. Content-neutral restrictions (e.g., "you can say that but not here, right now, or at that volume"), on the other hand, are subject to a slightly more relaxed standard. Also called "time, place, and manner restrictions," these laws must be "justified without reference to the content of the regulated speech, . . . narrowly tailored to serve a significant governmental interest, and . . . leave open ample alternative channels for communication of the information."[43]

A ban on costumed adventuring seems more like a content-

---

39. See, e.g., Cohen v. California, 403 U.S. 15 (1971) (holding a jacket with a protest slogan to be protected), Tinker v. Des Moines Independent Community School Dist., 393 U.S. 503 (1969) (holding that wearing a black armband as a form of protest is protected).

40. Texas v. Johnson, 491 U.S. 397, 404 (1989).

41. NAACP v. Alabama, 357 U.S. 449 (1958).

42. Austin v. Mich. Chamber of Commerce, 494 U.S. 652 (1990).

43. Ward v. Rock Against Racism, 491 U.S. 781, 791 (1989).

neutral regulation than a content-based one. After all, the Keene Act does not ban the wearing of costumes but rather the wearing of costumes *while fighting crime.* The justification for the law does not depend on the content of the speech (i.e., the superhero alter ego expressed by the costume) but rather the need to be able to identify and prosecute criminals. Preventing crime is certainly a significant governmental interest,[44] and many costumed adventures in *Watchmen*—such as Rorschach—had become anonymous criminals, so a ban on costumed adventuring would serve to prevent crime. And the Act does not prevent alternative channels for communication of the information, such as Halloween parties or even walking down the street.

Furthermore, at least one real-life law banning the wearing of identity-concealing masks has been upheld.[45] The Second Circuit—including now–Supreme Court Justice Sotomayor—noted "the Supreme Court has never held that . . . the right to engage in anonymous speech entails a right to conceal one's appearance in a public demonstration. Nor has any Circuit found such a right."[46] A court could find that costumed adventuring is similar to a public demonstration, and so there is no right to anonymous crime fighting.

The Superhuman Registration Act and the Draft

The Marvel Universe also has a version of an act like the Keene Act. In its 2006–2007 *Civil War* storyline, Congress finally passed a version of the long-rumored Superhuman Registration Act ("SHRA").

---

44. Hynes v. Mayor and Council of Oradell, 425 U.S. 610, 616–617 (1976) ("the Court has consistently recognized a municipality's power to protect its citizens from crime and undue annoyance by regulating soliciting and canvassing").

45. Church of the Am. Knights of the Ku Klux Klan v. Kerik, 356 F.3d 197 (2004).

46. *Id.* at 209.

This will be the last sensible thing Tony Stark says for almost two years. Brian Michael Bendis et al., NEW AVENGERS: ILLUMINATI (Marvel Comics 2008).

Unlike the Keene Act, the SHRA did more than ban unauthorized superheroes; it requires that superpowered individuals register with the government and, if asked, serve as a superhero on behalf of the government. Could Congress do this?

The Constitution empowers Congress to "raise and support Armies, . . . to provide and maintain a Navy; to make Rules for the Government and Regulation of the land and naval forces."[47] In other words, Congress has the power to raise armed forces for the national defense, and there is very little limit on its powers in this area. So if, as is sometimes indicated in the comic books, the SHRA was intended to form a kind of special branch of the federal armed forces, under the auspices of S.H.I.E.L.D. or something else, Congress has a lot of authority here. It certainly has the ability to authorize and fund a superhuman branch of the military.

But does it have the ability to force superhumans to register and work for the government? Maybe. Conscription is not directly addressed by the Constitution, but it has long been held that conscription is part of Congress's power to raise armies, and the Supreme Court tends to make unusually strong statements of congressional power when faced with this particular issue.[48] As John Quincy Adams said in a speech before the House of Representatives, "[The war power] is tremendous; it is strictly constitutional; but it breaks down every barrier so anxiously erected for the protection of liberty, property and of life."[49]

But while the power of Congress to draft people into the armed services is generally beyond question, the power of Congress to draft specific individuals is something different. For the most part, since World War II the draft has basically applied to all men equally. Prior to World War II, there was significant class discrimination, most exemplified by the paid substitute system of the American Civil War. But directly targeting specific individuals raises due process implica-

---

47. U.S. CONST., art 1, § 8, cl. 12–14.

48. See, e.g., Lichter v. U.S., 334 U.S. 742 (1948) ("The constitutionality of the conscription of manpower for military service is beyond question. The constitutional power of Congress to support the armed forces with equipment and supplies is no less clear and sweeping.").

49. CONG. GLOBE, 24th Cong., 1st Sess. 4038 (1836).

tions far beyond the skewed drafts of the nineteenth and early twentieth centuries. The draft is a pretty huge imposition upon civil rights, and while it is an imposition Congress is permitted to make, the Supreme Court might balk at permitting Congress to go so far as to shed even the pretense of fairness.

The Thirteenth Amendment, which prohibits involuntary servitude, is perhaps the most obvious potential constitutional issue with the draft, but the federal courts have unanimously and consistently held that it does not limit the draft power at all: "[T]he power of Congress to raise armies by conscription is not limited by either the Thirteenth Amendment or the absence of a military emergency."[50]

Similarly the federal courts have held that the First Amendment's protection of religious belief is no barrier to the draft. Conscientious objector status is the product of statute, not the Constitution: "The conscientious objector is relieved from the obligation to bear arms in obedience to no constitutional provision, express or implied; but because, and only because, it has accorded with the policy of Congress thus to relieve him."[51] In other words, conscientious objectors don't have to serve in the armed forces, not because the Constitution says so, but because Congress has passed a law to that effect. If Congress wanted to, it could conscript everyone, regardless of any religious or moral objection.[52] It's unlikely it would do so given that it would likely lead to civil disobedience, but it's a theoretical possibility. The Court has listed a whole host of constitutional rights that may be superseded by the war power, culminating in "other drastic powers, wholly inadmissible in time of peace, exercised to meet the emergencies of war."[53]

---

50. United States v. Chandler, 403 F.2d 531 (D.C. Cir. 1968).

51. United States v. Macintosh, 283 U.S. 605, 623 (1931).

52. Congress could also decide to draft women as well. The only reason women are not required to register for Selective Service is because Congress has not yet imposed the requirement. There's no reason it couldn't.

53. *Macintosh*, 283 U.S. at 622.

However, this is still an untested area of law, because as far as we can tell Congress hasn't actually tried to do this, there being no compelling reason to use the draft power this way. The only times a draft has been imposed have been in times of incredible demand for manpower—it is a drastic step, after all—so going after a handful of specific individuals wouldn't make sense in the real world. In the case of superheroes, however, it may well be that the courts would permit such an action, as the draft power is pretty sweeping, and the courts have not really displayed any willingness to limit that power before. If Congress thinks it needs the assistance of a uniquely capable citizen, the courts would most likely not object.

Mutants and Civil Rights

Although most superheroes and supervillains have unique origin stories, the mutants of the Marvel Universe all share a common origin: the X gene mutation. This common origin has made mutants a frequent target of discrimination in the Marvel Universe since the 1960s, sometimes at the hands of the government and sometimes at the hands of private actors. The X-Men have struggled against this discrimination in many ways, but could strategic civil rights lawsuits have prevented many of these problems? There are two major constitutional arguments that would likely be raised in a mutant rights lawsuit: equal protection and substantive due process.

The Equal Protection Clause of the Fourteenth Amendment
The Equal Protection Clause of the Fourteenth Amendment states, "No State shall . . . deny to any person within its jurisdiction the equal protection of the laws."[54] As the Supreme Court has explained,

---

54. U.S. CONST., amend. XIV, § 1.

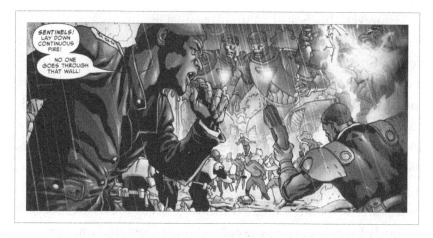

Sentinel robots are often used by the government to capture or kill mutants. David Hine et al., CIVIL WAR: X-MEN 1 (September 2006).

The general rule is that legislation is presumed to be valid and will be sustained if the classification drawn by the statute is rationally related to a legitimate state interest. . . . The general rule gives way, however, when a statute classifies by race, alienage, or national origin. These factors are so seldom relevant to the achievement of any legitimate state interest that laws grounded in such considerations are deemed to reflect prejudice and antipathy—a view that those in the burdened class are not as worthy or deserving as others. For these reasons and because such discrimination is unlikely to be soon rectified by legislative means, these laws are subjected to strict scrutiny and will be sustained only if they are suitably tailored to serve a compelling state interest.[55]

This strict scrutiny standard is the highest standard used by federal courts when evaluating legislation.

The Court has also held that other classifications (e.g., sex and legitimacy of birth) are subject to a lesser standard called intermediate scrutiny.

[W]hat differentiates sex from such nonsuspect statutes as intelligence or physical disability . . . is that the sex characteristic frequently bears no relation to ability to perform or contribute to society. Rather than resting on meaningful considerations, statutes distributing benefits and burdens between the sexes in different ways very likely reflect outmoded notions of the relative capabilities of men and women. . . . Because illegitimacy is beyond the individual's control and bears no relation to the individual's ability to participate in and contribute to society, official discriminations resting on that characteristic are also subject to somewhat heightened review.[56]

"So far, so good," you may be thinking. After all, discrimination on the basis of mutant status is often based on "prejudice and antipathy" and unlikely to be rectified by legislative means because

---

55. Cleburne v. Cleburne Living Center, 473 U.S. 432, 440 (1985).

56. *Id.* at 440–41 (internal citations and quotations omitted).

Pixie is attacked by members of the Hellfire Cult in an example of violent anti-mutant prejudice. Matt Fraction et al., *All Tomorrow's Parties*, in UNCANNY X-MEN 501 (Marvel Comics August 2008).

mutants are such a small minority. Or, at the very least, mutant status is "beyond the individual's control and bears no relation to the individual's ability to participate in and contribute to society," at least inasmuch as many mutants are equal to or superior to typical humans when it comes to their ability to function as citizens.

Alas, it is not that easy. All forms of discrimination are not created equal. Certain classifications protected by the text of the Constitution itself—race, national origin, and religion[57]—are subject to "strict scrutiny," meaning that the courts look very, very closely at anything that is even suspected to discriminate on those bases. When the courts apply strict scrutiny, they will strike down any law that is not absolutely necessary to achieve a compelling state interest and actually advances that interest. Once a court decides to apply strict scrutiny, it is almost a foregone conclusion that it will wind up striking down the law in question.

Some classifications are "quasi-suspect," in that while the Constitution does not provide explicit protection, they are similar enough to suspect classes that the Constitution implicitly provides similar, albeit reduced, protection. Quasi-suspect classes include biological sex, citizenship status, and legitimacy of birth.[58] Discrimination on the basis of a quasi-suspect class receives what is known as "intermediate" scrutiny by the courts. Intermediate scrutiny requires that the courts strike down any laws that do not serve a compelling state interest and are at least substantially related to the interest. This is a more relaxed standard than strict scrutiny, and cases go both ways here.

But every other classification is subject to mere "rational basis" review. Here, the government just has to show that the law in question is rationally related to *some* state interest. The interest doesn't have to be particularly important, and the relationship between the interest and the law doesn't have to be particularly close. In fact, the interest in question doesn't even have to be the one the legislature had in mind; "any conceivable rational basis" will do.[59] As one might

---

57. The Thirteenth and Fourteenth Amendments protect against discrimination on the basis of race or national origin, and the First Amendment protects against religious discrimination. These are the only "suspect clauses" actually in the text of the Constitution.

58. Sometimes memorably but crassly referred to as "women, aliens, and bastards."

59. Bd. of Trs. of the Univ. of Ala. v. Garrett, 531 U.S. 356, 367 (2001).

imagine, it is very rare for the courts to strike down a law using rational basis review, but it is not unheard of.[60]

Turning specifically to the question of mutation, discrimination on the basis of mutation is a relatively new phenomenon, only a few decades old, in marked contrast to discrimination on the basis of race, national origin, religion, gender, etc.[61] A court may be unwilling to conclude that legislative means of rectifying the problem will prove inadequate without giving the issue more time to develop. Second, from a legal perspective mutation could indeed bear a relation to an individual's ability to participate in and contribute to society. For example, one could easily imagine jobs that particular mutants could do much better than a typical human.[62] Let's continue with the *Cleburne* case for an example of the Supreme Court declining to grant heightened protection to a class and see if mutation fits the mold.

The *Cleburne* case was about discrimination against people with mental disabilities; the City of Cleburne had an ordinance that required a special zoning permit for the operation of a group home for the mentally disabled. The Fifth Circuit held that mental disability was a quasi-suspect-classification due at least some heightened scrutiny, but the Supreme Court disagreed. First, it held that mental disability was a highly variable condition requiring carefully tailored solutions not befitting the judiciary.[63] Second, it held that cities and states were addressing mental disabilities in a way that did not demonstrate antipathy or prejudice.[64] Third, the existence of specific leg-

---

60. The *Cleburne* case is one such example. Romer v. Evans, 517 U.S. 620 (1996) is another.

61. Although a handful of long-lived mutants have been around for centuries or even millennia (e.g., Apocalypse), most mutants began to appear after the advent of nuclear weapons testing. Mutants have sometimes been referred to as "children of the atom."

62. For a discussion of situations in which mutation is actually a drawback, see the discussion of the Americans with Disabilities Act in Chapter 7.

63. *Id.* at 442.

64. *Id.* at 443.

islation indicated that the mentally disabled were not politically powerless.[65] Fourth, if the Court recognized mental disability as a suspect class it would have to do the same for

> "a variety of other groups who have perhaps immutable disabilities setting them off from others, who cannot themselves mandate the desired legislative responses, and who can claim some degree of prejudice from at least part of the public at large[, such as] the aging, the disabled, the mentally ill, and the infirm. We are reluctant to set out on that course, and we decline to do so."[66]

Some of the Court's decision cuts in favor of mutants: Cities and states aren't really addressing the problem and there is very little legislation on the subject to indicate mutant political power. However, other aspects cut against mutant rights. Mutation is a "highly variable condition," and arguably it is "a difficult and often a technical matter, very much a task for legislators guided by qualified professionals and not by the perhaps ill-informed opinions of the judiciary."[67] And making mutation a suspect class would open a door the Supreme Court explicitly declined to open in *Cleburne*. Given the Court's current reluctance to embrace homosexuality as a suspect classification,[68] it's questionable whether it would do so for mutants. Discrimination on the basis of mutation would thus likely receive only rational basis review and likely survive an Equal Protection challenge.

---

65. *Id.* at 445.

66. *Id.* at 445–46.

67. *Id.* at 443.

68. *See* Lawrence v. Texas, 539 U.S. 558 (2003) (overturning an antisodomy law on the basis of substantive due process rather than the Equal Protection Clause).

Substantive Due Process

The second argument that might apply to mutant rights, substantive due process, is derived from the Due Process Clauses in the Fourteenth Amendment[69] ("nor shall any State deprive any person of life, liberty, or property, without due process of law") and Fifth Amendment[70] ("No person shall be . . . deprived of life, liberty, or property, without due process of law"). While we ordinarily think of due process as being about procedural rights (e.g., the right to a hearing), substantive due process protects rights held to be "fundamental to our scheme of ordered liberty" or "deeply rooted in [American] history and traditions."[71] An example of such rights that is relevant here are "the rights of 'discrete and insular minorities'—groups that may face systematic barriers in the political system."[72] When a law implicates such a right, the courts apply a strict scrutiny standard.

The courts do not recognize new substantive due process rights lightly. "Recognizing a new liberty right is a momentous step. It takes that right, to a considerable extent, outside the arena of public debate and legislative action."[73] However,

> [s]ometimes that momentous step must be taken; some fundamental aspects of personhood, dignity, and the like do not vary from State to State, and demand a baseline level of protection. But sensitivity to the interaction between the intrinsic aspects of liberty and the practical realities of contemporary society provides an important tool for guiding judicial discretion.[74]

---

69. U.S. CONST., amend. XIV, § 1.

70. U.S. CONST., amend. V.

71. McDonald v. City of Chicago, 130 S. Ct. 3020 (2010).

72. *McDonald*, 561 U.S. at 24 (Stevens, J., dissenting) (citing United States v. Carolene Products Co., 304 U.S. 144, 153, n. 4 (1938)).

73. *Id.*

74. *Id.*

So the questions are raised: Are mutants a discrete and insular minority? Do they face systematic barriers in the political system? Do anti-mutant laws threaten fundamental aspects of personhood or dignity that demand a baseline level of protection? We think the answer to all of these questions is yes. Although anti-mutant discrimination is a relatively new phenomenon, it has existed essentially as long as mutants have. Such discrimination is pervasive, sometimes violent (remember Pixie?), and often backed by the authority of the state. In the case of Genosha (an island off the coast of Africa and thus admittedly not part of the United States) it has even lead to the wholesale enslavement of mutants.[75] This discrimination goes to the mutants' very humanity, and there can hardly be a more fundamental aspect of personhood or dignity than that.

Anti-Mutant Hate Crimes

If mutant rights were embraced by society, could the federal or state governments pass hate crime laws that give mutants additional protections? Hate crime laws take many forms, but generally they enhance the penalty for an existing crime if the victim was chosen because of his or her race or other protected status. These kinds of laws are constitutional, as they do not punish a person for having a certain belief. Instead, the laws punish a motivation for a crime in much the same way that punishment may be enhanced when a crime was motivated by financial gain.[76] As the Supreme Court explained,

"bias-motivated crimes are more likely to provoke retaliatory crimes, inflict distinct emotional harms on their victims, and incite community unrest. The State's desire to redress these perceived harms provides an adequate explanation for

---

75. At the time (i.e., the late 1980s and early 1990s), Genosha served as an allegory for apartheid-era South Africa.

76. Wisconsin v. Mitchell, 508 U.S. 476, 485 (1993).

its penalty-enhancement provision over and above mere dis-
agreement with offenders' beliefs or biases."[77]

However, a law that targeted bias-motivated expression, such as
a law prohibiting anti-mutant signs or slogans, would not be constitutional.[78] The First Amendment protects such expression, loath-
some though it may be. States and cities may criminalize hate *crimes*
but not hate *speech*.

The federal government is another matter altogether. As discussed, the federal government's powers are constrained by the Constitution, and while the Commerce Clause is broad, it does have
limits. The Supreme Court has held that part of the Violence Against
Women Act of 1994[79] that prohibited "crimes of violence motivated
by gender" was unconstitutional because it exceeded the reach of the
Commerce Clause.[80] These limitations make a federal anti-mutant-
hate-crime law unlikely.

The Consequences of Mutant Rights

Mutants may be protected from discrimination by substantive due
process, but legal protection can be a double-edged sword for organizations that cater to mutants exclusively or that would like to preferentially hire people with superpowers. An example of the former
would be the Xavier Institute, which is a school for, and only for,
young mutants.[81] An example of the latter would be superpowered

---

77. *Id.* at 487–88.

78. *See* R.A.V. v. St. Paul, 505 U.S. 377 (1992) (striking down city ordinance banning the
display of symbols such as burning crosses with knowledge that it would arouse anger,
alarm or resentment in others on the basis of race, color, creed, religion or gender).

79. Pub. L. No. 103-322, 108 Stat. 2038, codified as amended at 4 U.S.C. §§ 40001–
40703.

80. United States v. Morrison, 529 U.S. 598 (2000).

81. We realize that the Xavier Institute no longer exists as such, so assume for the
sake of argument that mutant rights were established prior to the Messiah Complex
storyline.

CONSTITUTIONAL LAW • 33

law enforcement organizations like The Fifty State Initiative and the Department of Extranormal Operations.

If the Xavier Institute is a private school that takes no public funding, then it has more leeway to discriminate, albeit with potential repercussions such as loss of its tax-exempt status.[82] If the Institute takes public funding, however, then it will generally be required not to discriminate:

> The private school that closes its doors to defined groups of students on the basis of constitutionally suspect criteria manifests, by its own actions, that its educational processes are based on private belief that segregation is desirable in education. There is no reason to discriminate against students for reasons wholly unrelated to individual merit unless the artificial barriers are considered an essential part of the educational message to be communicated to the students who are admitted. Such private bias is not barred by the Constitution, nor does it invoke any sanction of laws. But neither can it call on the Constitution for material aid from the State.[83]

It could be argued that mutant status is related to individual merit, and that the special curriculum of the Xavier Institute would be of little use to a nonmutant student, but that argument cuts both ways. If it is permissible for the Xavier Institute to discriminate in favor of mutants because it is a school for special students, then it would also be permissible for a regular school to discriminate against mutants because it is a school for typical students.

A more likely result is that the Xavier Institute would have to rely on private funding or open its doors to nonmutant children. Given society's attitude towards mutants, few parents would send

---

82. *See* Bob Jones Univ. v. United States, 461 U.S. 574 (1983).

83. Norwood v. Harrison, 413 U.S. 455, 469 (1973).

their nonmutant children there, especially since much of the curriculum would be of no use to them (e.g., Northstar's flying class) and the super-genius mutants would probably wreck the grading curve for the normal classes.

S.H.I.E.L.D. and the DC Universe's Department of Extranormal Operations (DEO) are a different story altogether. Unlike most superhero groups, S.H.I.E.L.D. is often written as a part of the United States government, and the DEO is a federal agency. Groups like the X-Men and the various instantiations of the Justice League of America are presumably private organizations that do not even employ their members, so they are free to discriminate as they wish. Private clubs can even avoid the requirements of the Americans with Disabilities Act.[84] But if S.H.I.E.L.D. or the DEO (and the United States government) want to avoid a discrimination suit, then they will have to take some precautions.

The federal government has specific rules that it must follow when employing people. These rules are part of the civil service or "merit system." The first principle is

> Recruitment should be from qualified individuals from appropriate sources in an endeavor to achieve a work force from all segments of society, and selection and advancement should be determined solely on the basis of relative ability, knowledge, and skills, after fair and open competition which assures that all receive equal opportunity.[85]

As you can see, S.H.I.E.L.D. has room to prefer those with superpowers where such powers are relevant to the job (i.e., a "bona fide occupational qualification"). The problem is that superhuman abilities are not actually a requirement of being an agent of

---

84. *See* 42 U.S.C. § 12187 (exempting private clubs from the Americans with Disabilities Act).

85. 5 U.S.C. § 2301 (b)(1).

S.H.I.E.L.D. Numerous S.H.I.E.L.D. agents, although plainly very skilled, are not superhuman, at least not inherently (e.g., Nick Fury, Tony Stark, Clay Quartermain). The DEO has the same problem. This may make it difficult for S.H.I.E.L.D. or the DEO to preferentially hire people with superpowers or other unique abilities except when a position requires a particular ability (e.g., the S.H.I.E.L.D. Psi-Division).

There is an outlet, though. Not all civil service positions are covered by the merit system: "'covered position' . . . does not include any position which is . . . excluded from the coverage of this section by the President based on a determination by the President that it is necessary and warranted by conditions of good administration."[86] As long as the President signs off on a given position before a new agent is brought on board, S.H.I.E.L.D. is free to hire whomever it wishes.

Supervillain Sentencing and the Eighth Amendment

What if the state attempted to imprison an immortal supervillain for life? Or tried to execute a nigh-invulnerable supervillain? And what about special supervillain prisons? Finally, could a supervillain's powers be forcibly removed? Besides the practical problems involved with imprisoning an immortal, all-powerful villain like, say, Galactus, there are also constitutional issues to consider. The Eighth Amendment of the Constitution prohibits "cruel and unusual punishment." In the examples above, how would the courts rule?

Immortal Supervillains and Life Imprisonment

Life imprisonment appears to have emerged in the nineteenth century as an alternative to the death penalty. The Supreme Court for-

---

86. 5 U.S.C. § 2302 (a)(2)(B).

mally recognized it as constitutional in 1974.[87] For most people, a sentence of life without parole is really just a sentence of a few decades. The issue is not limited simply to life without parole either: courts can and do hand down consecutive life sentences. A defendant convicted of multiple serious crimes that do not reach the level in which life without parole is permitted may still be sentenced to enough prison time to guarantee that he'll never be released, e.g., six twenty-year terms to be served consecutively. He'd have to come up for and be paroled for each one in turn, which amounts to a life sentence.

But what about an immortal (or at least very long-lived) supervillain like Apocalypse? Even a very young man who gets life without parole will rarely see more than five decades in prison. Which is bad, but it's an entirely different kettle of fish from seeing fifty decades or five *hundred* decades. Is this cruel and unusual punishment?

It may very well be, especially given the ongoing debate about the practice of incarceration in general. There have been cases in which judges have ordered the release of large numbers of convicts due to prison conditions, especially overcrowding.[88] But that aside, it seems plausible that the Supreme Court might well rule that imprisoning someone for centuries, in addition to being completely impractical and phenomenally expensive, is crueler than simply killing him or her. Thus, if capital punishment is unavailable as an alternative to an eternity in prison, whether because no capital crime was committed or because the jurisdiction does not allow capital punishment, then a very long but finite sentence—or at least the possibility of parole—may be constitutionally required.

---

87. Schick v. Reed, 419 U.S. 256 (1974) (holding that reversing the Presidential pardon which reduced a death sentence to life without parole would be unconstitutional).

88. *See, e.g.,* Brown v. Plata, 131 S. Ct. 1910 (2011).

Nigh-Invulnerable Characters and the Death Penalty

While many superpowered characters are tough, most can be killed through conventional means when it comes right down to it. However, others may either be unkillable (e.g., Doomsday, Dr. Manhattan) or extremely difficult to kill (e.g., Wolverine). In the case of a character with a healing factor like Wolverine's, none of the most common modern methods of execution would work: shooting, hanging, lethal injection, electrocution, or the gas chamber. Decapitation might work (Xavier Protocol Code 0-2-1 mentions this as a possibility for Wolverine), but no one's tried it.

This uncertainty is problematic, because while the Supreme Court has repeatedly upheld the constitutionality of the death penalty and has never specifically invalidated a method of punishment on the grounds that it was cruel and unusual,[89] it has stated "[p]unishments are cruel when they involve torture or a lingering death."[90] Decapitation has been specifically cited as a form of execution that is likely unconstitutional for being too painful.[91] Another hypothetical example is "a series of abortive attempts at electrocution," which would present an "objectively intolerable risk of harm."[92] Since we don't know if a given method of execution would actually work for a regenerating or nigh-invulnerable supervillain, trial and error would be the only way to determine an effective method. Since regenerating characters are often unaffected by drugs, it may not be possible to mitigate pain. It seems likely, then, that the courts would rule that trying to carry out the death penalty would be unconstitutional for those who are unkillable or almost unkillable.

---

89. *See* Baze v. Rees, 553 U.S. 35, 48 (2008) ("This Court has never invalidated a State's chosen procedure for carrying out a sentence of death as the infliction of cruel and unusual punishment.").

90. *Id.* at 46.

91. *Id.*

92. *Id.*

Letting Wolverine know you're coming is *not* part of the plan. Warren Ellis et al., *London Burning,* in EXCALIBUR 100 (Marvel Comics August 1996).

Supervillain Prisons

Many supervillains could easily break out of a normal prison, so many comic books have developed special methods of incarceration to handle people who can fly or walk through walls. One example is the Marvel Universe's Negative Zone, which housed a prison during the Marvel Civil War. Although conditions at the Negative Zone prison were similar to a normal prison, the Zone itself seemed to negatively affect some people's emotions and mental health. Is it cruel and unusual to imprison people in such a place?

In short, probably not. Even regular prisons are seriously depressing, so it's already going to be difficult to prove that a prison in the Negative Zone is worse enough to be considered cruel or unusual punishment. As the Supreme Court has said:

> The unnecessary and wanton infliction of pain . . . constitutes cruel and unusual punishment forbidden by the Eighth Amendment. We have said that among unnecessary and wanton inflictions of pain are those that are totally without penological justification. In making this determination in the context of prison conditions, we must ascertain whether the officials involved acted with deliberate indifference to the inmates' health or safety.[93]

Furthermore, to be "sufficiently serious" to constitute cruel and unusual punishment, "a prison official's act or omission must result in the denial of the minimal civilized measure of life's necessities."[94] *Minimal* is the right word; prison officials "must provide humane conditions of confinement; prison officials must ensure that inmates receive adequate food, clothing, shelter, and medical care, and must

93. Hope v. Pelzer, 536 U.S. 730, 737–38 (2002) (holding that handcuffing an inmate to a hitching post outdoors for several hours with inadequate water and restroom breaks violated the Eighth Amendment) (quotations and citations omitted).

94. Farmer v. Brennan, 511 U.S. 825, 834 (1994).

Not Mr. Fantastic's finest hour. J. Michael Straczynski, Stan Lee et al., *Some Words Can Never Be Taken Back*, in FANTASTIC FOUR (VOL. 1) 540 (Marvel Comics November 2006).

take reasonable measures to guarantee the safety of the inmates."[95] This is a very low bar.

The emotional effects of the Negative Zone are not really part of the punishment but rather a side effect of the place. Because the

---

95. *Id.* at 833.

Negative Zone is the only suitable prison for many supervillains, the side effect is arguably necessary. Further, the side effects are not controlled or intentionally inflicted by anyone. Thus, the effects are not inflicted wantonly (i.e., deliberately and unprovoked). Offering the inmates adequate living conditions and mental health care to offset the effects of the Negative Zone could probably eliminate a charge of deliberate indifference. Finally, it would be difficult to argue that imprisonment in the Negative Zone denies the minimum civilized measure of life's necessities. "The Constitution does not mandate comfortable prisons," as the *Farmer* court noted,[96] only humane ones, and the Negative Zone is probably not bad enough to run afoul of the Eighth Amendment under the circumstances.

Forcible Removal of Superpowers

The DC supervillain Timothy Karnes had the power to transform into a demonic superbeing (Sabbac) by uttering a word of power. After being caught by Captain Marvel and transformed back into his human form, Karnes's larynx was surgically removed in order to prevent him from turning back into Sabbac. Is this cruel and unusual?

A real-world parallel is chemical castration, where convicted sex offenders, usually pedophiles, are treated with a hormonal drug routinely used as a contraceptive in women. While it has four side effects in women, in men the drug results in a massively reduced sex drive.

About a dozen states use chemical castration in at least some cases, and there does not appear to have been a successful challenge on constitutional grounds. This may in part be due to the fact that a significant percentage of the offenders who are given the treatment volunteer for it, as it offers a way of controlling their urges. If the person being sentenced does not object, it's hard for anyone else to

---

96. *Id.*

"WHEN HE WAS IN CUSTODY AT *IRON HEIGHTS* IN KEYSTONE CITY--"

"AW, JESUS, THAT PLACE IS A *HELLHOLE.* LIKE A *GULAG* WITHOUT THE SNOW."

"NO KIDDING. ANYWAY THEY *REMOVED* HIS *LARYNX* SO HE COULDN'T SPEAK AND SUMMON THE POWER OF SABBAC."

The government performed an involuntary laryngectomy on Timothy Karnes in order to prevent him from summoning the power of the demon Sabbac. Judd Winick et al., *Devil's Work: Part One: Sacrifice*, in OUTSIDERS (VOL. 3) 8 (DC Comics March 2004).

come up with standing for a lawsuit.[97] Either way, despite health and civil rights concerns, this appears to be a viable sentence in the United States legal system.

But it should not be hard to see that physically and permanently removing someone's ability to speak is not exactly the same as putting a reversible (or even permanent) chemical damper on their sex drive. It's entirely possible to live an otherwise normal life with a low sex drive, but being mute interferes with essential daily activities in a far more intrusive way. So while the idea of physical modification to the human body is not unconstitutional on its face, it remains to be seen whether this degree of modification would be permitted. For example, while chemical castration appears to be

---

97. "Standing" is essentially having the right status to bring a lawsuit. Under Article III of the Constitution, courts only have jurisdiction over "cases and controversies," and the Supreme Court has interpreted this to mean that the plaintiff has to have suffered some kind of actual injury. So a person can bring a lawsuit on the basis of injury to himself, but generally lacks "standing" to bring a lawsuit on the basis of injuries to someone else. The injured person has to do it. In this case, the mutant being sentenced would have to bring the lawsuit on his own behalf, so if he consents to the procedure, no one else is going to be sufficiently injured to have "standing."

constitutional, it's pretty likely that physical castration would not be. We can only say "pretty likely" because *Buck v. Bell*, a 1927 Supreme Court case that upheld (eight to one!) a Virginia statute instituting compulsory sterilization of "mental defectives," has never been expressly overturned, and tens of thousands of compulsory sterilizations occurred in the United States after *Buck*, most recently in 1981.[98]

On the other hand, Karnes isn't your run-of-the-mill offender. He's possessed by six demonic entities and capable of wreaking an immense amount of destruction. Part of the analysis in determining whether or not a punishment is cruel and unusual is whether or not the punishment is grossly disproportionate to the severity of the crime.[99] This is, in part, why the Supreme Court has outlawed the death penalty for rape cases. If the crime as such doesn't leave anyone dead, execution seems to be a disproportionate response.[100]

The Eighth Amendment also prohibits "the unnecessary and wanton infliction of pain," including those "totally without penological justification."[101] Here, though, there is a clear penological justification, namely the prevention of future crimes, and the laryngectomy, a routine medical procedure frequently used in those suffering from throat cancer, could be carried out in a humane manner without the infliction of unnecessary pain.

There are other criteria by which a punishment is judged, in-

---

98. Buck v. Bell, 274 U.S. 200 (1927); PAUL A. LOMBARDO, THREE GENERATIONS, NO IMBECILES: EUGENICS, THE SUPREME COURT, AND *BUCK V. BELL* (2008) (documenting the history of compulsory sterilization in the United States); *Eugenics Victims to Get Apology*, EUGENE REGISTER-GUARD, Nov. 16, 2002, at 2B (noting that sterilizations occurred in Oregon through 1981).

99. Ewing v. California, 538 U.S. 11, 21 (2003).

100. Kennedy v. Louisiana, 554 U.S. 407 (2008) ("As it relates to crimes against individuals . . . the death penalty should not be expanded to instances where the victim's life was not taken.").

101. Hope v. Pelzer, 536 U.S. 730, 737–38 (2002).

cluding whether it accords with human dignity and whether it is shocking or contrary to fundamental fairness. But in a case like this, necessity goes a long way, especially because the purpose of the operation is not retributive punishment but rather incapacitation. If the only way to prevent Karnes from assuming his demonic form is to render him mute, then it's possible that the courts would go along with that, particularly if it proved impossible to contain him otherwise and the operation was carried out in a humane manner.

However, what if taking away someone's powers could be done with no other side effects? In *X-Men: The Last Stand* and various stories in the comic books, someone develops a "cure" for mutation, which removes or mitigates a mutant's powers without really affecting them in any other way. This is far more like the chemical castration situation, but unlike that, a "cure" wouldn't even remove any functions a normal human has. It's very unlikely that a court would recognize this as being unconstitutionally inhumane, provided their offense was serious enough to justify this rather harsh sentence.

Superpowers and the Second Amendment

Although some superheroes and villains have powers that are harmless or at least not directly harmful to others (e.g., invulnerability, superintelligence), many have abilities that have no or only limited uses apart from harm (e.g., Superman's heat vision, Havok's plasma blasts). Although the government may be limited in its ability to discriminate on the basis of mutant status or innate superpowers, could the federal government or the states regulate superpowers as weapons without running afoul of the Second Amendment?

The Supreme Court has relatively recently addressed the Second

Amendment in two cases: *DC v. Heller*[102] and *McDonald v. City of Chicago*.[103] The first case dealt with the District of Columbia's ability to regulate firearms, and (broadly speaking) the second case applied the same limits to the states via the Fourteenth Amendment. In particular, *Heller* held that the District of Columbia's ban on the possession of usable handguns in the home violated the Second Amendment. From those decisions we can get a sense of how a comic book universe court might address the issue of superpowers as arms.

The Scope of the Second Amendment

First, let us begin with the text of the amendment: "A well regulated Militia, being necessary to the security of a free State, the right of the people to keep and bear Arms, shall not be infringed."[104] This is a notoriously difficult sentence to interpret, but here is how the Court defined the individual terms.

"[T]he people" refers to people individually, not collectively, and not only to the subset of the people that could be a part of the militia.[105] "Arms" refers broadly to "weapons of offence, or armour of defence" and "any thing that a man wears for his defence, or takes into his hands, or useth in wrath to cast at or strike another," and it is not limited to weapons in existence in the eighteenth century.[106] Interestingly, this suggests that defensive powers may also be protected by the Second Amendment, but for the sake of brevity we will only consider offensive powers as those are the kind most likely to be regulated.

"To keep and bear arms" means "to have weapons" and to

---

102. 554 U.S. 570 (2008).

103. 561 U.S. 3025, 130 S. Ct. 3020 (2010).

104. U.S. Const., amend. II.

105. *Heller*, 554 U.S. at 581.

106. *Id.* at 582.

"wear, bear, or carry . . . upon the person or in the clothing or in a pocket, for the purpose . . . of being armed and ready for offensive or defensive action in a case of conflict with another person."[107] Taken together, the Second Amendment guarantees "the individual right to possess and carry weapons in case of confrontation," but the right does not extend to any and all confrontations—there are limits.[108]

The Court first addressed limitations established by past precedents: "the Second Amendment confers an individual right to keep and bear arms (though only arms that 'have some reasonable relationship to the preservation or efficiency of a well regulated militia')."[109] Further, "the Second Amendment does not protect those weapons not typically possessed by law-abiding citizens for lawful purposes, such as short-barreled shotguns."[110]

Beyond that, there are lawful limits on concealed weapons as well as "prohibitions on the possession of firearms by felons and the mentally ill, or laws forbidding the carrying of firearms in sensitive places such as schools and government buildings, or laws imposing conditions and qualifications on the commercial sale of arms."[111] Perhaps most importantly for our purposes, there is a valid, historical limitation on "dangerous and unusual weapons."[112]

With the scope of the right established, let us now turn to whether the government could regulate superpowers under the Second Amendment.

---

107. *Id.* at 584 (quoting Muscarello v. United States, 524 U.S. 125 (1998) (Ginsburg, J., dissenting)).

108. *Id.* at 591–96.

109. *Id.* at 595 (quoting United States v. Miller, 307 U.S. 174, 178 (1939).

110. *Id.* at 625.

111. *Id.* at 627.

112. *Id.*

Regulating Superpowers as Weapons

We may start with the presumption that a superpower may be possessed and used for lawful purposes such as self-defense. The question is whether a given power fits into any of the exceptions that limit the Second Amendment right.

"Concealed Weapons"

First, many superpowers could be considered "concealed weapons." Before the Human Torch shouts "flame on!" and activates his power, he appears to be an ordinary person. Could the government require a kind of Scarlet Letter to identify those with concealed superpowers? The answer is a qualified yes. The Constitution would not tolerate requiring innately superpowered individuals to identify themselves continuously. That would seem to violate the constitutional right to privacy and the limited right to anonymity. Furthermore, simply keeping concealed weapons is allowed (e.g., a hidden gun safe in a home). The real objection is to concealed weapons borne on the person in public.

Thus, the calculus changes when a superhero sets out to bear his or her powers against others in public (e.g., goes out to fight crime). Luckily, many superheroes already identify themselves with costumes or visible displays of power (e.g., Superman, the Human Torch). Beyond that, most states offer concealed carry permits to the public, usually after a thorough background check and safety & marksmanship training. It may well be that the Constitution requires that if a state will grant a concealed carry permit for a firearm then it must do the same for an otherwise lawful superpower.

"Typically Possessed by Law-Abiding Citizens for Lawful Purposes"

Whether this limitation encompasses a given superpower may depend on the number of superpowered individuals in a given universe and the balance of lawful superheroes to unlawful supervillains. If superpowered individuals are relatively common, which seems to be the case in the Marvel Universe, for example, and superpowered individuals are generally law-abiding and use their powers for lawful purposes, then superpowers would seem to be protected by the Second Amendment. If, on the other hand, superpowers are very unusual or if they are typically used unlawfully, then the government may be able to regulate such powers more extensively.

In most comic book universes powers are both relatively common and normally used for good, suggesting that they do not fall under this exception. However, if certain kinds of powers are more commonly associated with law breaking, then perhaps those powers in particular may be regulated, though in our experience powers of all kinds seem evenly distributed between heroes and villains.

"Dangerous and Unusual Weapons"

Here we come to the catchall. Superpowers are certainly unusual in an historical sense,[113] and they are unusual in the sense that in most comic book universes superpowered individuals are a minority. But perhaps it is the nature of the power that counts. If a superpowered individual is approximately as powerful as a normal individual with a handgun (though perhaps one with unlimited ammunition), is that really so unusual?

Wherever the line is drawn, it seems clear that at least some superpowers would qualify as dangerous or unusual weapons (e.g., Cyclops's optic blasts, Havok's plasma blasts). These are well beyond the power of weapons allowed even by permit, and their nature is unlike any weapon typically owned by individuals or even the police and military.

---

113. Not counting the *Marvel Earth-311* continuity, in which superpowers appeared in the Elizabethan era. NEIL GAIMAN, MARVEL: 1602 (2006).

The Nature and Scope of Regulation

Given that some powers are likely to fall outside the protection of the Second Amendment, how could the government regulate them? We've already discussed the issue of concealed powers, but what about powers that fall into the other two exceptions?

The government would take a page from the way it regulates mundane firearms. First, all possessors of potentially harmful powers could be subject to a background check if they did not have the powers from birth. If they failed the background check, they could be forbidden to use the power (although use in self-defense might still be allowed by the Constitution). A registration scheme would be likely, subject to the limits discussed in reference to the Keene Act.

Second, exceptional powers could be subject to a permitting system including more thorough background checks and training requirements. Some powers could be expressly prohibited outside police or military use.

Third, superpowered individuals who have committed crimes—with or without using their powers—may be forbidden from using them or even be required to have their powers deactivated, if possible, in keeping with the Eighth Amendment issues discussed earlier. Following the decision in *United States v. Comstock*[114] it may even be permissible to indefinitely detain a superpowered criminal after his or her prison sentence was completed if it was not otherwise possible to prevent future criminal acts.

What about uncontrolled powers, for which merely forbidding the use isn't enough? This probably falls outside the scope of the Second Amendment and is closer to the law of involuntary commitment. If a superpowered individual is a danger to himself or others, then he could be required to undergo de-powering treatment or be incarcerated for the individual's protection and the protection of society.

There may be an alternative to incarceration or de-powering.

---

114. 560 U.S. (2010), 130 S.Ct. 1949.

In the real world, specialized drug courts offer treatment and reha-bilitation rather than punishment for nonviolent offenders. "Super courts" could work with institutions like the Xavier Institute, which aims to teach mutants to control their powers and use them safely.

Thus, the Supreme Court's current view of the Second Amend-ment, though politically contentious, would give superpowered indi-viduals significant protection to keep and use their powers largely free from government regulation or interference, with some impor-tant limitations.

No Man's Land and the Limits of Government Power

The 1999 Batman story arc *No Man's Land* centered around a mas-sive earthquake and fire that left Gotham City devastated. Rather than pay to rebuild the city, the federal government decided to man-date an evacuation, thereafter declaring it no longer part of the United States. The bridges to the mainland were demolished and the waters surrounding the island were mined. The result was (in the-ory) a legal no man's land where survivors, criminals, die-hard police officers, and a few superheroes were left to sort through the rubble. But could the government really toss off part of a state like that?

The comic books do not clearly define the process by which Go-tham was evacuated and quarantined, but we know three things for certain. First, Congress refused to grant Gotham additional federal aid (this much is certainly within congressional authority). Second, the President issued an executive order, invoking "some half-forgotten loophole about national security," which is apparently what actually set the evacuation and quarantine in motion. Third, Congress then enacted a law that made Gotham no longer part of the United States. It's these second and third issues that we'll be taking a closer look at.

Isn't Gotham City sometimes part of New Jersey? Bob Gale et al., *No Law and a New Order—Part One: Values*, in BATMAN: NO MAN'S LAND 1 (DC Comics March 1999).

The Limits of Executive Orders

An executive order is a formal declaration by the President, which can be made pursuant to one of two sources of authority. First, the authority can be an inherent constitutional power, such as the power to pardon. Second, the authority can be derived from a statute (i.e., a grant of power to the executive branch by the legislature). If an executive order is unconstitutional or otherwise invalid, those adversely affected by it can challenge the order.[115]

So given that Congress acted after the executive order was given, what source of power could the President possibly use to justify the order to evacuate and quarantine Gotham? One possibility is the Insurrection Act,[116] which makes particular sense given that we know that the military was called in to keep order, and it was the military that eventually demolished the bridges connecting Gotham to the mainland and also mined the river and harbor.

Typically, invoking the Insurrection Act requires a request from the governor or state legislature, but we can reasonably assume that the governor of whatever state Gotham is in did so. This could arguably give the President the power to "order the insurgents to disperse" to some place other than Gotham. Ordinarily the insurgents must be ordered to "retire peaceably to their abodes within a limited time," but it's conceivable that the whole of Gotham was seized by eminent domain, so the insurgents' "abodes" would no longer be in Gotham.

Invoking eminent domain would require compensating the property owners, but since the earthquake and fire drastically reduced the value of the property, the compensation would likely be

---

115. *See, e.g.*, Reid v. Covert, 354 U.S. 1 (1957).

116. 10 U.S.C. §§ 331–335. This Act, dating back to 1807, gives the President authority to deploy federal troops on domestic soil to put down rebellion, insurrection, and even unrestricted lawlessness. It's been on the book for two centuries now, but it's only rarely invoked. The most recent use was the deployment of federal troops to Los Angeles to control the riots after the Rodney King beating in 1992.

significantly less than the cost of rebuilding. While it would make more sense for Congress to act first, it's not inconceivable that the President's actions could be more or less justified under existing law.

Giving Up Territory

Here's where we come to the sticky part. There's no explicit constitutional provision for acquiring new territory, much less giving it up. This fact has been something of an elephant in the room ever since the Louisiana Purchase. Thomas Jefferson wanted to amend the Constitution to spell out the process for acquiring new territory, but the Purchase was pushed through without it. Various ad hoc and ex post facto justifications for acquiring new territory have since been invented, typically resting on the treaty power. The treaty power is also the mechanism by which territory can be given up (or "alienated"), which is something the United States has done several times in the twentieth century.[117]

However, not all United States territory is equal. There are five different kinds of US territory: unincorporated & unorganized, unincorporated & organized, incorporated & unorganized, incorporated & organized, and states. These kinds of territory differ in how they may be alienated, but we don't have to go into all of the details because Gotham, of course, is part of a state (traditionally New Jersey). In fact, it's not clear how the US would go about giving up part of a state, since that has never happened before.

Making it possible to surrender part of a state would require a constitutional amendment. "The Constitution, in all its provisions, looks to an indestructible Union, composed of indestructible States. . . . There was no place for reconsideration, or revocation, except through revolution, or through consent of the States."[118] If Gotham were part

---

117. For example, ceding the Panama Canal Zone back to Panama under the Torrijos-Carter Treaty of 1978 and granting independence to the Philippines in 1946.

118. Texas v. White, 74 U.S. 700 (1868).

of an unincorporated territory (e.g., Puerto Rico), then it's at least arguable that Congress would have the power to "deannex" it.[119] But once something becomes an incorporated part of the United States (organized or not), it's essentially part of the United States forever. While it might be possible to evacuate and quarantine Gotham, it's probably not possible to go so far as to declare it no longer part of the United States.

Even if the United States could give up Gotham, the remaining people living there would not cease to be United States citizens. This has an interesting side effect: Federal courts would still have jurisdiction over federal crimes committed by or against US nationals in Gotham. The United States "special maritime and territorial jurisdiction" extends to "Any place outside the jurisdiction of any nation with respect to an offense by or against a national of the United States."[120] Because Gotham was outside the jurisdiction of any nation, the United States would actually retain jurisdiction over many crimes committed there. So much for the idea of a legal no man's land!

---

119. *See* Christina Duffy Burnett, *United States: American Expansion and Territorial Deannexation*, 72 U. Chi. L. Rev. 797 (2005).

120. 18 U.S.C. § 7 (7).

CHAPTER 2

Criminal Law

Superpowers have rather surprising effects on substantive criminal law.[1] Consider the many questions raised by psychic powers, for example. Psychic supervillain Dr. Psycho was once put on trial for causing a crowd of bystanders to commit murder. This raises two questions: can he be held liable for doing so, and what defense do the bystanders have? Or consider Wonder Woman, who was charged with the murder of Maxwell Lord after killing him in order to stop him from causing Superman to attack his friends. If her case had gone to trial, could she have invoked self-defense or defense of others? More fundamentally, is reading someone's mind itself a crime? This chapter deals with these kinds of questions.

While some may think of crimes as a kind of general "doing bad stuff" with particular kinds of bad stuff associated with particular crimes, this will not suffice as a legal analysis. Crimes are carefully and specifically defined as consisting of "elements," just like molecules are composed of atoms. This careful specification is important because serious ambiguities in the definition of a crime can be inter-

---

1. For criminal procedure, see chapter 4.

preted in favor of the defendant, per the rule of lenity.[2] These elements are divisible into two main categories: *"actus reus"* and *"mens rea,"* Latin for "guilty act" and "guilty mind," respectively. These are basically the same as "act" and "intent."

The act element is probably the one that most people identify with intuitively. Murder involves killing, theft involves taking other people's stuff, etc. But the level of detail with which criminal acts are defined may come as a surprise. For example, the act element of murder is the "unlawful killing of another." All three of the main words in that definition are important. For starters, there must be a killing. No murder if the victim isn't dead. But that killing must be "unlawful," as there are a number of circumstances under which killing is legally justified.[3] The most obvious example is killing in self-defense, but we can also include soldiers killing in wartime or police officers killing a fleeing violent felon. Lastly, the killing must be "of another." Suicide may be morally problematic, and it's even a crime in some jurisdictions, but it isn't *murder* because it doesn't fit the definition. Implied in the "of another" element is that the victim must be a person.[4] Slaughtering pigs isn't murder, and the legal system is pretty resistant to classifying people as anything other than human.

On the other hand, the intent element is not something that most people immediately think of when discussing criminal law, but it is intuitive enough that most people will recognize its validity almost right away. People recognize a difference between doing

---

2. *See, e.g.,* Muscarello v. United States, 524 U.S. 125 (1998).

3. There are certain traditions ethical, philosophical, and religious, which view any and all killing as impermissible, but we are concerned here not with ultimate moral significance but the current state of the legal system. A pacifist may think that killing in warfare or even self-defense is *wrong*, but that doesn't make it *illegal*.

4. This will come up again when we talk about the status of non-human intelligences in chapter 13. For now, the law only recognizes the killing of a human being as murder, but that would likely change if genuine non-human intelligence, particularly in the form of a non-human civilization, were ever encountered.

something on purpose and doing something accidentally. As the great American jurist Oliver Wendell Holmes put it, "Even a dog distinguishes between being stumbled over and being kicked."[5] The law generally recognizes five different "levels" of intent: intentional/ purposeful, knowledgeable, reckless, negligent, and strict liability.[6] "Purposeful" actions are done with the "conscious object" that the act be accomplished and the consequences occur. "Knowledgeable" actions are done with the knowledge that a particular result is a practical certainty, but they are not specifically intended by the actor. "Reckless" acts are done with conscious disregard of known risks in a way that a normal, law-abiding person would not have done. "Negligent" acts are those that involve a risk that a reasonable person *should have* perceived but did not *actually* perceive. Lastly, there are some crimes for which there is no intent element at all, i.e., liability is "strict." For instance, it doesn't matter whether or not you *meant* to speed, if you did it, you're guilty.

With those definitions out of the way, we can explore how throwing superpowers into the mix does odd and sometimes unexpected things to the elements of particular crimes.

Actus Reus

There are a number of different crimes whose *actus reus* might be affected by superpowers.

Murder
Let's start with the big one: murder. As discussed, murder requires that someone die. But what if the dead don't *stay* dead? Take Ra's al

---

5. Oliver Wendell Holmes, The Common Law 3 (1909).

6. Though these distinctions were latent in the common law for centuries, they were only formalized in this spectrum in the 1960s with the introduction of the Model Penal Code, one of the most successful legal reforms in history.

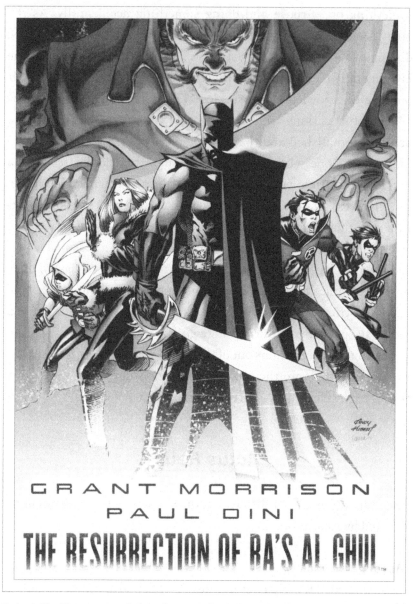

Ra's al Ghul has a nasty habit of coming back from the dead, even more so than most comic book villains. Grant Morrison et al., THE RESURRECTION OF RA'S AL GHUL (2008).

Ghul. In DC's 2007–08 *The Resurrection of Ra's al Ghul* event, Ra's, having been killed by his daughter Nyssa some years prior, is returned to life by a "Fountain of Essence," similar in function to the

Lazarus Pits that Ra's had used to keep himself alive for centuries. In this particular story, killing Ra's does not seem to have been a crime, but what if the circumstances had been different? What if it was Batman who was killed and brought back to life while his killer sat languishing in Arkham Asylum? In short, does the subsequent resurrection of a murder victim undermine the validity of the original conviction?

With one minor caveat, the answer is "almost certainly not." The caveat is that we need to be talking about actual, honest-to-goodness *resurrection*, not one of the myriad ways that comic book writers use to explain why a particular character wasn't really dead. "I got better!" may be a decent hand-wave reason for bringing a beloved (or hated!) character back into the story, but if it turns out that the victim was never actually *dead*, then any convictions related to their death will need to be overturned. The law already knows how to deal with that one, as someone seeming to be dead but coming back later is an uncommon but understood phenomenon. While there are no *criminal* cases on point, there have been a number of civil cases in which someone faked his or her own death for insurance purposes then reappeared some years later.[7]

But if the victim *did* die, then the fact that they later return to life does not matter. The *actus reus* for murder is simply that the victim has died as a result of the defendant's actions. The victim's *staying* dead is not actually an element of the crime. This is probably the right result too, because unless resurrection becomes some kind of commonly available service, we don't want the convictions of known murderers to be overturned because there's been what amounts to a miracle.

Resurrection isn't the only comic book story element that is in play here. What about Multiple Man? Jamie Madrox has the ability to create duplicates of himself using absorbed kinetic energy. Does

---

7. *See, e.g.,* Southern Farm. Bureau Life Ins. Co. v. Burney, 590 F. Supp. 1016 (E.D. Ark. 1984). See discussion in chapter 12.

killing a "dupe" constitute murder? This one is a much harder call, especially given the fact that Madrox himself can "reabsorb" dupes at any time. The law currently has no mechanism for dealing with this kind of ability, but if we apply a "looks like a duck" analysis, it seems like someone else killing a dupe might well be found guilty of murder. Each dupe is said to possess all of Madrox's memories up to the point the dupe was created, they are capable of independent thoughts and actions, including making more dupes, and can live separately from the original for an indefinite period of time. Furthermore, killing a dupe leaves a corpse, so it isn't hard to see a prosecutor taking an interest in pursuing that case. Madrox himself might have an interest in that too, because if it *weren't* murder, he would seem to be in constant mortal peril, as who's to know which is a dupe and which is the original? If it's open season on dupes, it winds up being open season on Madrox "Prime" too.

Deciding the dupes are people is not without side effects, however, both in criminal law and other areas.[8] For example, it's an interesting question whether Madrox reabsorbing a dupe is itself murder. If the dupes control the process, then it would seem to be a form of suicide, which is generally legal.[9] If the original controls the process, however, then it's arguably murder, except perhaps in the case of a terminally ill dupe being absorbed in a jurisdiction that explicitly allows assisted suicide. It's not enough that the dupes want to be reabsorbed: "The lives of all are equally under the protection of the law, and under that protection to their last moment. . . . [Assisted suicide] is declared by the law to be murder, irrespective

---

8. For example, Madrox's ability manifested from birth, unlike most mutants. If Madrox creates a duplicate while a minor, is he essentially foisting another child upon his parents or is he legally and financially responsible for the dupe himself? If Madrox typically has at least one dupe around at all times but not necessarily continuously, can he (or his parents) claim the dupe as a dependent?

9. Note that while suicide is generally legal, assisting, aiding, and counseling suicide generally are not.

Jamie Madrox, the world's only *literal* one-man army. Peter David et al., *Trust Issues*, in X-FACTOR (VOL. 3) 9 (Marvel Comics July 2006).

of the wishes or the condition of the party to whom the poison is administered."[10]

Attempted Murder

Attempting a crime, part of what are known as the "inchoate" (i.e., incomplete) offenses, is still a crime, and the punishment for attempted murder can be just as severe as for actual murder, though the death penalty is generally off the table. The layman's definition of attempted murder is something like "trying to kill someone," and that's accurate, roughly speaking. But the technical definition is somewhat more precise. For example, one state statute defines attempted murder as follows:

> a. A person commits an attempt when, with intent to commit a specific crime, he does any act which constitutes a substantial step toward the commission of that crime.
> b. It shall not be a defense to a charge of attempt that because of a misapprehension of the circumstances it would have been impossible for the accused to commit the crime attempted.[11]

What we have here is a rigorous definition for what counts as attempt and what doesn't, as well as a provision that so-called factual impossibility is not a defense to a charge of attempt.

Let's break that down a bit. The *mens rea* for attempt is intentional. Fair enough. It doesn't make sense to convict someone for trying to do something they weren't actually trying to do. But the *actus reus* element is a bit more interesting. It has to be a "substantial step" towards the commission of that crime. Shooting at some-

---

10. Cruzan v. Director, Mo. Dept. of Health, 497 U.S. 261, 296 (1990) (quoting Blackburn v. State, 23 Ohio St. 146, 163 (1873)).

11. Pa. Cons. Stat. §901.

one and missing would count under most circumstances. It's even possible that lying in wait might work too, though the lack of any actual shooting would hurt the prosecution's case. But buying a gun? Not enough. That's a step alright, but it's a perfectly legal activity in and of itself, and doesn't constitute a concrete step towards a crime.

But what if you shoot Wolverine? That's not going to kill him. It isn't even necessarily going to incapacitate him for all that long. Getting shot in the head in *X2* seems to have knocked him out for a few minutes at best, and being *completely incinerated* by Nitro seems to have lasted for only a few minutes, hours at most. So can it truly be said that shooting Wolverine counts as a "substantial step" towards killing him?

At this point we need to look at subsection (b). There, it says that it is *not* a defense that the act in question would not have accomplished the intended goal as long as the defendant *thought* that it would. Sneaking into someone's home after midnight and trying to kill him by emptying a clip into his bed is still attempted murder if the defendant finds out after the fact that the intended victim wasn't home. But if a defendant realizes that the person isn't home and empties a clip into the bed out of frustration, that's a different situation. If the defendant actually knows that what he's going to do isn't going to kill the victim, how is that a "substantial step" towards accomplishing the crime? Courts are generally looking for some action that the defendant believes will succeed, regardless of whether or not it could. Believing that an action will not succeed would seem to be a defense to an attempt charge.

So turning back to Wolverine, the question becomes whether the person doing the shooting knows that Wolverine isn't going to die as a result of being shot. If the assailant is someone who has just met him or is unaware of his abilities, he probably believes that shooting Wolverine will kill him, so the fact that it won't will not serve as a defense. But if we're talking about someone with whom Wolverine has tangled before, someone from the Brotherhood of Evil Mutants

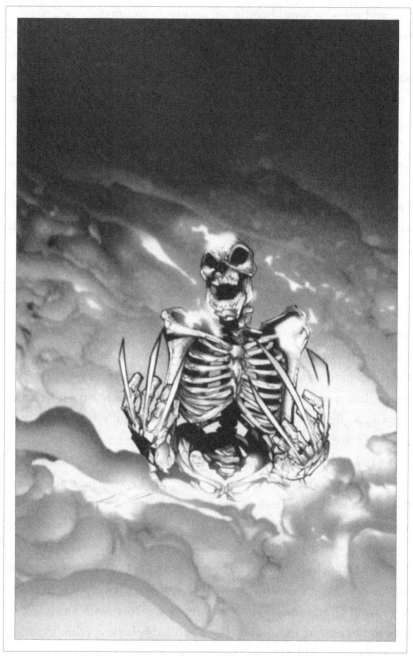

He gets better. Marc Guggenheim et al., *Vendetta Part 2, Revenge,* in WOLVERINE (VOL. 3) 43 (Marvel Comics August 2006).

say, the bad guy should know quite well that anything he does isn't going to kill Wolverine. As such, though any attack would definitely count as an assault, it would not count as attempted murder, because they knew they weren't going to succeed.

Assault

Assault is another crime whose act element is implicated by super-powers. Most jurisdictions distinguish between simple assault and aggravated assault or between different degrees of assault. Simple assault is typically a misdemeanor, whereas aggravated assault is typically a felony. For example, here's how the Model Penal Code defines simple and aggravated assault:

1. Simple Assault. A person is guilty of assault if he:
    a. attempts to cause or purposely, knowingly or recklessly causes bodily injury to another; or
    b. negligently causes bodily injury to another with a deadly weapon;
2. Aggravated Assault. A person is guilty of aggravated assault if he:
    a. attempts to cause serious bodily injury to another, or causes such injury purposely, knowingly or recklessly under circumstances manifesting extreme indifference to the value of human life; or
    b. attempts to cause or purposely or knowingly causes bodily injury to another with a deadly weapon.[12]

Thus, the same intentional act (causing bodily harm) is a misdemeanor if done without a deadly weapon and a felony if done with

---

12. Model Penal Code § 211.1; *See also, e.g.*, N.Y. Penal Law §§ 120.00, 120.05 (distinguishing between third degree and second degree assault).

one. Two issues present themselves: (1) can superpowers count as deadly weapons, and (2) what about telekinetic or psychic powers?

As to the first, Wolverine's claws would seem to count as a deadly weapon, as would most of the gadgets ginned up by Forge and Batman. But in the end of the "Fatal Attractions" crossover in the early 1990s, Magneto stripped the adamantium from Wolverine's skeleton, revealing that his claws are actually bone. Do *they* count as deadly weapons? The question here is whether a natural part of a person's body counts as a "weapon" in terms of the law. If so, it's plausible that any significant deviation from the human norm might lead to aggravated assault charges. This would include things like the Hulk's strength and even Cyclops's energy beams. It seems plausible that a court might well find that they do count as "deadly weapons."[13] The theory here is that assaulting someone with a weapon is inherently worse than assaulting someone barehanded for two reasons. First, weapons enable even ordinary people to cause serious harm. The use of a weapon greatly increases the stakes in any conflict.

The second reason is related to the first. Using something other than one's bare hands also suggests a different sort of mental state. *Actus reus* can sometimes act as a proxy for *mens rea*, the latter being more difficult to prove. A defendant who attacks with a gun wants to do more damage and has put more thought into doing so than someone who simply throws a punch. As most superpowered characters didn't ask for their abilities—the vast majority were either born that way or were powered up as the result of an accident—it seems kind of unjust to hold them to a higher standard just because they can do stuff the rest of us can't. On the other hand, superhero stories make much of the with-great-power-comes-great-responsibility idea. So ultimately, how a court would rule on whether assault by a superpowered individual constitutes aggravated assault *per se* would probably wind up depending on the facts of the specific case.

Then there's the issue of psychic powers, especially telekinesis.

---

13. Which raises the Second Amendment concerns discussed in chapter 1.

EXACTLY SIX SECONDS!
THAT BEATS YOUR PREVIOUS
TIME! NOW GET IT DOWN...
LET'S EXAMINE IT!

Jean Grey demonstrates her powers of telekinesis by levitating two small objects. Due to the inflation of superpowers over the years, this display looks positively quaint by today's standards. Stan Lee, Jack Kirby et al., *The Uncanny Threat of . . . Unus, the Untouchable!, in* X-MEN (VOL. 1) 8 (Marvel Comics November 1964).

A number of superpowered individuals, including Jean Grey, Legion, and Magneto, can exert force on physical objects, including the bodies of others, without actually *touching* them. This ability can take a variety of forms including telekinesis and the control of magnetic fields, but they all have in common the mental projection of force. Although it might seem strange that a noncorporeal force could cause an assault, courts have recognized that even something as insubstantial as a low-power laser beam can cause an assault.[14]

Another kind of psychic power is the manipulation of thoughts or memories. This is also arguably an assault, as manipulating someone's mind necessarily requires manipulating his or her physical neurons. In the DC Universe, this process even leaves trace evidence in the brain, which has been used as evidence in court to prove psychic manipulation.

Theft

While we're on the subject of superpowers being treated in unexpected ways, there are numerous characters whose powers have been stolen or removed by another, for example by the mutant Rogue. While this

---

14. *See, e.g.,* Adams v. Com., 534 S.E.2d 347 (Ct. App. Va. 2000).

So . . . workers' compensation claim? Stan Lee, Jack Kirby et al., *The Fantastic Four!*, in FANTASTIC FOUR (VOL. 1) 1 (Marvel Comics November 1961).

almost always involves some kind of assault, is it also theft? Comic book stories certainly use the language of theft to describe these interactions, but would they be viewed as such in the eyes of the law?

It's actually hard to say. The *actus reus* of theft is the taking of another person's property without permission. At common law there were a variety of different kinds of theft—larceny by trick, larceny by false pretenses, embezzlement, robbery, and the like—but they all have one common element: appropriating another person's *property*. Which is where we run into problems, because the courts are pretty clear that while we certainly have an interest in our own bodies, that interest is not actually a property interest.[15]

---

15. *See, e.g.*, Moore v. Regents of the University of California, 793 P.3d 479 (Cal. 1990) (*en banc*) (holding that a patient does not have a property right in his cells).

Property is generally considered a "bundle of rights," including the right to control and use the property, obtain any benefits related to it, transfer or sell it, and to exclude others from it, along with other more technical rights we will not get into here. We generally think that we have those rights in our own bodies, right? So why are our rights in our bodies not considered property rights? We have actuarial tables for how much losing an arm, a leg, or an eye is worth, so why aren't they property?

Largely because the courts, reflecting their perception of societal mores, are a little squeamish about assigning property rights in human bodies, in no small part due to the idea that recognizing such rights might create a market in human organs. Which is generally considered to be kind of gross. In addition, if we view the human body as being the property of its owner, we get into a pretty bizarre tax situation. For example, would the Fantastic Four's gaining superpowers while in orbit suddenly become a taxable event? They've acquired new "property," and those sorts of transfers or acquisitions generally require tax reporting. This does not seem to be the way that we want to go.

But more than that, most people's intuition seems to be that whatever our relationship with our bodies, the relationship is more significant than that of mere ownership. Spitting in someone's face is somehow morally different from spitting on someone's lawn, even if the monetary damages are both purely nominal. So "stealing" superpowers is probably better categorized as an assault than as a theft.

Mens Rea

As mentioned in the beginning of the chapter, the law already has a pretty sophisticated way of analyzing intent and mental states ranging from deliberate, intentional actions all the way down to consequences that, while not intended or even anticipated, should have

Actually, compared to some real-life "experts," this is pretty unremarkable testimony. Marc Andreyko et al., *Psychobabble—Part Two: Mind Over Morals*, in MANHUNTER (VOL. 3) 21 (DC Comics June 2006).

been if a defendant was acting reasonably. As with *actus reus* super-powers can do some pretty unexpected things to the intent element.

Mind control and illusions

Let's start with a pretty obvious one: mind control. The X-Men's Professor Xavier has demonstrated on numerous occasions that he is able to induce people to perform actions they might not otherwise do. So has the Martian Manhunter, J'onn J'onzz. Other characters, like Mastermind, can generate mental illusions, causing people to see things that aren't there. Apart from the fact that using such powers may be an assault, we are also presented with a question as to whether people who commit criminal acts while under the influence of such powers possess the required mental state to be convicted.

The answer probably depends on the nature of the mental powers at work. On one hand, the law recognizes that truly involuntary actions do not generally confer criminal liability. For example, the driver of a car who suffers an unexpected seizure cannot be held

No points for subtlety. Stan Lee, Jack Kirby et al., *The Stronghold of Doctor Strange!*, in TALES OF SUSPENSE (VOL. 1) 41 (Marvel Comics May 1963).

criminally liable for killing someone while in the throes of the sei-zure.[16] Or take the most basic example: If someone physically forces you to shoot someone else, actually pushing your finger on the trig-ger, the other person is responsible for the resulting death, not you. In *Tales of Suspense #41*, Dr. Strange[17] uses a device he made to control Tony Stark's mind, forcing Stark to break him out of pris-on.[18] Breaking someone out of jail is obviously against the law, but it would be very difficult to convict Stark under these facts, assum-ing he could prove he was being controlled. Yes, he did bad things, but intent is just as much an element of criminal definitions as ac-tions are.

Illusions are a slightly different case. Here we have people acting under their own power and initiative, but faced with circumstances that are not as they appear to be. Under these circumstances the doctrine of "transferred intent" comes into play. If a defendant in-tends to commit a crime against victim A but somehow manages to victimize B instead, his intent is said to "transfer" from A to B.[19] If you think about it, given that the requirements for a crime are a guilty act combined with a guilty mind, the fact that the act and intent are not directed at exactly the same person doesn't actually matter because both mind and act are still guilty.

This may sound bad for our heroes, but all is not lost. The question of whether a person acting under Mastermind's influence could be guilty of a crime may actually depend on what the person *thought* was going on. If he was deceived into believing that he was acting in self-

---

16. Of course, if the driver knew he was prone to seizures, the result is very different.

17. No relation to the master magician from later Marvel stories!

18. Stan Lee, Jack Kirby et al., *The Stronghold of Doctor Strange!*, in Tales of Suspense (Vol. 1) 41 (Marvel Comics May 1963).

19. People v. Bland, 48 P.3d 1107 (Cal. 2002) ("[T]he doctrine of transferred intent applies when the defendant intends to kill one person but mistakenly kills another. The intent to kill the intended target is deemed to transfer to the unintended victim so that the defendant is guilty of murder.").

defense, then it could be difficult to convict him, assuming he is capable of convincing a jury that that's what was going on. Almost this exact situation occurred when Maxwell Lord mentally manipulated Superman into thinking that Batman and Wonder Woman were actually Doomsday attacking Lois Lane. Superman tried to kill each of them as a result. In the end, Wonder Woman killed Lord in order to prevent future attacks. Superman's belief in the necessity of the use of force may have been mistaken, but it was a reasonable and good faith belief caused by Lord's mental manipulation.

Going one step further, what about effects that merely influence a person's mind without controlling it, such as the Scarecrow's fear gas or the alien symbiote that caused Eddie Brock to become the supervillain Venom? People under the influence of such effects could claim the defense of involuntary intoxication. As the Model Penal Code describes it, involuntary intoxication is "a disturbance of mental or physical capacities resulting from the introduction of substances into the body" and "is an affirmative defense if by reason of such intoxication the actor at the time of his conduct lacks substantial capacity . . . to appreciate its criminality."[20] Note, however, that *voluntary* intoxication is not a defense: if someone puts on the symbiote suit knowing that it will affect his mind, any crimes he commits under its influence are on him.[21]

Insanity

A large percentage of Batman's rogues gallery are characterized as insane: the Joker, the Riddler, Poison Ivy, Two-Face, etc. The list goes on, and this phenomenon isn't limited to the DC Universe either. A

---

20. MODEL PENAL CODE §§ 2.08(5)(a) and 2.08(4).

21. Technically some jurisdictions recognize a limited defense of voluntary intoxication in that it may defeat the specific intent required for some crimes. For example, a drunken person may not be capable of forming the level of intent required for premeditated murder but could still be charged with involuntary manslaughter. If, however, the person became drunk knowing they would lose control, then they could be found guilty of premeditated murder.

frequent motivation for supervillains is that they've been driven mad by something in their past.

The specifics of this madness are usually not worked out all that well, certainly not in any way that the psychological or psychiatric establishments would recognize as describing any particular pathology. Regardless, this does raise the issue of whether such characters could successfully raise the insanity defense.

Insanity comes into play because it affects *mens rea*, the mental state with which acts are committed. Insanity and mental disturbances have been known to human society since ancient times, but in 1843, the English House of Lords—the English supreme court at the time—handed down what have become known as the M'Naghten Rules.[22] The M'Naghten test (or something like it) is still what many American courts use to decide whether a given defendant is insane or not. The scope of the insanity defense widened during the first half of the twentieth century, as psychology and psychiatry came into their own as disciplines, but the attempted assassination of President Ronald Reagan by John Hinckley, Jr.—who was found not guilty by reason of insanity—prompted Congress to tighten things up, largely restoring the status quo from the late nineteenth century. Many states followed the federal example.

The core of the M'Naghten test is to determine whether "the party accused was labouring under such a defect of reason, from disease of the mind, as not to know the nature and quality of the act he was doing; or, if he did know it, that he did not know he was doing what was wrong."

In other words, if a defendant can prove that as a result of some mental condition either (1) he didn't know what he was doing, or (2) he didn't know what he was doing was wrong, then he should be found not guilty by reason of insanity.

The "nature and quality" part of the test asks whether the defen-

---

22. M'Naghten's Case, 8 Eng. Rep. 718 (H.L. 1843).

dant actually knew what was going on. The classic example is cutting a woman's throat under the delusion that it was a loaf of bread. If a person truly were suffering from such a delusion (not an easy thing to prove!), then no conviction will lie, because there is no intent to kill. There isn't even negligence, because a reasonable person exercising due care will not have any qualms about slicing himself some toast.

Likewise, if people simply lack the capacity to string together actions and consequences, there are procedural problems with holding them accountable for their actions. The mental state of children is a useful analogy. Just as very young children are not held responsible for the acts they commit because they simply cannot understand the implications and consequences of what they do,[23] a mentally disabled adult might be found not guilty for the same reasons.

Note that either prong of the test, if proved, will result in an acquittal guilty verdict, but both of the prongs require that the defendant be operating under a "disease of the mind" or a "defect of reason." Being drunk won't cut it, as the courts generally impute knowledge to voluntarily intoxicated people so as to avoid drunkenness becoming a complete defense to crimes. But similarly, simply being mistaken about what it was you were doing will not cut it either.

Also note that while a clinical diagnosis can certainly help here, whether or not the defendant has been diagnosed as mentally disturbed is, in a sense, irrelevant. Legal insanity and clinical mental illness are only loosely related. A defendant with no psychiatric history, if he can make out either prong of the test, can be found not

---

23. For example, at common law, children below the age of seven are conclusively presumed to be incapable of committing a crime, children between seven and fourteen are rebuttably deemed incapable of committing a crime, and those fourteen or over are presumed capable. 21 Am. Jur. 2d Crim. Law § 34. Some states have statutory minimum ages rather than following the common law rule.

guilty, and a defendant with a schizophrenia diagnosis can be convicted.

It is worth mentioning two other tests for insanity: the irresistible impulse test and the Model Penal Code's substantial capacity test.[24] In short, the "irresistible impulse" test excuses a defendant acting under an irresistible impulse, and the substantial capacity test excuses a defendant if "as a result of mental disease or defect he lacks substantial capacity either to appreciate the criminality of his conduct or to conform his conduct to the requirements of the law."[25]

The irresistible impulse test has been rejected by most jurisdictions, often vigorously. As the Supreme Court of Pennsylvania put it: "Moreover, the 'defense' offered in this case is simply an attempt to once again foist the 'irresistible impulse' concept upon this Court under different nomenclature, an attempt which we have consistently rejected and will continue to resist."[26] However, it is available in some jurisdictions, such as Virginia: "The irresistible impulse defense is available where the accused's mind has become so impaired by disease that he is totally deprived of the mental power to control or restrain his act."[27] It is possible that many comic book supervillains could be excused by the irresistible impulse test if it were available in Gotham, since many supervillains seem to labor under an irresistible compulsion to commit crimes, often in a specific way (e.g., the Riddler's compulsive riddling).

The Model Penal Code's substantial capacity test has been adopted by a few jurisdictions, including Illinois, Massachusetts, and Rhode Island. It, too, is broader than the M'Naghten rule, and it

---

24. The Model Penal Code is a model criminal law that has been adopted in many states. Although it is often modified by adopting states, it is nonetheless common to refer to the model law rather than individual state versions.

25. MODEL PENAL CODE § 4.01 (1962).

26. Com. v. Cain, 503 A.2d 959 (Pa. 1986).

27. Morgan v. Com., 646 S.E.2d 899, 902 (Ct. App. Va. 2007).

might excuse supervillains where M'Naghten does not. But it is definitely a minority position; the majority of United States jurisdictions, including federal courts, use the M'Naghten test.

Since we don't know what test the comic book worlds use for insanity, we will focus on the M'Naghten test, as it is the majority position. Under the M'Naghten test, a lot of so-called criminally insane supervillains are not actually insane, or at least not insane in such a way as would render them not guilty.

Take the Joker for example. In addition to occasionally denying that he is crazy—as he does at several points in the 2009 film *The Dark Knight*—the Joker does not actually display any likelihood, in most continuities anyway, of being eligible for an insanity defense. He almost always knows exactly what he is doing, and almost always knows that what he is doing is illegal. That, right there, means that he cannot successfully assert an insanity defense.

Perhaps the most detailed examination into the Joker's "insanity" can be found in Alan Moore's story *Batman: The Killing Joke*: "When you're loo-oo-oony, then you just don't give a fig. Man's so pu-uu-uny, and the universe so big! If you hurt inside, get certified,

Scary? Yes. Crazy? No. Alan Moore et al., THE KILLING JOKE (1988).

and if life should treat you bad, don't get ee-ee-even, get mad!"[28] Disturbed? Certainly. Evil even. But actually insane? It sounds as if the Joker has been reading too much Foucault and Nietzsche, but not as if he's actually *disoriented*. And since it is that which the law is interested in when assessing mental culpability, simply adopting an abhorrent coping mechanism will not excuse the Joker from criminal guilt. It is this very line of reasoning that Heath Ledger's Joker adopts when he confronts Harvey Dent in the hospital: "Introduce a little anarchy." This is awful, but it isn't actually unhinged.

The same can likely be said of almost all the characters in Arkham Asylum. Very few if any of them are under the illusion that blowing up buildings is anything other than blowing up buildings. The Riddler commits crimes, knowing they are crimes, as a demonstration of his alleged intellectual superiority.[29] Black Mask is motivated by revenge. So, arguably, is Poison Ivy (at least in certain continuities). All of them know exactly what they're doing, and most of them display extraordinary planning and strategic capabilities. They certainly are capable of forming the requisite mental state to be guilty of a crime. Many of them might be found not guilty under an irresistible impulse doctrine, but again, that doctrine has proved to be both judicially and politically disfavored, only operating in a small minority of jurisdictions.

But there are at least two characters that can probably never be found guilty of a crime even under the M'Naghten test: the Hulk and Doomsday.

The Hulk is going to be mostly immune from criminal prosecution, as when Bruce Banner goes into Hulk mode in most stories, he loses all ability to reason or plan. In those stories where the Hulk is a mindless ravaging beast, holding him criminally liable for his ram-

---

28. Alan Moore et al., BATMAN: THE KILLING JOKE (1988).

29. The Riddler might have an argument to make under the "irresistible impulse" test, but would fail the M'Naghten test.

pages will prove difficult, because he simply can't form the mental state necessary for criminal culpability. In those stories where Banner remains more or less in control during his Hulk phases, the insanity defense should be unavailable, or at least a lot harder to prove. Of course, if Banner commits a crime while himself, his situation would be no different than any other criminal defendant.

Doomsday, on the other hand, is an almost elemental destroyer, possessing neither language nor reason, bent only on destruction. Exactly how that's supposed to work is left as an exercise for the imagination, but it's pretty clear from all of his appearances in comics that Doomsday isn't really capable of forming *any* mental state, and not having a mind to speak of would certainly count as a "defect of reason." In the story where Doomsday gains some modicum of awareness, the insanity defense would be unavailable, but he lost that awareness pretty quickly.[30]

Then again, that would go for any of those villains who lack a sentient mind. Animals, machines, and other non-sentients would never be tried in open court. It does not require a court order for the dogcatcher to put down a rabid dog. Neither would it require a court order for a truly mindless enemy to be "punished" or otherwise dealt with. Whether or not rogue artificial intelligences would count is a discussion for another chapter, but to the extent that they are not considered persons, they would not be tried in court.

---

30. Jeph Loeb et al., *Doomsday Rex, in* SUPERMAN (VOL. 2) 175 (DC Comics December 2001).

CHAPTER 3

Evidence

Can a superhero testify while masked? Could Professor X testify about what he learns via telepathy? What effect would Mystique or another shape-shifter have on trial testimony? More importantly, what do all of these questions have to do with one another?

The answer is that they all touch on different aspects of the law of evidence. Evidence is a fairly complicated legal subject and has significant overlap with constitutional law: the reason a goodly number of potential kinds of evidence are inadmissible is because they are unconstitutional.[1] More generally speaking, admitting inadmissible evidence (or excluding admissible evidence) is a violation of the constitutional right to due process.[2] But here we're going to focus on those aspects of evidence that do not directly implicate any specific constitutional provisions. And believe us, there's a bunch.[3]

---

1. For example, a forced confession.

2. *See, e.g.*, Crane v. Kentucky, 476 U.S. 683 (1986).

3. Throughout this chapter we will be using the Federal Rules of Evidence and related cases as our guidelines. Although these rules only explicitly apply in federal cases, most states have adopted similar rules.

Masked Testimony

In *She-Hulk* (Vol. 1) #4, a lawyer needs to put Spider-Man on the stand.[4] While masked. This, to put it mildly, is a problem. If it were a criminal case, there would be Sixth Amendment issues, which we discuss in chapter 1, but this is a civil trial. Even so, putting anyone on the stand while they're wearing a mask would likely violate Fed. R. Evid. 602, which reads, in part,

> A witness may not testify to a matter unless evidence is introduced sufficient to support a finding that the witness has personal knowledge of the matter. Evidence to prove personal knowledge may, but need not, consist of the witness' own testimony.

The thing is, if the person is masked, how is the judge or jury supposed to evaluate whether or not the person is telling the truth about possessing personal knowledge? It could be anyone under there, and there can't be any witnesses who can confirm that the person here, in court, right now, is the same person who was at the scene of the incident. Indeed, the judge and jury can't really even confirm that the person on the stand is the same before and after a court recess!

The argument that this would be hard to do, or is unlikely, isn't really enough here. The mere fact that the court simply has no way *at all* of verifying who's under the mask would probably make masked testimony inadmissible.

Interestingly enough, the few times that comic book writers have put a masked character on the stand, they seem to have gotten this. So in *She-Hulk* (Vol. 1) #4, the lawyer produces an "Avengers scanner," borrowed from Stark Tower and part of the security system

---

4. Dan Slott et al., *Web of Lies*, in SHE-HULK (VOL. 1) 4 (Marvel Comics August 2004).

Even if he's right, isn't J. Jonah Jameson rich enough to afford a lawyer to make these objections for him? Dan Slott et al., *Web of Lies*, in SHE-HULK (VOL. 1) 4 (Marvel Comics August 2004).

at Avengers' Mansion. The scanner can identify any current or former Avengers, like Spider-Man, and compare them with a federal database.

The comic book is wrong that this could just sort of be produced in court, on the spot, without any problems. We're potentially looking at months, even years of legal battling to get that particular stunt admitted. But it probably is the right way to go about it, and it's certainly possible for such a thing to satisfy the court that Spider-Man's identity is verified, mask and all. The opposing attorney might still attack the idea that Spider-Man actually witnessed what he says he did—the scanner simply verifies that he's Spider-Man, not that he was at the scene—but that's true of any witness.

Verifying a witness's identity may still not be enough, however. A mask, particularly a full-face mask, makes it difficult for the judge and jury to read facial expressions and other nonverbal cues that are considered important for judging a witness's credibility. Federal Rule of Evidence 403 permits a judge to exclude evidence "if its probative value is substantially outweighed by the danger of unfair prejudice, confusion of the issues, or misleading the jury." A witness testifying in a mask is potentially both unfair and misleading. Masked testimony is unfair because other witnesses must testify with their faces exposed, and it is misleading because the jury may find it difficult to judge the witness's credibility or may even assume that the witness is lying.

The DC Universe handles this a little differently. In *The Flash* (Vol. 2) #135, an attorney mentions the "Twelfth Amendment," which permits "registered meta-humans" to testify while masked.[5] The real Twelfth Amendment was passed in 1803 and changed the procedure about the way we elect the President and Vice-President, but whatever. Note two things here. First, a constitutional amendment really might be necessary here, given the problems with masked testimony interacting with the Sixth Amendment,[6] but second, DC seems to have sneaked in superhuman registration, the very thing that sparked the Marvel *Civil War* in 2006! So while the DC workaround would be effective in the courts, it does not seem as if that universe has fully dealt with the implications of that solution.[7]

---

5. Mark Millar, Grant Morrison et al., *Death at the Top of the World Part 3*, in FLASH (VOL. 2) 135 (DC Comics March 1998).

6. Again, see chapter 1.

7. Not that *Civil War* fully dealt with much of anything, when it comes down to it, but at least the authors realized that federal registration is kind of a big deal.

Sometimes making up fictional constitutional amendments is just the way to go. Mark Millar, Grant Morrison et al., *Death at the Top of the World Part 3*, in FLASH (VOL. 2) 135 (DC Comics March 1998).

Hearsay and Telepathy

At first glance, a psychic would seem like the perfect solution to many evidentiary problems such as lying on the stand or failing to tell the whole truth. But would using a mind reader to verify a witness's testimony actually stand up in court?

Relevance

First we must ask "is the evidence relevant?" Only relevant evidence is admissible, and Federal Rule of Evidence 401 defines relevant evidence as "evidence having any tendency to make the existence of any fact that is of consequence to the determination of the action more probable or less probable than it would be without the evidence." This is a very low bar, and Federal Rule of Evidence 402 provides that relevant evidence presumptively admissible. But the question must still be asked, "Is a psychic's claim about the contents of another person's head relevant?"

We think the answer is yes. The psychic could be lying, but that's true of any witness, and the jury must judge the psychic's credibility just like any other witness's. The psychic could be a fraud, but the judge could require that the psychic's powers be proved prior to offering the substantive evidence. Federal Rule of Evidence 901(a) provides "the requirement of authentication or identification as a condition precedent to admissibility is satisfied by evidence sufficient to support a finding that the matter in question is what its proponent claims." By way of example, Federal Rule of Evidence 901(b)(9) gives "Evidence describing a process or system used to produce a result and showing that the process or system produces an accurate result." The accuracy and reliability of a psychic's power fits that example.

Exclusion under Federal Rule of Evidence 403

Relevance is only the beginning of the analysis, however. Relevant evidence may be excluded under Federal Rule of Evidence 403 "if its probative value is substantially outweighed by the danger of unfair prejudice, confusion of the issues, or misleading the jury." Of these, unfair prejudice is the greatest risk here.

The notes on Federal Rule of Evidence 403 state that "'unfair prejudice' within its context means an undue tendency to suggest decision on an improper basis, commonly, though not necessarily, an emotional one." A fact finder might unfairly prejudice a party by giving undue weight to the testimony of a psychic, possibly completely ignoring the testimony of the original witness. Psychics, after all, have supranormal abilities, and juries might be somewhat awed by them to the detriment of other testimony. However, "in reaching a decision whether to exclude on grounds of unfair prejudice, consideration should be given to the probable effectiveness or lack of effectiveness of a limiting instruction." It may suffice for the judge to remind the jury that it should also consider the testimony of the original witness.

Personal Knowledge

As discussed, Federal Rule of Evidence 602 requires that a witness have personal knowledge of the matter being testified about. This means that a fine but important distinction should be made. The psychic would not be testifying as to the actual events the original witness had personal knowledge of. Instead, a psychic would testify about his or her personal knowledge of what he or she read in the original witness's mind. It's the difference between Professor X's saying "Magneto killed Jean Grey" and his saying "I believe the original witness remembers seeing Magneto kill Jean Grey." This is a great example of why a psychic verification of a witness's testimony does not mean that the witness's testimony is necessarily accurate. Everything the psychic testifies about is ultimately coming through the lens of the original witness's senses, understanding, and memory.

In fact, Magneto was once suspected of killing Jean Grey, but the killer was actually an imposter, Xorn, who was killed by Wolverine for his trouble.[8] This is a great example of why a psychic's verification of a witness's testimony does not necessarily mean that the witness's testimony is accurate.

Hearsay

Now we come to one of the biggies. The general rule under Federal Rule of Evidence 801 is that " 'hearsay' is [an oral or written assertion or nonverbal conduct of a person, if it is intended by the person as an assertion], other than one made by [the person who made the statement] while testifying at the trial or hearing, offered in evidence to prove the truth of the matter asserted."

It's a complicated definition, to be sure, but maybe we don't have to address it. A person's thoughts are not an oral or written assertion, nor are they a nonverbal action intended as an assertion. Of course,

---

8. *See* Chuck Austen et al., *Of Darkest Nights*, in Uncanny X-Men (Vol. 1) 442–43 (Marvel Comics June–July 2004).

it is likely that in a universe with psychics and telepaths the Federal Rules of Evidence would be amended to include such things. Given that, let's complete the hearsay analysis.

Assuming thoughts fit the first part of the definition (i.e., they are an assertion), then we know the second part fits as well, since the psychic is not the person who made the statement. The final part is whether the psychic's testimony is offered to prove the matter asserted. For example, when Professor X says, "The witness remembers that Magneto killed Jean Grey," is that being offered to prove that Magneto did, in fact, kill Jean Grey? We think the answer is no; rather than being offered to prove that Magneto killed Jean Grey, the psychic's statement is only offered to prove that the witness is not lying. In lawyer-speak, we would say that the statement goes to the witness's credibility, not the truth of the matter asserted.

The Fifth Amendment

So far we have assumed that the psychic was being used to verify a witness's truthfulness. But what about using psychic powers to extract information from a witness who refuses to testify, such as a witness invoking the Fifth Amendment right against self-incrimination? For the answer to that, see chapter 1 on constitutional law.

Shape-shifters

Related to the issue of masked testimony, shape-shifters pose a potentially destabilizing effect on trial testimony, not to mention legal proceedings in general. The Marvel character Mystique can impersonate anyone, down to his or her voice. What's to stop her from replacing a witness on the stand? Even worse, couldn't she perfectly frame someone else for a crime by committing it while looking like them?

As to whether she might be able to frame people, whether or not it would *work* depends on how much forensics she's able to fake, which probably depends on the imagination of the comic book writer. But shape-shifters in court are less of a problem than it might seem at first glance.

One can perhaps think of technical means, perhaps similar to the Avengers scanner mentioned earlier, that a court could impose to verify the identity of witnesses given the possibility of a changeling impersonating them. Certain superheroes might even find some side work this way, as could enterprising inventors. But even aside from the potential cost and inconvenience, this is not something the court system would probably impose.

Why? Because juries are *already* tasked with evaluating the credibility of witnesses. No special care is taken to make sure that witnesses aren't lying, so why should special care be taken to ensure that they are who they appear to be? Indeed, witnesses must already identify themselves, and we trust juries to tell if a witness is lying about their identity. Perjury is also already a crime—and impersonating another to give testimony under oath is certainly perjury. So if we already trust juries to weigh the credibility of testimony, including the witness's claimed identity, it would seem that the problem of shape changers is an issue of degree rather than kind.

Note that this is a slightly different issue from simply testifying with a mask on. In that case, the court knows for a fact that it cannot tell who is under there. But a true shape-shifter would be able to fool it completely, never giving rise to the issue that the person testifying might not be who he says he is.

The reason that the legal system puts such faith in juries and takes so few preventive steps to prevent perjury is the system's reliance on cross-examination. Cross-examination is the part in a trial in which a witness is questioned by the opposing attorney, a process that witnesses universally report is No Fun At All. The attorney is deliberately attempting to catch and exploit inconsistencies, however minor, in the witness's testimony, and even an entirely truthful, honest witness can be made to appear pretty silly by a skilled trial lawyer. A good discussion of how this works and the ways in which a cross-examiner can accomplish his or her objectives can be found in Irving Younger's "Ten Commandments of Cross-Examination."[9]

The reliance placed upon cross-examination is so great that it underpins one of the most fundamental rights in criminal procedure: the right to confront witnesses. If an attorney is not able to convince a jury through cross-examination that a witness is either lying or unreliable or is a changeling in disguise, that's basically just too damn bad.

This is because testifying in court is different from having a discussion with friends over a few beers; there are stringent rules for what can be said and what cannot be said, and the attorney not doing the questioning has every interest in seeing that they are enforced. Remember how in all those law shows attorneys are always yelling "Objection!" That's because they're trying to draw the judge's attention to what they believe (or would like the judge to believe) is a violation of the rules of evidence, although in the real world the reason for the objection also has to be given.

Even an honest witness can be tripped up by a skilled attorney. How much more a witness who does not actually have first-hand knowledge of the testimony being offered? Even a shape-shifting telepath is going to have a really hard time slipping one past an attorney who knows what he or she is doing. By the time a witness appears on the stand, particularly in a case of any significance, both attorneys pretty much know what their respective witnesses have to say. They will all have given extensive depositions, and the trial process is less a revelation of new evidence than it is a formal way of entering that evidence into the record. Any deviation from a deposition is likely to be noticed by the examining attorney and immediately pounced on, assuming the attorney is adequately prepared. It will quickly become

---

9. The commandments were published in IRVING YOUNGER, THE ART OF CROSS-EXAMINATION (1976), but they are also readily available online.

clear to the judge and the jury that something fishy is going on, and at that point the jig is up; either the doppelgänger will be revealed, or the damage to the case intended by the shape-shifter will be avoided.

At this point, other laws come in to play. "Subornation of perjury"[10] is itself a crime, so a party or an attorney who solicited the shape-shifter to replace a witness is in big trouble, and tampering with evidence in this way could well be a violation of discovery rules. Federal Rule of Civil Procedure 37 and its state equivalents permit a judge to impose a variety of sanctions on a party that does not cooperate with the discovery process, up to and including both contempt of court and ruling that the record treat the issue in question as conclusively established for the opposing party. The attorney could also be sanctioned directly under Federal Rule 11, particularly if he or she knew about the scheme.

---

10. A fancy way of saying "asking someone else to commit perjury."

CHAPTER 4

Criminal Procedure

"Look, I know what you're here for. Think you gonna scare us out. Like we're gonna start shakin' and sayin' 'Oh, Superman, don't hurt us! Don't zap us with your eye-beams!' You can't do **squat**, S. You got to abide by the law same as everybody else. You can't go **inside** any of our cribs, you can't **take** anything, you can't force us to **move**, you can't do **jack**."

So says the rather courageous drug dealer in the first issue of the *Superman: Grounded* story arc.[1] It turns out that the guy is probably *wrong*, but rather than correct him or simply move on, Superman makes the rather counterintuitive move of trading up from a misdemeanor trespass, what the thug says is off limits, to full-on felony arson. Way to go, Supes.

What Superman and this guy are fighting about is the body of law known as "criminal procedure." This is distinct from what lawyers refer to as "criminal law," the subject of chapter 2, in that "criminal

---

1. J. Michael Straozynski et al., *Grounded Prologue: The Slap Heard 'Round the World*, in Superman (Vol. 1) 700 (DC Comics August 2010).

Stymied by an incorrect interpretation of criminal procedure, Superman decides to engage in a little harmless felony arson. J. Michael Straczynski et al., *Grounded Prologue: The Slap Heard 'Round the World*, in SUPERMAN (VOL. 1) 701 (DC Comics September 2010).

law" has to do with the definitions and elements of various crimes, while "criminal procedure" has to do with the mechanics of prosecuting and defending criminal charges. Although the word "procedure" suggests tedious detail and arcane rules, criminal procedure is actually an important area of the law that you probably know more about than you might think. Criminal procedure encompasses such vital safeguards as the right to a jury trial, the right to remain silent, and the prohibition against double jeopardy. In fact, it's such a fundamental part of the law that much of it comes from the Constitution, and the authors of the Constitution got many of the ideas from Magna Carta, the English feudal charter which dates all the way back to AD 1215. But while you may have heard about many of these topics in high school civics class (or while watching *Law & Order* episodes), the details—and limitations—of these rules may surprise you.

First, a Brief Word About State Action

A recurring theme in this chapter will be the difference between how the law treats the government and how it treats private actors. Most of criminal procedure is about limitations on what the *government* can do, and the flip side is that private actors generally aren't subject to the same limitations. This is part of the "state action requirement," and as we saw in chapter 1, this works in favor of freelance superheroes, but superheroes that work for the government will have to follow the same rules as regular police. This is really where the State Action section of chapter 1 comes into play in a big way.

Investigation and the Fourth Amendment

Let's turn back to the confrontation between Superman and the drug dealer for a minute. The dealer is essentially asserting that Superman can't do anything about the drug dealer's activities without violating rules of civil procedure, specifically those having to do with criminal investigations. Investigations can occur while a crime is still being planned, while it's in progress, or after it's been committed. Most superheroes deal with the first two scenarios, although sometimes they investigate crime scenes to figure out where a villain might strike next. But regardless of the circumstances of the investigation, the biggest issue is, as the drug dealer suggests, whether the evidence gathered during the investigation will be admissible in court after the villain is arrested. This brings us to the Fourth Amendment.[2] The text of the amendment is short and relatively straightforward:

> The right of the people to be secure in their persons, houses, papers, and effects, against unreasonable searches and seizures, shall not be violated, and no Warrants shall issue, but upon probable cause, supported by Oath or affirmation, and particularly describing the place to be searched, and the persons or things to be seized.[3]

---

2. One could be excused for wondering why this subject wasn't covered in chapter 1, when we talked about constitutional law. It turns out that "criminal procedure" is sometimes called "constitutional criminal procedure," because so many of the issues have their origin in the Constitution. But legal scholars generally recognize criminal procedure as being a distinct subset of constitutional law and treat it as its own subject. Generally speaking, "constitutional law" refers to the size and powers of the federal government, its interaction with state governments, and civil rights other than those involving criminal law.

3. U.S. Const. amend. IV.

There are really two separate ideas here. First, there is the general rule that unreasonable searches and seizures are prohibited. Second, an otherwise unreasonable search or seizure can be made after obtaining a warrant, which in turn requires probable cause. The exact definition of probable cause is slippery, but "the substance of all the definitions of probable cause is a reasonable ground for belief of guilt."[4] It is something "more than bare suspicion" but also "less than evidence that would justify . . . conviction."[5]

Finally, bear in mind that the limitations of the Fourth Amendment generally only apply to state actors. Superheroes who work closely with the police (e.g., Batman) and superpowered police officers (e.g., agents of S.H.I.E.L.D., certain versions of the Avengers) must abide by the Fourth Amendment, but superheroes acting as private citizens do not. However, we will discuss the rules for citizen's arrest in this chapter, which of course do apply to private citizens, and all of the procedural rules for trials (such as pleading the Fifth) apply whether a cop or a superhero arrested the supervillain.

Searches

As noted, the Constitution protects people from *unreasonable* searches, and there is a two-part test for determining whether a given search is reasonable or not. "[F]irst that a person have exhibited an actual (subjective) expectation of privacy and, second, that the expectation be one that society is prepared to recognize as 'reasonable.'"[6] For the Fourth Amendment to apply, both of these requirements must be met. The person in question must actually believe he or she had an expectation of privacy, and "society" (e.g., jurors and judges) must agree that the belief was reasonable.

So what does this mean for superheroes? Two superpowers that

---

4. Brinegar v. United States, 338 U.S. 160, 175 (1949).

5. *Id.*

6. Katz v. United States, 389 U.S. 347, 361 (1967) (Harlan, J., concurring).

police would love to use when investigating crimes are X-ray vision and psychic powers. Unfortunately, using such powers would probably be an unreasonable search.

X-ray vision is often used to look through walls and inside containers. It's not much of a stretch to imagine that when people put something behind a wall or inside a box, they intend for it to be private, and that expectation of privacy is reasonable since most people can't see through walls. In fact, the Supreme Court has held that the police need a warrant to use special thermal imaging cameras to see warm objects through walls (e.g., marijuana growing lights).[7] The Court held that "obtaining by sense enhancing technology any information regarding the interior of the home that could not otherwise have been obtained without physical intrusion into a constitutionally protected area constitutes a search—at least where . . . the technology in question is not in general public use."[8]

X-ray vision is not a sense-enhancing *technology*, but it is an unusual ability not in general public use. For example, even though Superman can see through the walls of a house, people in Metropolis still have a reasonable expectation that what goes on in their homes is private. Thus, if Superman or another character with X-ray vision (e.g., the Martian Manhunter) works for the police, they'll need a warrant to use that power to investigate crime.

So it turns out the drug dealer in the example at the beginning of the chapter is partially right and partially wrong. If Superman was a police officer, he probably couldn't use his X-ray vision to locate the drug stashes. Or, at least, any evidence obtained using X-ray vision in the absence of a warrant or justification for a warrantless search would be inadmissible. In that sense, from a perspective of being used to dealing with mundane law enforcement agencies, the dealer is right. But in this particular story, Superman doesn't have any particular connection with any particular government agency,

---

7. Kyllo v. United States, 533 U.S. 27 (2001).

8. *Id.* at 34–35.

official or otherwise. So there probably wouldn't be a problem with him using his powers to locate the stashes and then calling in an anonymous tip. This sort of thing happens all the time, and the police don't really need much more than that in most cases.

The same is true of psychic powers like the mind reading powers of Professor X. If there is anywhere that people have a reasonable expectation of privacy it is in their own thoughts. Believe it or not, the Supreme Court has indirectly addressed this issue! Justice Brandeis, dissenting from the (later overturned) decision that wiretaps were not a search, said, "Advances in the psychic and related sciences may bring means of exploring unexpressed beliefs, thoughts and emotions. . . . Can it be that the Constitution affords no protection against such invasions of individual security?"[9] Just as the Supreme Court later recognized that wiretaps are a form of search,[10] no doubt the Court would hold that mind reading likewise requires a warrant.

Two other powers that technology already provides the police are superhearing and highly acute visible light vision, in the form of powerful directional microphones and devices such as binoculars and telescopes. Just like their technological equivalents, both superpowers are likely to require a warrant when observing the inside of a home[11] but not when searching outside the home (e.g., a backyard or a public place).[12]

---

9. Olmstead v. United States, 277 U.S. 438, 474 (1928) (Brandeis, J., dissenting).

10. *Katz*, 389 U.S. at 347.

11. *Kyllo*, 533 U.S. at 35 (comparing a "powerful directional microphone" with the thermal imager at issue in the case); United States v. Agapito, 620 F.2d 324, 330 (2d Cir. 1980) (making a distinction between permissible eavesdropping by the naked human ear and the impermissible warrantless use of listening devices); United States v. Taborda, 635 F.2d 131, 139 (2d Cir. 1980) ("[O]bservation of objects and activities inside a person's home by unenhanced vision from a location where the observer may properly be does not impair a legitimate expectation of privacy. However, any enhanced viewing of the interior of a home does impair a legitimate expectation of privacy.").

12. *See, e.g.*, Fullbright v. United States, 392 F.2d 432, 434 (10th Cir. 1968) (holding the use of binoculars to observe a backyard shed did not violate the Fourth Amendment).

Exceptions

There are several exceptions to the general rule that a search warrant is required, and we will discuss four of them: "stop and frisk" situations, searches incident to an arrest, exigent circumstances, and airports and other special environments. These searches have all been held to be reasonable by the Supreme Court, which means that a warrant is not required. However, they are each limited in the circumstances in which they are allowed and in the scope of what may be searched.

Stop and Frisk

First, and perhaps most importantly, is the "stop and frisk" exception. This exception allows a police officer who reasonably suspects "that criminal activity may be afoot and that the persons with whom he is dealing may be armed and dangerous" to identify himself as a police officer, make reasonable inquiries, and, if still reasonably fearful of his own or others' safety, to "conduct a carefully limited search of the outer clothing of such persons in an attempt to discover weapons which might be used to assault him."[13]

The "outer clothing" limitation suggests that the use of X-ray vision may be permitted so long as it is limited to the outer clothing. On the other hand, a general mind-reading search would probably not be permitted, since

> [t]he sole justification of the search in the present situation
> is the protection of the police officer and others nearby, and
> it must therefore be confined in scope to an intrusion reason-
> ably designed to discover guns, knives, clubs, or other hidden
> instruments for the assault of the police officer.[14]

---

13. Terry v. Ohio, 392 U.S. 1, 30 (1968).

14. *Id.* at 29.

Mind reading may be too broad unless it is limited to scanning for thoughts about hidden weapons or intent to assault the officer.

Searches After an Arrest

The police may search a person after arresting them, although there are again limits to the scope of the search. The arresting officer may "search the person arrested in order to remove any weapons that the latter might seek to use in order to resist arrest or effect his escape" and "search for and seize any evidence on the arrestee's person in order to prevent its concealment or destruction."[15]

Even given these limitations, both X-ray vision and limited mind reading could be used here. X-ray vision is useful as a way to quickly search for concealed weapons or evidence, and mind reading may reveal the arrestee's plans to attack the arresting officer, attempt an escape, or destroy evidence.

Exigent Circumstances

A warrant is not required "when the exigencies of the situation make the needs of law enforcement so compelling that a warrantless search is objectively reasonable under the Fourth Amendment."[16] Over the years the courts have established several examples of such exigent circumstances, including rendering emergency assistance,[17] pursuing a fleeing suspect,[18] and preventing the imminent destruction of evidence.[19] These exceptions are available even when the police created the exigent circumstances, as long as the police acted lawfully.[20] An example of this might be a police officer's entering a bystander's

15. Chimel v. California, 395 U.S. 752, 763 (1969).

16. Kentucky v. King, 131 S. Ct. 1849, 1856 (2011).

17. Michigan v. Fisher, 130 S. Ct. 546, 548 (2010).

18. United States v. Santana, 427 U.S. 38, 42–43 (1976).

19. Brigham City v. Stuart, 547 U.S. 398, 403 (2006).

20. *King*, 131 S. Ct. at 1862.

house if the officer thinks a stray bullet from a firefight may have hurt someone inside.

As you might imagine, this is an important exception for superheroes, who often find themselves rendering emergency assistance and pursuing suspects through buildings. The exigent circumstances doctrine allows superpowered police to make use of evidence of other crimes they discover while doing so.

Airports and Other Special Environments

Routine searches are allowed at airports, subway stations, border crossings, prisons, and other special environments: "where the risk to public safety is substantial and real, blanket suspicionless searches calibrated to the risk may rank as 'reasonable'—for example, the searches now routine at airports and at entrances to courts and other official buildings. But where . . . public safety is not genuinely in jeopardy, the Fourth Amendment precludes the suspicionless search, no matter how conveniently arranged."[21] Such searches are also called "special needs searches" because they serve "special governmental needs, beyond the normal need for law enforcement."[22] In such cases "it is necessary to balance the individual's privacy expectations against the Government's interests to determine whether it is impractical to require a warrant or some level of individualized suspicion in the particular context."[23] That balancing test is based on four factors: "(1) the weight and immediacy of the government interest, (2) the nature of the privacy interest allegedly compromised by the search, (3) the character of the intrusion imposed by the search, and (4) the efficacy of the search in advancing the government interest."[24]

---

21. Chandler v. Miller, 520 U.S. 305, 323 (1997). See also United States v. Aukai, 497 F.3d 955 (9th Cir. 2007) (upholding airport searches even without consent); MacWade v. Kelly, 460 F.3d 260 (2d Cir. 2006) (upholding random subway searches).

22. Nat'l Treasury Employees Union v. Von Raab, 489 U.S. 656, 665 (1989).

23. Id. at 665–66.

24. MacWade, 460 F.3d at 269 (citing Bd. of Educ. v. Earls, 536 U.S. 822 (2002)).

One can easily imagine the tremendous value that X-ray vision and mind reading would have at an airport or subway station. The constitutionality of searches by X-ray vision seems well established by the constitutionality of existing X-ray searches, including modern body scanners.

The case for mind reading is somewhat harder to make. Following the four-factor test, the weight and immediacy of the government interest is the same as for other searches. As the Second Circuit put it, "We need not labor the point with respect to need; the success of the FAA's anti-hijacking program should not obscure the enormous dangers to life and property from terrorists [and] ordinary criminals."[25] On the other hand, a person undoubtedly has a reasonable expectation of privacy in his or her own thoughts. The constitutionality of mind reading in the security context likely hinges on the third and fourth factors: the character of the intrusion and the efficacy of the search. If mind reading is painful, lengthy, stigmatizing, or ineffective then a court might hold that, on balance, it does not meet constitutional muster, even in the airport security context.

Fourth Amendment Violations

So what happens when the police violate the Fourth Amendment? There are two major consequences. The first is the exclusionary rule, under which evidence obtained in violation of the Fourth Amendment may not be admitted at trial.[26] Furthermore, any evidence derived from such tainted evidence is "fruit of the poisonous tree" and likewise cannot be admitted.[27] There are several exceptions to

---

25. United States v. Edwards, 498 F.2d 496, 500 (2d Cir. 1974).

26. The exclusionary rule has its origin in the English common law. *See, e.g.,* Roe v. Harvey, 98 Eng. Rep. 302 (K.B. 1769). However, it was not until Weeks v. United States, 232 U.S. 383 (1914), that the rule as we know it today came into existence in the United States.

27. Silverthorne Lumber Co. v. United States, 251 U.S. 385, 391–92 (1920). The phrase "fruit of the poisonous tree" comes from Nardone v. United States, 308 U.S. 338, 341 (1939).

this rule, however. Tainted evidence may still be admitted if it can also be derived from an untainted source,[28] if it would have been discovered inevitably,[29] or if the connection between the lawless conduct and the discovery of the tainted evidence has become so attenuated as to dissipate the taint.[30]

The second consequence is a civil lawsuit. Local and state police may be sued under 42 U.S.C. §1983, and federal officers may be sued directly under the Constitution in what is known as a *"Bivens* action."[31] The standard for these suits is a high one, though. The official may invoke a qualified immunity, which requires that the plaintiff prove that the official "knew or reasonably should have known that the action he took within his sphere of official responsibility would violate the constitutional rights of the [plaintiff], or if he took the action with the malicious intention to cause a deprivation of constitutional rights or other injury."[32]

Arrest

Once a superpowered police officer or citizen superhero has gathered evidence of a crime, under what circumstances can they arrest the suspect? As with searches, the rules are different depending on whether a warrant has been obtained or not. The rule for arrest warrants is simple: Like search warrants, they require probable cause. Also, like search warrants, there are exceptions to this rule. Thankfully, the exceptions are simpler.

First, though, we should briefly define what *arrest* means. "[A]

---

28. *Silverthorne Lumber,* 251 U.S. at 392.

29. Nix v. Williams, 467 U.S. 431 (1984).

30. *Nardone,* 308 U.S. at 341.

31. Bivens v. Six Unknown Named Agents, 403 U.S. 388 (1971).

32. Harlow v. Fitzgerald, 457 U.S. 800, 815 (1982). This is also known as the "good faith" defense.

A reasonable person would probably not feel free to leave after Captain America tells them "you're under arrest." Then again, Daredevil may not fit in most people's definition of "reasonable person." Mark Waid, Paolo Rivera et al., *Red, White, Black and Blue*, in DAREDEVIL (VOL. 3) 2 (Marvel Comics October 2011).

person has been 'seized' [i.e., arrested] within the meaning of the Fourth Amendment only if, in view of all of the circumstances surrounding the incident, a reasonable person would have believed that he was not free to leave."[33] There's no requirement to say "you're under arrest" or to slap handcuffs on the suspect. As long as a reasonable person would not feel free to leave, he or she is under arrest as far as the Constitution is concerned. However, most reasonable people would not feel free to leave if they are told "you're under arrest."

Warrantless Arrests for Police and Citizens

The general rule is that a police officer may arrest any person without a warrant if the officer has probable cause to believe that the person committed a crime. In some states, the police officer must have observed the crime firsthand unless it was a felony.[34]

Private citizens, on the other hand, are more restricted. The most common restriction is that a private citizen can only lawfully arrest someone when that person has in fact committed a crime.[35] If the private citizen is wrong, then they may be liable for false arrest, whereas the police would not be. Some states go further, only allowing citizen's arrest in felony cases or in cases where the crime was committed in the arresting person's presence.[36]

The practical upshot is that superheroes had better know their legal environment. They risk criminal and civil liability if they arrest someone who hasn't actually committed a crime, so they need to be sure of the situation before swinging into action. And this is

---

33. United States v. Mendenhall, 446 U.S. 544, 554 (1980).

34. *See, e.g.,* Cal. Penal Code § 836. New York makes a similar distinction between offenses (i.e., anything punishable by imprisonment or a fine) and crimes (i.e., misdemeanors and felonies). N.Y. Crim. Proc. Law § 140.10. Offenses include minor violations such as traffic tickets.

35. *See, e.g.,* Cal. Penal Code § 837; N.Y. Crim. Proc. Law § 140.30.

36. *See, e.g.,* Ind. Code Ann. § 35-41-3-3 (only felony arrests allowed); C.R.S.A. § 18-1-707 (crime must be committed in arresting person's presence).

probably a good thing; we wouldn't want superheroes smashing heads or tying people up in webs on a hunch. Superheroes need to know what kind of crime has been committed, what evidence is required (because if the suspect isn't convicted the superhero may face charges), and what kind of force the superhero can use. The rules for the use of deadly force are another state-by-state patchwork, so to be on the safe side, superheroes should stick to non-deadly force. Luckily many of them do that already.

Miranda Rights

You are probably familiar with the *Miranda* warning:

> "You have the right to remain silent. Anything you say or do can and will be held against you in a court of law. You have the right to speak to an attorney. If you cannot afford an attorney, one will be appointed for you. Do you understand these rights as they have been read to you?"[37]

But what does this warning really mean? There are three parts to the warning. First, the suspect is reminded of his or her Fifth Amendment right to silence.[38] That is, the suspect has a right to be silent during interrogation and a right not to incriminate himself or herself at trial. Second, the suspect has a Sixth Amendment right to an attorney. Third, in order for the warning to be meaningful, the suspect must understand it.[39]

---

37. The exact wording of the warning can vary, but this example is typical.

38. The Fifth Amendment states that "No person . . . shall be compelled in any criminal case to be a witness against himself," which the courts have interpreted as including a right to remain silent. U.S. CONST., Amend. V.

39. In *Miranda v. Arizona*, 384 U.S. 436 (1966), the Supreme Court required that "[p]rior to any questioning, the person must be warned that he has a right to remain silent, that any statement he does make may be used as evidence against him, and that he has a right to the presence of an attorney, either retained or appointed. The defendant may

So that's what the warning means, but what are the consequences if the police don't give the warning, as Captain America didn't when he arrested Daredevil? If the police do not give the warning—or if the suspect did not understand it—then testimonial evidence from the suspect resulting from police interrogation is inadmissible against the defendant in a criminal case.[40] However, because this is a product of the Fifth Amendment, not the Fourth, the doctrine of the fruit of the poisonous tree (discussed earlier) does not apply. As a result, the police can use the information for other purposes, such as continuing the investigation, and evidence derived from the suspect's testimony may be admitted as well.

Thus, in the Daredevil case, nothing Daredevil said to Captain America could be used against Daredevil. However, Captain America could use Daredevil's claim that Daredevil was "turned into a hand puppet" to continue his investigation into the crimes Daredevil allegedly committed, and the admissibility of any evidence that he found during that investigation would not be affected by his failure to give Daredevil a *Miranda* warning.

Criminal Procedure at Trial

We have already discussed how the Fourth Amendment exclusionary rule and *Miranda* affect the admissibility of evidence at trial, but there are other constitutional rights that come into play during the trial phase, including the right not to testify at all and the right not to testify against oneself. Both of these rights are derived from the Fifth Amendment.

Just as in the real world, comic book superheroes that find them-

---

waive effectuation of these rights, provided the waiver is made voluntarily, knowingly and intelligently."

40. *Miranda*, 384 U.S. at 476–77.

Vance Astrovik (a.k.a. Marvel Boy) made use of his Fifth Amendment rights and declined to testify in his own defense. Smart move. Fabian Nicieza et al., *Nothing But the Truth Part Two*, in NEW WARRIORS (VOL. 1) 23 (Marvel Comics May 1992).

selves accused of a crime rarely waive these rights and take the stand in their own defense. Also just as in the real world, sometimes superhero defendants want to take the stand and must be talked out of it by their attorneys.[41] Once a defendant takes the stand, the prosecution can ask a lot of uncomfortable questions. It is often better to force the prosecution to find other ways of proving issues, such as where the defendant was at the time of the alleged crime—remember,

---

41. Ultimately, the decision to testify is the defendant's, and an attorney must let a client take the stand even if the attorney believes it would harm the client's case. MODEL RULES OF PROF'L CONDUCT R. 1.2(a).

Captain America tried to convince Bucky Barnes's attorney, Bernie Rosenthal, to put Bucky on the stand. In the end, Bucky followed his attorney's advice and did not testify. Ed Brubaker et al., *The Trial of Captain America Part 2*, in CAPTAIN AMERICA (VOL. 1) 612 (Marvel Comics January 2011).

innocent until proven guilty. Taking the stand means that the prosecution can ask the defendant directly.

However, even though a defendant has agreed to testify, that does not waive the right not to incriminate oneself. A defendant can still "plead the Fifth" and refuse to answer questions that would tend to incriminate himself or herself. In fact, the right not to incriminate oneself applies to all witnesses in court, even civil cases, and even to nonparties (i.e., people who are not a plaintiff or defendant). The government can get around this by imposing immunity on the witness: If the witness is immune to prosecution, then he or she can be compelled to answer questions that would otherwise incriminate him or her.[42] This method is often used to force a member of a conspiracy to testify against the other coconspirators.

---

42. Kastigar v. United States, 406 U.S. 441 (1972).

CHAPTER 5

Tort Law and Insurance

In *She-Hulk* (Vol. 1) #4, Spider-Man sues J. Jonah Jameson for libel.[1] In #6, Hank Pym is threatened with a lawsuit for injuries allegedly caused by exposure to Pym particles, including violent mood swings and cancer.[2] More generally speaking, superheroes and supervillains do all kinds of things, which, if you or I did them, would tend to land us in civil court. This chapter focuses on the implications of tort law for comic books.

A "tort" is simply a wrong that is the grounds for a *civil* lawsuit, as opposed to a wrong that is the grounds for a *criminal* lawsuit. Criminal prosecutions are brought by the state for violations of the law and if a defendant is found guilty, the state can impose fines and jail time. But in many cases, the victim of a crime can bring his own lawsuit seeking compensation for his damages. For example, if a person injures someone in a bar fight, they can be both prosecuted by the state for assault *and* sued by the injured party for bodily in-

---

1. Dan Slott et al., *Web of Lies*, in She-Hulk (Vol. 1) 4 (Marvel Comics August 2004). This does not go exactly as planned, but more on that later.

2. Dan Slott et al., *Minor Complications*, in She-Hulk (Vol. 1) 6 (Marvel Comics October 2004).

jury. This chapter focuses exclusively on the latter, civil side of the equation.

Privacy

We discussed telepathy in chapters 1 and 3, but what about civil liability? When Professor X or Jean Grey read a person's mind, are there grounds for a lawsuit based on the invasion of privacy? Similarly, many superheroes take great pains to keep their mundane identities secret. If a superhero was "outed" against his will, would he have a cause of action against the person who revealed his identity?

Both of these questions, and many more, have to do with privacy rights.[3] The Restatement (Second) of Torts describes the general principle of the right to privacy as follows:

1. One who invades the right of privacy of another is subject to liability for the resulting harm to the interests of the other.
2. The right of privacy is invaded by
   a. unreasonable intrusion upon the seclusion of another . . . ; or
   b. appropriation of the other's name or likeness . . . ; or
   c. unreasonable publicity given to the other's private life . . . ; or

---

3. Note that this is entirely different from the "right to privacy" recognized by the Supreme Court in *Griswold v. Connecticut*, 381 U.S. 479 (1965), in which the Court recognized a constitutional right to privacy. That case, and the cases that stem from it, have to do with governmental intrusion into arguably private affairs. Here, we discuss the law related to individual intrusion into the privacy of other individuals. The Constitution does not really apply to these cases. Remember the state actor doctrine.

>   d. publicity that unreasonably places the other in a
>   false light before the public. . . . [4]

So right away we see there are a number of different ways the law recognizes that privacy may be invaded. Simply prying into another's affairs can be actionable. But so is using another person's "name or likeness" in unauthorized ways, or publicizing the details of their private life. This is especially true when the publicity might lead to false inferences about a person.

There is an Alabama case, *Phillips v. Smalley Maintenance Services, Inc.*,[5] which, while obviously not dealing with telepathy, contains a number of holdings that are of interest here. The court focused its analysis on the "Intrusion upon Seclusion" privacy tort, which the Restatement defines as follows: "One who intentionally intrudes, physically or otherwise, upon the solitude or seclusion of another or his private affairs or concerns, is subject to liability to the other for invasion of his privacy, if the intrusion would be highly offensive to a reasonable person."[6] In considering that tort, the court held, first, that "acquisition of information" is not actually necessary to ground an invasion of privacy tort. Second, there can be liability even when information about the plaintiff's private life is not communicated to a third party. Third, the "wrongful intrusion" tort does not require that the defendant be ignorant of the intrusion when it occurs. Perhaps most significantly, "One's emotional sanctum is certainly due the same expectations of privacy as one's physical environment."[7]

---

4. RESTATEMENT (SECOND) OF TORTS § 652A. Restatements of the law are scholarly works that attempt to set forth the majority position on particular areas of law or recommended changes to the majority position. They mostly cover subjects that are still primarily common law rather than those based on legislation. The Restatements are not laws themselves, but courts often find them persuasive, and many sections of various Restatements have been adopted as law by state courts.

5. 435 So. 2d 705 (1983).

6. RESTATEMENT (SECOND) OF TORTS at § 652B.

7. *Id.* at 711.

An important thing to remember here is that while superheroes may seem different from ordinary people, this may not matter in assessing their privacy rights. The offensiveness of an intrusion is judged by the standard of an ordinary, reasonable person, not a superhero.[8] Furthermore, "the intrusion must be of such a character as would shock the ordinary person to the point of emotional distress."[9]

Let us then consider the issue of telepathy. The *Phillips* ruling will be particularly important here. For starters, involuntary telepathic reading would certainly seem to be an "intrusion" on one's "solitude" or "seclusion," particularly into one's "emotional sanctum," and this is usually presented as "highly offensive" in most comic book stories where the issue arises. But more than that, the *Phillips* ruling might even apply to mere empathic gifts, where the user can determine another's emotional state. Prying into other people's hearts is just as problematic as prying into their thoughts. The telepath/empath does not even need to tell anyone about what he learns; the mere fact that the person who was read knows about the intrusion is enough.

Granted, some of these things will probably be important in determining damages. In the *Phillips* case, a woman was wrongfully terminated when she resisted the sexual advances of her boss and suffered chronic anxiety for which she underwent psychological treatment. The damages there are pretty easy to understand. But while a character who is briefly "read" by Professor X but who suffers no ill effects may be able to win a lawsuit, the character is going to need to introduce some evidence as to the nature of his injury if he wants to win more than nominal damages or an injunction against future mind reading.[10]

---

8. William Prosser, *Privacy*, 48 CALIF. L. REV. 383, 397 (1960).

9. Roe ex rel. Roe v. Heap, 2004 Ohio 2504, (Ohio Ct. App. 2004).

10. Note that if the telepath violated the injunction, then he or she could be found in contempt of court and subjected to a substantial fine, even if the actual damage done was still minimal. The fine would be paid to the court, however, and not the victim.

But telepathy isn't the only kind of privacy that comes up in comic books, and the issue of secret identities implicates a number of potential privacy torts. A superhero might be able to sue someone who is intruding into the superhero's secret identity for invasion of privacy, if the intrusion was big enough. Merely asking about or even forcefully demanding to know a superhero's identity would probably not "shock the ordinary person to the point of emotional distress." However, actions like ripping off a superhero's mask or demanding the answer at gunpoint likely would qualify, even if the superhero was impervious to bullets.[11] So might engaging in a consistent pattern of intruding into or investigating the secret identity at every opportunity in a stalker-ish way. One way to consider it is, would an ordinary, reasonable person feel coerced into giving up his or her secret identity? Given the danger posed to a superhero and his or her family by exposure, such coercion would cause severe emotional distress.

Or consider the situation in *The Dark Knight*, where the Joker puts pressure on Batman to reveal his true identity by threatening not only Rachel Dawes, but also random civilians. It is not hard to argue that a public figure of the sort that Batman had become in the film would reasonably feel coerced—Wayne would have revealed himself if Dent had not stepped in—by a threat like that one. So if anything, the unusual situation most superheroes find themselves in, particularly those who are more or less explicitly dedicated to public service, means the range of potential coercion adequate to ground such a tort would appear to be quite broad.

Even more, the scope of this tort is not limited to supervillains. A subplot of *The Dark Knight* involves a consultant threatening to go public with Batman's real identity. While the Joker probably wouldn't care all that much about being served with a civil lawsuit (Any volunteers for that job? No?), trying to blackmail someone like

---

11. The ordinary person standard strikes again.

Bruce Wayne by threatening to go public is a spectacularly bad idea, even aside from the do-you-really-want-to-blackmail-Batman? bit.

Similarly, in the *She-Hulk* issue where Spider-Man sues J. Jonah Jameson for libel, it would have made sense to include a claim for invasion of privacy as well. Not only is it simply good sense to include as many potential claims as possible,[12] but that particular claim would probably have led to a very different outcome. In the story, Peter Parker is put on the stand because Spider-Man's lawyer does not know that Parker is actually Spider-Man.[13] The attorney then names Parker as a codefendant in the suit against Jameson and the *Daily Bugle*,[14] convincing Spider-Man to settle, as there was an excellent argument that Parker was involved in the libelous conduct of the *Bugle*. But the invasion of privacy claim would probably have turned out differently because although Jameson had expressed a dedicated and obsessive interest in exposing Spider-Man to the world, Parker had expressed no such intention and had simply taken the kind of pictures that any public figure could expect to be taken.

All of that being the case, it is important to remember that the law makes a distinction between intruding on someone's privacy and publicizing private information about someone's personal life. The two are independent torts. And, unfortunately, most superheroes will likely have trouble pursuing the second one. The Restatement defines the publicity tort as follows:

> One who gives publicity to a matter concerning the private
> life of another is subject to liability to the other for invasion
> of his privacy, if the matter publicized is of a kind that

---

12. If they aren't included then they may be waived.

13. This is just another reason why masked superheroes are problematic for the Rules of Evidence.

14. Which is probably a violation of the rules of civil procedure. Any potential defendants need to be named in the pleadings and properly served. Trial is far, far too late in the litigation process to be naming additional parties.

a. would be highly offensive to a reasonable person, and

b. is not of legitimate concern to the public.[15]

The reason for (b) is the First Amendment. A 1983 California case discussed the issue in some detail:

[T]he right to privacy is not absolute and must be balanced against the often competing constitutional right of the press to publish newsworthy matters. The First Amendment protection from tort liability is necessary if the press is to carry out its constitutional obligation to keep the public informed so that they may make intelligent decisions on matters important to a self-governing people. However, the newsworthy privilege is not without limitation. Where the publicity is so offensive as to constitute a "morbid and sensational prying into private lives for its own sake, . . ." it serves no legitimate public interest and is not deserving of protection.[16]

Note the phrase "matters important to a self-governing people." The courts are interested in protecting the freedom of the press, in no small part because that is viewed as an essential ingredient in a democratic society. As a result, whether or not a particular superhero can recover for someone publishing the details of his secret identity probably depends on the superhero. Bruce Wayne is a billionaire industrialist who is involved in politics through donations and fundraising, and his secret identity as Batman might well be a "matter important to a self-governing people" about which the public should be informed. But Spider-Man's alter ego is just a working stiff, a news photographer and, perhaps most importantly, is often written as a minor. The public probably doesn't have as much of an interest

---

15. Restatement (Second) of Torts § 652D.

16. Diaz v. Oakland Tribune, 139 Cal. App. 3d 118, 126 (Cal. Ct. App. 1983).

in knowing those details. Thus, whether or not a particular masked character will be able to recover for someone publicizing his secret identity will likely be a fact-intensive analysis wherein the court would balance the First Amendment interests in freedom of the press against the privacy interests of the individual in question.

There is another kind of invasion of privacy about which super-heroes might be concerned: appropriation of one's name or likeness, particularly in the context of advertising or merchandising. The Fan-

Booster Gold discovers the perils of signing over his right of publicity. Dan Jurgens et al., *When Glass Houses Shatter,* in BOOSTER GOLD (VOL. 1) 11 (DC Comics December 1986).

tastic Four actually run their own *gift shop*, and would probably take it quite ill if someone else started to sell goods with their names, faces, or logos.[17] And there are several examples of superheroes endorsing products (e.g., Booster Gold and the Boostermobile), so it's important to consider what could be done about it if a false endorsement were attributed to a superhero. Here we have two distinct torts to discuss: appropriation and the right of publicity. As the Nevada Supreme Court opined:

> The distinction between these two torts is the interest each seeks to protect. The appropriation tort seeks to protect an individual's personal interest in privacy; the personal injury is measured in terms of the mental anguish that results from the appropriation of an ordinary individual's identity. The right to publicity seeks to protect the property interest that a celebrity has in his or her name; the injury is not to personal privacy, it is the economic loss a celebrity suffers when someone else interferes with the property interest that he or she has in his or her name. We consider it critical in deciding this case that recognition be given to the difference between the personal, injured-feelings quality involved in the appropriation privacy tort and the property, commercial value quality involved in the right of publicity tort.[18]

Unlike intrusion and disclosure, appropriation does not concern private facts. Instead, appropriation is defined by the Restatement thusly: "One who appropriates to his own use or benefit the name or likeness of another is subject to liability to the other for invasion of

---

17. The logo would probably be protected by trademark, which is discussed in Chapter 9, but (real) names and faces are not, and in the context of the Marvel Universe, the Fantastic Four are real, rather than fictional, people.

18. PETA v. Bobby Berosini, Ltd., 895 P.2d 1269 (Nev. 1995) (emphasis in original).

his privacy."[19] Since private facts aren't at issue here, this tort could apply to the appropriation of the name or likeness of the superhero identity, the secret identity, or both. Note, however, that many states have specific statutes for appropriation, and the definition given in the Restatement does not necessarily track the statutes or even state-by-state common law.

As one can probably guess, appropriation is related to the right of publicity, but it concerns different kinds of harm. One commentator puts it this way: "[A]n infringement of the right of publicity focuses upon injury to the pocketbook, while an invasion of 'appropriation privacy' focuses upon injury to the psyche."[20] Note, though, that an invasion of appropriation privacy may be caused by commercial exploitation of someone's name or likeness (and indeed many state statutes require it), but the measure of damages is still the mental anguish and physical distress caused by the appropriation.

Given the effort that many superheroes put into maintaining a sterling reputation in the community, one can see how they might suffer significant mental and physical distress upon seeing their name or likeness used without their permission, particularly if the use was unsavory (e.g., using the image of the Human Torch and his "Flame On!" catchphrase to sell cigarettes).

As mentioned, the right of publicity has more of a property right quality to it. And indeed, unlike the right of privacy, the right of publicity may be assigned or licensed to others. And this makes sense because privacy is inherently personal; it cannot really be divorced from the individual in question. The commercial use of one's name and likeness, however, can be licensed or assigned to others, and so the right to sue for infringement of that right follows.

This is where we come back to the Fantastic Four gift shop and the Boostermobile. Superheroes, particularly well-known ones, are

19. Restatement (Second) of Torts § 652C.

20. McCarthy, 1 Rights of Publicity and Privacy § 5:60.

likely to have significant commercial value in their identity or persona. Superhero product endorsements, movie and TV appearances, and other uses are probably at least as valuable in the comic book world as the real one. Thus, the right of publicity is an extremely important one for a superhero, whether it's used as a carrot to fund an otherwise cash-strapped superhero or as a stick to fend off inappropriate use of a superhero's name and likeness.

But where Spider-Man can *really* go after Jameson is for so-called "false light" defamation. Jameson uses the *Daily Bugle* to paint Spider-Man as a menace to society. More generally speaking, an article on the abuse of superpowers accompanied by the picture of a superhero who either doesn't have such powers or who has never hurt anyone would invite the public to draw an unfair inference about the person in the picture.

False light is a relatively new tort, but it has been adopted by a majority of jurisdictions. Most states have adopted the Restatement's definition:

> One who gives publicity to a matter concerning another that places the other before the public in a false light is subject to liability to the other for invasion of his privacy, if
>
> a. the false light in which the other was placed would be highly offensive to a reasonable person, and
> b. the actor had knowledge of or acted in reckless disregard as to the falsity of the publicized matter and the false light in which the other would be placed.[21]

Note that many jurisdictions have held that mere negligence is sufficient if the victim is not a public figure, but in this case most superheroes are public figures, so knowledge of or reckless disregard

---

21. Restatement (Second) of Torts § 652E.

of falsity is required. Examples of false light highly offensive to a reasonable person and potentially applicable here include drug use, teenage crime, police brutality, and organized crime. News stories or other publicity that falsely connect a superhero to such things could give rise to a false light case, and the *Daily Bugle's* consistent depiction of Spider-Man as a threat to public safety almost definitely counts. This, combined with the fact that Jameson has reason to know that Spider-Man is *not* a menace to society and routinely and recklessly disregards that knowledge, should be enough to base a false light claim on.

Excessive Force and Assault

Batman, Superman, Daredevil, and Spider-Man habitually patrol the streets of their respective cities, looking for crimes being committed and intervening to prevent them and apprehend the criminals. On the whole, this is a noble endeavor, but there's a potential problem here: excessive force.

Basically, the question is whether using superpowers to prevent the commission of crimes can subject the superhero to civil liability *from the criminal.* The answer here is "Quite possibly." Remember the discussion in chapter 2 of whether or not Wolverine's claws count as a deadly weapon for the purposes of aggravated assault? This is similar, only here, the idea is that injuring someone to prevent a property crime is generally legally problematic.

This is not an idle question. In the summer of 2011, a jury in El Paso County, Colorado, awarded about $300,000 to the family of a man who was killed while attempting to rob a used car lot.[22] Robert Johnson Fox was a methamphetamine user who, along with a com-

---

22. *Burglar's family awarded $300,000 in wrongful death suit*, COLORADO SPRINGS GAZETTE (August 26, 2011), available at http://www.gazette.com/articles/jury-123946-burglar-lot.html.

panion, scaled the fence to steal stereos. But the owner of the lot had already been robbed a few times that month and was waiting for them—with a semiautomatic Heckler & Koch rifle. Fox was shot through the heart and died on the scene, and the jury determined that this was a wrongful death for which the lot owner was liable. The reason this is the right result is because using deadly force to prevent property crimes is *never* justifiable. One is only permitted to use deadly force to prevent death or serious bodily injury to one's self or to another, but not to protect property. Even "Make My Day" or "Castle Doctrine" laws, which permit the use of deadly force to prevent trespassing in one's home, won't work here, because the theory there is really that trespass to a residence always carries with it the threat of violence, particularly at night. This just isn't true when the property in question is a business or personal property.

The parallels to Batman and other superheroes are pretty easy to see. If Superman injures a robber while preventing a bank robbery, he could actually get in big trouble. His superstrength and heat vision arguably constitute deadly force, and if the robbers weren't using guns or otherwise posing a threat to the lives of others, this would be unjustified. Spider-Man, on the other hand, will probably have an easier time of it here, because his powers, even if he uses them, aren't the sort that cause injury unless Spidey really goes out of his way to hurt someone. Being shot with webbing is unpleasant, but not actually *harmful*. Wolverine, on the other hand, had better watch his step. The fact that his claws are naturally occurring almost doesn't matter: he has a choice whether or not to use them.

Accidental Superpowers

Quite a number of superheroes were not born with their superpowers, receiving them either accidentally or deliberately, somewhere along the way.[23] The Fantastic Four were bombarded with cosmic rays during a test flight. Spider-Man was bitten by a radioactive or genetically engineered spider, depending on the origin story. Bruce Banner was exposed to gamma rays during a physics experiment. The question arises, "Can these characters sue anyone for the changes to their bodies?"

Assumption of Risk

The answer depends strongly on the facts of the case. Consider the case of Ben Grimm, who first appears in *Fantastic Four* #1.[24] Dr. Reed Richards is planning a space mission and feels a sense of urgency because the Communists are apparently on the verge of launching their own. The story was published at the height of the Cold War, and this issue came out mere months after Cosmonaut Yuri Gagarin became the first human being to leave the earth's atmosphere. Richards is discussing the flight with his team when the following exchange occurs:

Grimm: If you want to fly to the stars then you pilot the ship! Count **me** out! You **know** we haven't done enough research into the effect of cosmic rays! They might kill us all out in space!

Susan Storm: Ben, we've got to take that chance . . . unless we want the Commies to beat us to it! I— I never thought that **you** would be a coward!

Grimm: **A coward!! Nobody** calls **me** a coward! Get the ship! I'll fly her no matter what happens!!

---

23. We focus here on characters whose powers are somehow part of their bodies, not technological in nature. Batman and the Punisher, for example, are really just ordinary men in peak physical condition who happen to have access to awesome technology. This is quite different, legally speaking, from having one's body affected by an accident.

24. Stan Lee, Jack Kirby et al., *The Fantastic Four!*, in Fantastic Four 1 (Marvel Comics November 1961).

Ben Grimm provides a textbook example of assumption of risk. Stan Lee, Jack Kirby et al., *The Fantastic Four!*, in FANTASTIC FOUR 1 (Marvel Comics November 1961).

If Grimm were then to act as a plaintiff—presumably against Reed Richards for organizing the flight without adequately research-ing it first—this little conversation would come back to haunt him. Why? Because assumption of risk is a defense in tort law. The basic idea is that if a plaintiff is aware of a specific risk related to a par-ticular activity and engages in that activity anyway, a defendant would be absolved of any duty to protect the plaintiff from that par-ticular risk.[25] This is not a blanket protection, however; the specific nature of the risk generally needs to be contemplated by the plaintiff, but in Grimm's case, there's a good argument to be made that he has assumed the risk of flying Richards's ship.

First, the comic indicates that in addition to being a test pilot

25. For example, think of signing a waiver before going skydiving. Note, though, that there are some things that can't be waived or consented to, such as *intentional* serious harm or death caused by the defendant, which is something that will come up when we discuss the Hulk's origin.

and thus familiar with the risks associated with piloting experimental craft, he specifically knows about the risk of cosmic rays. Granted, he did not know that they would turn him into the Thing. Everyone involved was consciously aware that they had no idea what the effects of exposure to cosmic rays might be, but they did know that death was a distinct possibility. So because there was an apprehension of some kind of serious bodily injury, up to and including death, the fact that Grimm turns into the Thing rather than receiving an ordinary injury doesn't matter. Besides, "I'll fly her no matter what happens," is a pretty broad statement.

Second, both Grimm and Richards seem to possess the same mental state with respect to the risks involved. Assumption of risk will not protect a reckless defendant against a negligent plaintiff, but it may well protect a reckless defendant against a similarly reckless plaintiff. The idea here is that the law does not want to protect a party that acted with a lower degree of care over one who acted with a higher degree. When the playing field is equal, the argument that everyone involved knew the risks of the activity and voluntarily engaged in it is a lot stronger.

Third, Grimm was not a mere passenger. He was a pilot. As such, he had a significant role in the planning and execution of the test flight, and was in fact the only person even potentially capable of steering the craft out of danger. So unlike a passive participant or even someone participating in an event organized by others, Grimm had ample opportunity to mitigate the risks involved both before and during the incident. It's even theoretically possible that the Storm siblings might have a cause of action against Richards and Grimm as the joint organizers of the project! However, neither of them seems to have been affected negatively, so their "damages" may be nominal.

Ben Grimm knew as well as anyone what he was getting into. He knew that the trip involved the risk of cosmic rays, and he knew that exposure to those rays posed a risk of serious bodily injury or death. No one seems to have known more about the risks than he did, even Richards, though that's more a matter of shared ignorance than anything else. What Richards did was arguably incredibly foolish, but to quote a non-comic-book character for a minute, "Who's the more foolish? The fool, or the fool who follows him?"[26]

Workplace Accidents

So if a character goes into a dangerous situation with full knowledge of the danger, that's going to be a problem. But many superhero and supervillain origin stories involve situations where this doesn't really apply. For instance, She-Hulk encounters an "accidental superpowers" situation in *She-Hulk* (Vol. 1) #2. Dan "Danger-Man" Jermain falls into a vat of experimental chemicals while working for the company Roxxon[27] and comes out with unspecified "atomic powers."[28] There's a real question as to whether or not "bodily injury" includes being made "larger, stronger, and more powerful,"[29] but more than that, the fact that the injury took place at work is significant, and not just for the question of suing over accidental superpowers. Injuries that occur while on the job are treated very differently from injuries that happen outside the workplace.

The rise of industrialization was accompanied by the rise of severe workplace injuries, as people started working around machines more often, sometimes incredibly dangerous ones. In the nineteenth and early twentieth centuries, it was commonplace for factory workers to lose fingers and even whole limbs to machinery. This was hugely problematic, especially for plaintiffs, because the "master-servant" relationship required that they prove negligence or even *malice* on the part of the employer to be able to recover anything. This was a very high burden, and courts ruled for employers far more

---

26. Obi-Wan Kenobi in *Star Wars: A New Hope* (1977).

27. Probably a thinly veiled reference to Exxon.

28. Dan Slott et al., *Class Action Comics!*, in SHE-HULK (VOL. 1) 2 (Marvel Comics June 2004).

29. Which is probably a question of law for the court rather than a question of fact for the jury, contrary to the way the story goes in the comic.

often than not, leaving large numbers of industrial workers injured on the job with no recovery at all. Further, even if they were eventually able to recover, tort cases routinely take *years* to resolve, and if the injured person was unable to work because of their injury, they could very easily find themselves in a very bad way. But legal reforms favoring labor began in the late nineteenth century, and by 1949, every state and the federal government had instituted a "workers' compensation" regime.

Workers' compensation operates by creating a system for compensating workers for workplace injuries regardless of fault. What this means is that if you are injured while serving your employer, you get paid the vast majority of the time, even if your employer was completely without fault. This may seem very favorable to the workers, so to even things out, i.e., to make sure that employers weren't bankrupted every time someone broke an arm, workers' compensation regimes were limited in three ways.

First, unlike traditional tort cases where damages are awarded by juries, which can lead to unpredictable and occasionally massive awards, compensation for workplace injuries is computed based on actuarial tables created by state agencies rather than by juries. This rationalizes and limits compensation. Whereas a jury can award a basically arbitrary amount of money, workers' compensation payouts are known ahead of time and are thus a lot easier to plan for and insure. Second, compensation is limited to purely economic damages, i.e., medical bills, lost wages, lost future earnings, etc. There is very little provision for noneconomic damages like "pain and suffering" or punitive damages, which really drive up verdicts in traditional liability cases. Third, workers' compensation is an exclusive remedy, i.e., employees cannot choose to forgo participation in the workers' compensation program and sue their employers. Workers' compensation is their only way to recover. Likewise, employers cannot decide not to pay for workers' compensation insurance. It's just a cost of doing business.

So employees benefit because they almost always get paid, even if the accident was their fault, and they usually get paid in a fraction of the amount of time they'd have to wait if they sued. But employers benefit because their costs are controlled and employees can't turn around and sue them. Workers' compensation coverage is mandatory in just about every state for just about every employee. There are, of course, certain exceptions, but a worker in an industrial plant working with radioactive materials, e.g., Dan Jermain, would definitely be covered.

So what happened to Roxxon's workers' compensation carrier? How is Jermain able to sue at all? Sure, She-Hulk might act as plaintiff's counsel in the workers' compensation case (coverage can be disputed, leading to litigation, but this is much simpler than suing in open court), but workers' compensation is largely limited to economic damages. Danger-Man is basically uninjured, and even if we want to go with She-Hulk's argument and say that Dan Jermain is "dead" (more on that in a minute), workers' compensation only pays out a couple of hundred grand—at best—for wrongful death. Not $85 million, which is the settlement reached at the end of the issue.

Of course, the whole issue goes away if Jermain isn't an employee. If the writers had him be some random schmo who happened to get in a wreck with a Roxxon tanker truck, covering him in radioactive goo, he would not be covered by the workers' compensation regime and thus would be free to sue as he does in the comic. Oh well.

Damages for the Hulk

Bruce Banner's story contains another big difference. Banner is characterized as one of the world's most brilliant scientists, rivaling if not surpassing Reed Richards and Tony Stark. Banner is involved with a Defense Department project to develop a gamma ray bomb or "G-bomb" when he is accidentally exposed to gamma rays, which due to a fluke in his genetic structure transforms him—periodically—into the rampaging Hulk.

Sounds pretty similar to Ben Grimm, right? So far, yes. But there's a wrinkle that makes all the difference. In the case of the Fantastic Four, just about everyone involved is acting recklessly, and no one intends for anyone to get hurt. But Banner was actually a victim of attempted murder. The way the story is told in the comics, just before the test of the G-bomb, Banner notices that a teenager has breached security and is inside the blast zone. He orders the test to be delayed and runs to get the kid out of the way. Banner is able to get the kid to a protective trench when the bomb goes off, but does not make it himself, and he is exposed to gamma rays. But the reason the bomb goes off is because Igor Drenkov, a Russian agent, orders the test to continue, hoping that Banner would die in the resulting explosion. Assumption of risk will protect a defendant against a reckless plaintiff, but it will not protect a defendant who acts with malice. Indeed, Drenkov could be subject to civil and criminal liability, as attempted murder is a serious felony.

But wait a minute . . . doesn't this all happen while Banner is at work? And didn't we just talk about how that might not work out very well for a potential plaintiff? Banner's case is a little different from Jermain's because Banner works for the government. First off, Banner would probably not be able to sue the government directly, as he is the organizer of the project and the government is likely not liable for the actions of enemy infiltrators. Furthermore, depending on the nature of Banner's employment, either the Federal Employee Compensation Act (FECA), the federal equivalent of workers' compensation, or the Veterans Affairs Administration (VA) would provide compensation for his injuries, as he sustains them while executing his duties as a government employee. So he is theoretically entitled to some money, though only in proportion to his medical bills (nonexistent) and expenses related to mitigating his disability.[30] In practice, he's going to have trouble proving his damages, and as

---

30. See chapter 7 and, umm, good luck with that.

the FECA or VA would be an exclusive remedy, no other recovery would be available with respect to the government. He's still free to sue Drenkov, though, because while workers' compensation does shield employers from traditional liability, intentional tortfeasors[31] are pretty much on their own.

Property Damage and Insurance

If there's one thing that almost all comic books have in common, it's that at some point there is probably going to be an *absolutely insane* amount of property destruction. Nitro takes out a huge chunk of Stamford, Connecticut, in the first issue of Marvel's *Civil War* event, and the final battle does significant damage to downtown Manhattan. Doomsday carves a path of destruction through three states in DC's *Death of Superman* story back in the early 1990s. The Incredible Hulk does a complete number on Stark Tower in *World War Hulk* and causes Manhattan to be evacuated, disrupting the operations of tens of thousands of businesses on the island.[32] Even something as innocuous as the Flash's running across town can create sonic booms that leave a trail of broken windows in his wake.

Liability isn't the only aspect of tort law. The other big part is damages. Most of the time when property is damaged, the property owner has insurance that will pay to restore the property to approximately the state it was in before the loss occurred.[33] But when the Joker blows up half of downtown Gotham just for the hell of it,

---

31. "Tortfeasor" is a fancy term for "someone who commits a tort."

32. "Business interruption insurance" is a real thing.

33. In theory the property owner could sue the tortfeasor, but there are several problems with this. For one thing, lawsuits are expensive, time-consuming, and uncertain. For another, many defendants are in no position to pay for their damages (i.e., they are "judgment proof"). Usually it's simpler to take out an insurance policy and let the insurance company sue the tortfeasor if it makes financial sense to do so.

insurers aren't actually going to want to pay for that, and there is reason to believe that under the terms of standard insurance contracts, they wouldn't have to. The reason has to do with the way insurance policies are written, which is a matter of contract as much at it is a matter of law.

Understanding this involves a little intro to insurance. Insurance, technically speaking, is a financial product whereby risk is transferred from one person, the "insured," to another, the "insurer," in exchange for a sum of money, called the "premium." Insurance policies are only written for "insurable risks." Generally speaking, an "insurable risk" is one where both the probability and magnitude of a particular kind of loss are measurable, where the occurrence of that loss is truly random, and where it is possible to transfer that risk to an insurer for an economically feasible premium. A common example of an insurable risk is one's house burning down. We know how often houses in a particular zip code burn down, we know what a particular house is worth, houses don't burn down at any predictable frequency, and as it turns out, it's possible to insure against the risk of fire for a premium that is both acceptable to the insured and profitable for the insurer. Keeping track of all of those statistics and figuring out the appropriate premium for a particular risk is what actuaries do for a living. Some fun, eh?

Flooding, on the other hand, is an example of an "uninsurable" risk. Floods do occur at random, and we know basically how often, but the magnitude of losses caused by flood are such that it is impossible to offer flood insurance at any price a homeowner can afford. Floods are considered "catastrophic" losses, because they cause both a high amount of damage to individual properties but also a high amount of damage to entire regions, making it impossible to adequately spread the cost to other property owners, since they all get hit too. We'll talk more about how uninsurable risks like flooding are covered later in this section.

The reason this is important for comic books is that the same is true of war, terrorism, civil unrest, revolution, etc. Discharge of nuclear weapons, intentional or accidental, is also uninsurable. This is starting to sound a lot like a comic book, isn't it? And here's the thing: uninsurable risks are generally excluded from insurance policies.

When a loss occurs, the claims adjuster is going to look to the policy to see if there's coverage. First, he'll look to see if there is coverage for this kind of loss on the declarations page, i.e., the coverage scheduled for this particular policy. For example, a liability policy is not going to have coverage for property losses, and vice versa. Then, he's going to check the insuring agreement to see if the loss results from a "covered peril."[34] Some policies cover losses from any peril that isn't excluded, others only cover losses from a particular list of perils. Then, he's going to check to see if there are any relevant conditions in the policy that have been breached, like failing to pay the premium or refusing to cooperate with the adjuster. Finally, he'll see if there are any relevant exclusions, e.g., fire is generally a covered peril, but there's no coverage if a homeowner burns down his own house.

Take the Doomsday example again, and let's assume that he has just leveled a private residence, insured by ABC Ins. Co., by throwing Superman through it. ABC's adjuster is first going to look at the declarations page for the insured's homeowner's policy. The house is insured for $100,000. So far so good. Then, he's going to look at the insuring agreement to see if there is anything of interest there. This policy covers everything not specifically excluded, so again, so far so good. Then he'll check conditions. The homeowner is current on his premium, gave timely notice of the claim, and is cooperating with the adjuster, so again, probably okay there.

But what's this? The homeowner didn't buy terrorism coverage?

---

34. In insurance terms, a "peril" is anything that causes loss. So lightning, fire, flood, etc. are all types of perils.

Hmm. That's going to be a problem because it's going to be pretty easy to argue that Doomsday is a terrorist. Even if he isn't, it isn't going to be difficult to fit this into either the war or civil unrest exclusions, both of which are part of every insurance policy. Any coverage attorney worth his salt would certainly make that argument, and it's hard to see why it wouldn't win. Heck, if Superman is working for the government, then it might be excluded under the "civil authority" exclusion.

In a world where central business districts are regularly leveled by marauding supervillains and the superheroes who fight them, this hardly seems like a positive result. If we're talking about a universe where superheroes and supervillains exist and unstoppable monsters do level significant sections of town every other Tuesday, it seems probable that the legal system or insurance industry would take this into account. But because the magnitude of losses caused by superhero battles are so great, it seems likely that the states would have to resort to what are called "residual market mechanisms."

And in fact, this is how flood insurance is currently offered on a national level: the Federal Emergency Management Agency operates the National Flood Insurance Program. This is pretty much the only way to buy flood insurance anymore. States have also set up residual markets for both high-risk drivers and properties with significant windstorm exposures (Mississippi, South Carolina, Texas, etc.), earthquake exposures (California), and for high-risk drivers (every state). Basically, state legislatures have decided that even though certain kinds of risk are impossible to insure against on the open market, we want people to take those risks anyway, for a host of possible reasons. We want high-risk drivers to be insured both for their protection and for others', and denying someone permission to drive because he cannot buy mandatory insurance seems unjust. People really want to live in earthquake- and hurricane-prone areas, and those people vote, so we're going to find some way of making that work, no matter how silly it is.

Residual markets can work in one of a number of ways. One is "assigned risk," an approach frequently used to ensure that high-risk drivers have access to at least the state minimum liability limits for personal auto insurance. Basically, every insurer that participates in the market is required to take its fair share of high-risk drivers as a cost of doing business in the state. It can then spread this cost to its other insurance customers, keeping the company profitable.

But it seems more likely that the states would create their own "Supervillain Pool" similar to the windstorm pools active in the Gulf and coastal states. The way windstorm pools work is that every insurance policy is assessed a tax, based on the premium, which goes into the residual pool. The pool then reimburses property owners for damages caused by hurricanes. Property owners in comic book stories would need to buy "Superhero/Supervillain Insurance" from a pool, set up for that purpose though that premium would be a good start because this truly is an uninsurable risk; the pool will probably need to be supported by taxpayer revenue as some windstorm pools are. The idea is that all but the biggest losses will be at least mostly absorbed by the pool but that the government will step in if things get really out of hand. The pool can theoretically up its rates in the years following a big loss to ensure that the government gets its money back, but this rarely happens.

In the Marvel Universe, this is basically how things work. Individuals and businesses can purchase Extraordinary Activity Assurance (EAA), which is essentially superhero insurance. In New York City, large claims or claims by people who can't afford EAA are backed up by the (fictional) Federal Disaster Area Stipend.

Of course, while we're modifying the law to account for superheroes, it would probably also be the case that insurance companies would include some kind of "superhero/supernatural/paranormal" exclusion, shifting that exposure more directly to the residual pool, as has been done with flood, earthquake, and windstorm exposures. However, as much as it might make sense to require superheroes to use their powers to help repair the damage they cause, the Thirteenth Amendment makes it pretty difficult for the states to impose forced labor on people not convicted of a crime or drafted into the military. On the flip side, if a superhero is sued for causing damage, he might be able to significantly reduce the settlement amount by voluntarily agreeing to use his powers in the repair efforts.

CHAPTER 6

Contracts

In the 1999 Batman story arc *No Man's Land*, Gotham City is rocked by a massive earthquake and fire. Low on options, Batman hires mobsters and thugs—mostly working for the Penguin—to help find and assist survivors. To ensure their cooperation, he writes a contract. Unfortunately, we don't see the whole contract, but the parts we do see are sound, if maybe a little questionably written. Under the circumstances Batman can probably be forgiven a little loose writing!

Over the course of the story, several details of the contract emerge. Ultimately the deal is simple: The villains help the survivors in exchange for payment, and Batman promises not to spend the rest of his life making their lives as miserable as he can. The contract is very specific about how the work is to be performed: the villains can't use guns, they have to work together, and they have to be careful not to harm the survivors or each other.

Contracts are an important part of our daily lives, but they come up more rarely for superheroes. Not too many superheroes and supervillains seem to have lease agreements for their secret hideouts, for example! But this contract in *No Man's Land*, as it turns out, is a

Batman used a contract to secure the help of the Penguin and his goons in the aftermath of the earthquake that destroyed Gotham. We might have advised him to leave off the "From the Desk of Bruce Wayne" part, though! Devin Grayson et al., *The Contract*, in BATMAN CHRONICLES (VOL. 1) 12 (DC Comics Spring 1998).

Batman offers the Penguin "good and valuable consideration" in the form of agreeing not to make his life miserable. We'd certainly take the deal. Alan Grant et al., *Cataclysm, Part Nine: The Naked City*, in BATMAN: SHADOW OF THE BAT 74 (DC Comics May 1998).

valid contract.[1] A contract has three major elements: an offer, an acceptance, and consideration. This contract has all three. The first two, together, are sometimes referred to as a "meeting of the minds," meaning, a mutual understanding between the parties about a particular subject, the consideration.

The Offer

An offer is a promise to do something in exchange for something else (i.e., the "consideration," more on that later). The offer must clearly manifest the intent of the offering party to be bound by the terms of the offer should the particular person to whom it is offered accept (more on that in a minute). So, for example, an advertisement to the general public simply saying that a particular product is available for a particular price is not an "offer" in the technical sense, because there is no particular person to whom the offer is made. But an advertisement that says that only five of an item are for sale and that the first five people to show up have a right to pay a particular price is different. That's definite enough to constitute an "offer," and the first five people who show up can demand that they be sold the item for the advertised price.[2]

Of particular interest for comic book stories is the issue of bounties. Bounties are advertisements that the government—or some other entity—is willing to pay a certain amount of money for the apprehension of a particular person.[3] But despite the fact that the offer is theo-

---

1. Notably, it is a contract for services (as opposed to goods), so it is governed by state common law rather than the Uniform Commercial Code's Article 2. Since we don't know what state Gotham is located in, we will refer to general common law principles.

2. Lefkowitz v. Great Minn. Surplus Store, Inc., 251 Minn. 188 (1957).

3. Note that most comic book "bounty hunters" (e.g. Deadpool, Lobo) are criminals who take jobs for hire. While they may talk about taking a contract, such agreements aren't legally enforceable because they are contracts for the commission of a crime. *See, e.g.,* McConnell v. Com. Pictures Corp., 7 N.Y.2d 465 (1960) ("It is the settled law of this State [and probably of every other State] that a party to an illegal contract cannot ask a court of law to help him carry out his illegal object, nor can such a person plead or prove in any court a case in which he, as a basis for his claim, must show forth his illegal purpose.").

retically made to the entire public, the fact that only the first person (or persons) who bring the criminal in can collect the bounty makes bounties definite enough to be offers in the contractual sense. This is significant for a number of superheroes, particularly Superman, who in one story[4] makes a significant amount of money (most of which he donates to charity) collecting bounties on various criminals.

In this case, Batman has made a clear offer to a particular group of people and has made it very clear that he intends to be bound by the terms of the contract. So whatever else we've got, we've got an offer.

The Acceptance

Once an offer is made, the contract isn't formed until the other party accepts the offer. Sometimes acceptance is verbal (e.g., saying "I agree"), sometimes it is written (e.g., signing a contract), and sometimes it is an action (e.g., showing up with a lost pet in order to collect a reward offered for its return). The person who makes the offer is generally permitted to set the means by which an acceptance can be made (e.g., requiring that acceptance be in writing). Because there is no contract until the offer is accepted, an offer can be revoked (almost) any time before the acceptance.

Note that the acceptance must be of the terms that are offered. If a party disagrees to the terms or suggests alternate terms, this is not a modification of the offer. It is a *rejection* of the offer and possibly a *counter*offer. The original offering party is now free to treat this as any other offer and may accept or reject it in turn.

Furthermore, the acceptance must be clear. If Batman says, "I'll pay you to help Gotham if you agree to these terms," and the villains say, "We'll think about it," that isn't acceptance. They have not objectively manifested their agreement and acceptance of the terms of the contract.

---

4. Robert Bernstein et al., *Superman Owes a Billion Dollars!*, in SUPERMAN (VOL. 1) 148 (DC Comics October 1961).

Lastly, remember that the person making the offer has the right to determine the means of acceptance. If Batman says that acceptance must be in writing, and the villains simply go out and start helping without signing anything, Batman doesn't have to pay them, because they did not accept the offer under the terms he laid out. If, on the other hand, Batman said that he would pay any villain who assisted and complied with certain terms, the villains could still accept in writing if they so chose, but they could also accept verbally— "I'll take it!" They could even just go out and start helping and then turn around and demand payment if they had complied with the terms, that is, accept by performance of the contract.[5]

In this case the contract was in writing and required a written acceptance by "the undersigned." When the villains signed the contract they became bound to uphold their end of the bargain.

The Consideration

You might think "consideration" has something to do with thinking about the contract before agreeing to it ("considering" it). But actually, "consideration" requires that the contract involve something of value on both sides. Think about how someone might say "In *consideration* of the payment specified, the undersigned agree to assist the citizens of Gotham as follows . . ." Consideration is what separates a contract from a gift. A promise to give someone something for nothing is generally not enforceable.[6]

Don't be confused by the word "value," though. Consideration

---

5. A peppercorn is the stereotypical example of nominal consideration, but as long as it does not appear that it is being included simply so that the contract will not fail for lack of consideration, it can still work. Courts usually do not examine the *adequacy* of consideration, i.e., whether the mutual promises are of similar objective worth, only the *existence* of consideration, i.e., whether something has, in fact, been promised by both parties.

6. There are ways around this, though. The doctrine of *promissory estoppel* allows someone to enforce a promise to make a gift if he has reasonably relied on the promise and suffered some loss because of it. *See, e.g.,* Grouse v. Group Health Plan, Inc., 306 N.W.2d 114 (Minn. 1981). This, however, is an equitable remedy based upon concepts of justice and fairness, not an enforcement of a contract as such.

does not have to be particularly valuable or even proportional. In fact, a single peppercorn can be sufficient; it only has to be acceptable to the other party (i.e., enough to make them accept the contract).[7] Consideration can even be something that is actually good for the person making the promise (e.g., "I will pay you $100 if you give up smoking.").[8] One catch, however, is that consideration cannot be something that the party was already legally obligated to do. So, for example, promising simply to obey the law is not enough (e.g., "I will pay you $100 if you promise not to run any red lights.").

Almost anything can be the subject of a contract, but there are some exceptions. For example, you can't make a contract to do something illegal,[9] so a contract to kill someone isn't an enforceable contract. If a supervillain hitman like Bullseye does the job but doesn't get paid, he can't go to court to enforce the contract. In this case, the villains are promising to help rescue survivors of the earthquake and fire, which is of course entirely legal. In fact, the contract specifies that they have to avoid breaking the law while doing so. Furthermore, the villains are paid money for the job, and the amount is apparently acceptable since they took the job. It's true that the contract requires the villains not to break any laws while carrying out the job, but they also have to promise to help survivors. They are already legally obligated to do the former, but not the latter, so the contract stands.

Breach and Damages

What happens when a party to a contract doesn't fulfill its end of the bargain? This is called "breach of contract," and the result is that the other party can sue for damages. In the case of Batman's contract

---

7. Weiner v. McGraw-Hill, Inc., 57 N.Y.2d 458, 464 (1982). Note, though, that the courts are pretty good at sniffing out "nominal consideration," i.e., a situation in which the parties *pretend* that something is valuable when they're really just trying to avoid some other aspect of the law, usually taxes but theoretically almost anything.

8. *See, e.g.,* Hamer v. Sidway, 124 N.Y. 538 (1891).

9. *See, e.g.,* Lloyd Corp. v. Henchar, Inc., 80 N.Y.2d 124, 127 (1992).

with the villains, one of the villains breaks the rule against using guns. But what would Batman's remedy be?

There are several ways that someone can be harmed by a breach of contract. For example, it may cost money in order to put things back the way they were before the contract was formed (e.g., Batman probably wants his money back). These are called "reliance damages." Or, it may cost money to complete the contract (e.g., Batman may have to spend time and money to find a replacement villain). These are called "consequential damages."

Alternatively, the parties can agree to damages ahead of time. Batman's contract with the villains might have said, "If a party breaches this contract, that party will pay the non-breaching party one thousand dollars." These are called "liquidated damages." Generally speaking, courts frown on liquidated damages when they are used to *penalize* a breaching party, but they are actually favored where the risks of a venture are difficult or impossible to estimate.[10] By agreeing to damages ahead of time, the parties can control risk, not to mention save themselves and the court a significant amount of time and effort trying to figure out exactly how much a particular breach costs.

Contracts with the Devil

Several comic book characters, including Ghost Rider and Spider-Man, have made deals with the Devil, or at least a demon. The Faustian bargain is a long-standing literary trope, and sometimes the demon is outsmarted and sometimes not. Ignoring for the moment the difficulty of bringing a suit against a supernatural being,[11] we

10. *See, e.g.,* Truck Rent-A-Ctr. v. Puritan, 41 N.Y.2d 420, 423–25 (1977).

11. This situation was indirectly addressed by a federal court in United States ex rel. Gerald Mayo v. Satan and His Staff, 54 F.R.D. 282 (W.D. Pa. 1971). The court observed that it is doubtful that the court could assert personal jurisdiction over the defendant, and in any case, the plaintiff gave no instructions as to how service of process might be perfected.

can consider whether these contracts are valid, at least by the standards of American law.

Ghost Rider and the Meeting of the Minds

In the classic Ghost Rider origin story, stuntman Johnny Blaze sells his soul to the demon Mephisto in exchange for Mephisto curing fellow stuntman Crash Simpson's cancer. As a traditional Faustian demon, Mephisto upholds his end of the bargain in a very literal way: Crash's cancer is cured, but he dies shortly afterward in an accident.

This raises a significant issue. Johnny thought selling his soul would save Crash's life, but he only changes the way in which he

This works out about as well as one might expect. Gary Friedrich et al., *Ghost Rider*, in MARVEL SPOTLIGHT (VOL. 1) 5 (Marvel Comics August 1972).

died. Could Johnny argue that Mephisto twisted his words and claim that Mephisto has breached the contract by not saving Crash's life?

The question comes down to whether this scenario constitutes a legitimate "meeting of the minds" as discussed earlier. That is, "there must be a manifestation of mutual assent sufficiently definite to assure that the parties are truly in agreement with respect to all material terms."[12] In other words, everyone needs to be on the same page.

So far that sounds good for Johnny, since he and Mephisto have different ideas in mind. However, it would be problematic if parties to a contract could so easily claim, "That's not what I meant!" after the fact. To solve this problem, the courts judge a contract by an *objective* standard rather than the *subjective* mindset of the parties. "In determining whether the parties entered into a contractual agreement and what were its terms, it is necessary to look . . . to the objective manifestations of the intent of the parties as gathered by their expressed words and deeds."[13] Johnny seems to understand and agree to the terms of the deal, so it is unlikely he could claim differently afterward.

All is not necessarily lost for Johnny, however. There are several ways to "avoid" a contract, and Johnny might claim mistake, undue influence, or unconscionability. Notably, he can't claim that the contract was made under duress because duress requires that the contract be induced by a wrongful threat.[14] In this case, Mephisto doesn't threaten to do anything illegal if Johnny doesn't agree to the contract, so no dice there.

---

12. Express Indus. & Term. v. Dept. of Trans., 93 N.Y.2d 584, 589 (1999).

13. Flores v. Lower East Side Serv., 4 N.Y.3d 363, 368 (2005).

14. *See, e.g., In re* Baby Boy O, 733 N.Y.S.2d 768, 770 (App. Div. 2001).

Mistake

Johnny could argue that Mephisto knew full well that Crash was doomed to die (in some versions of Ghost Rider's origin, Mephisto actually causes the accident). As a result, Johnny is laboring under the mistaken belief that selling his soul would save Crash's life. Prolonging Crash's life is Johnny's entire purpose in entering the contract, so when he dies at almost exactly the same time he would have if he'd just kept on with the cancer, Mephisto would be claiming Johnny's soul in exchange for essentially nothing. This would probably be considered "unconscionable" (more on that later).[15] Since Mephisto knows the truth, i.e., that Crash is going to die in a very short time regardless of whether or not the cancer is cured—and knows that Johnny didn't—the contract should be voided.[16] To do otherwise would unjustly enrich Mephisto.[17]

Undue Influence

Undue influence is not commonly used to void contracts because of the high burden of proof often placed on such claims.[18] Undue influence may be found when there has been "unfair persuasion of a party who is under the domination of the person exercising the

15. Long v. Fitzgerald, 659 N.Y.S.2d 544, 547 (App. Div. 1997) ("[A] contract may be voided for unilateral mistake of fact only where enforcement of the contract would be unconscionable, the mistake is material and was made despite the exercise of ordinary care."). There's a good argument to be made that just about any contract made with the Devil is going to be unconscionable, since it almost always involves someone's immortal soul. There's also good reason to think that the Devil probably won't care, being the Devil and all.

16. Application of David R., 420 N.Y.S.2d 675, 679 (Family Ct. New York Co. 1979) ("There is no contract where one party knew . . . that the other is laboring under a mistake.").

17. Cox v. Lehman Bros., Inc., 790 N.Y.S.2d 16, 17 (App. Div. 2005) ("A unilateral mistake can be the basis for rescission if failing to rescind would result in unjust enrichment of one party at the expense of the other and the parties can be returned to the status quo ante without prejudice.").

18. See, e.g., Dolloff v. Dolloff, 593 A.2d 1044, 1045 (Maine 1991).

persuasion."[19] Among the factors that may be considered in determining whether undue influence was present are the unfairness of the sale price, the absence of independent advice and counsel, and the susceptibility of the party.[20] In this case, the sale price was arguably unfair, Johnny doesn't have any independent advice or counsel, and his youth and concern for Crash makes him susceptible to influence, so there is a good argument for undue influence here.

But if we change the facts just a bit, we can see how undue influence might work in other contexts as well. Say Johnny does consult with a lawyer (and, heck, why not a priest too?), and the subject matter is not Crash's life, but something like success in an upcoming race. To make matters even more level, let's say that instead of Johnny's immortal soul, Mephisto only demands five years of service. We've got what looks like a level playing field, and there isn't a great argument that there's undue influence going on unless Mephisto uses some kind of supernatural power to somehow influence Johnny into taking the deal, which would obviously be undue influence. The same would go for any situation in which a telepath or empath plants a suggestion in the person's mind.[21]

Unconscionability

Moving on, unconscionability protects a party to a contract from terms that are "so grossly unreasonable as to be unenforceable because of an absence of meaningful choice on the part of one of the parties together with contract terms which are unreasonably favorable to the other party."[22] "The concept of unconscionability is re-

---

19. *Dolloff*, 593 A.2d at 1046.

20. *Id.*

21. Christopher Nolan's recent hit movie *Inception* (2010) contains another kind of potential undue influence. Putting the idea to sign a contract into someone's head, if such could be proven, would absolutely be grounds for voiding a contract.

22. King v. Fox, 851 N.E.2d 1184, 1191 (N.Y. Ct. App. 2006).

served for the type of agreement so one-sided that it shocks the conscience such that no person in his or her senses and not under delusion would make it on the one hand, and no honest and fair person would accept it on the other."[23]

Consigning one's eternal soul to hell is as unconscionable as you can get, yet if we may literally play Devil's advocate for a moment, we can imagine a counterargument. It would certainly be unconscionable if Mephisto demands *Crash's* soul in exchange for saving Crash's life, but asking for Johnny's soul is different. Can an act of self-sacrifice, no matter how extreme, be unconscionable? Is there some threshold past which an invitation to altruism becomes extortion? And if you like the idea of twisting altruism into a legal defense for the Devil, then you may have a bright future as a defense lawyer.

---

23. Kojovic v. Goldman, 823 N.Y.S.2d 35, 39 (App. Div. 2006) (quotations omitted).

CHAPTER 7

Business Law

Most superheroes and superhero teams don't operate as a business or formal legal organization, but there are some notable exceptions, such as the Avengers, which has had a charter since 1982. Could a superhero team ever qualify as a real business?[1] If so, which of the alphabet soup of business organizations (LLP, LLC, Inc., etc.) would be a good fit?[2] And what about the laws and regulations that affect businesses?

Business associations are significantly and arguably principally concerned with minimizing two things: taxation and personal liability. Superheroes aren't generally in it for the money, so the tax implications of their activities aren't really so important. But all

---

1. We discuss only superhero teams rather than supervillains in this section because a criminal conspiracy can't avoid liability by hiding behind a corporation. Forming an explicit organization also makes it that much easier to prosecute the organization under the Racketeer Influenced and Corrupt Organizations Act, which is often used to prosecute organized crime. That leaves tax avoidance as the major advantage to forming a business organization, and somehow we suspect that most supervillains (with some exceptions, such as Lex Luthor) aren't too concerned with paying income tax on their loot.

2. The terms "business organization," "business association," and "business entity" are used interchangeably here.

THE AVENGERS
CHARTER

ARTICLE ONE: ORGANIZATION

The Avengers is hereby chartered as a peace-keeping force of the security arm of the United Nations answerable only to the Security Council.

Headquarters shall be in New York City and there shall be established facilities for the use of the Avengers in the current eleven member nations of the Security Council.

ARTICLE TWO: JURISDICTION

The Avengers, as a group, are empowered to act as an agency of enforcement on duly recognized and approved missions in all lands, territories and protectorates of member states of the United Nations, providing that the threat in question is super-powered, extra-terrestrial, extra-dimensional, sub-terranean, sub-oceanic, or occult, and engaged in an invasion, infestation, limited incursion, piracy, enchantment or any flagrant violation of international law not instigated, sanctioned, or abetted by a member nation.

ARTICLE THREE: FUNDING

Major funding for the major operations of the Avengers—for upkeep of the New York headquarters, transportation, and equipment shall be provided by a grant from the Maria Stark Foundation—Anthony Stark, Director—with the understanding that the Foundation shall have no say in Avengers operations, policy, membership or the deployment of funds within the Avengers organization.

The stipends to serving members and active and inactive reserve members shall be drawn from the major pool of United Nations funding.

Costs for construction, maintenance, and staffing of subsidiary headquarters shall be absorbed by the host countries.

ARTICLE FOUR: OPERATIONS

The day-to-day operations of the Avengers shall be governed by a set of bylaws as put forth by the founding members.

AVENGERS bylaws

SECTION ONE: POLICY AND OPERATIONS

A: All Avengers shall, at all times, endeavor to adhere to the principles of the Avengers Charter and follow the rules and regulations of these bylaws.

1. The bylaws may be amended, when necessary, by the active members of the Avengers. Amendments may be proposed by any active Avenger. Amendments shall become a binding part of these bylaws upon approval by two-thirds of the active membership.

1a. Active membership shall be further defined to mean the seven serving members of the primary team and their seven specific reserve substitutes.

B. No Avenger shall be required to surrender knowledge of his or her civilian identity or personal affairs to the membership at large or the United Nations Security Council.

C. The Avengers shall be led by a duly elected chairbeing. It shall be the duty of this leader to coordinate all Avenger activities whether business or tactical in nature.

1. The position of Chairbeing shall be open to any active member who has passed his/her probationary period (see Section Two

—Membership).

2. The Chairbeing shall serve for a term of one year, with no limit to the number of successive terms a leader may serve.

3. It shall be a privilege of the Chairbeing to determine the format of meetings and to call special meetings as he/she sees fit.

4. In the event of the absence, incapacity or resignation of the Chairbeing, an interim leader shall be chosen by a two-thirds vote of the active membership.

5. In the event of incapacity or death during action, chairbeing-ship shall pass in orderly succession among the primary team in a predetermined chain of command arrived at by majority vote among the primary team.

SECTION TWO: MEMBERSHIP

A. Recognizing that the membership of the Avengers may be subject to, and, indeed, might profit from change, procedures for the addition of members shall be set forth.

B. Candidates for membership in the Avengers must be legal adults, possessing at least one skill, power, ability, or talent which is deemed valuable by a majority of the active membership.

1. Membership shall not be denied on account of race, color, creed, sex, or condition of birth or origin.

2. Candidates for membership must be nominated by one active member in good standing at a regular or special meeting. Election for membership must be held within one week of nomination and be attended by a simple majority of active members. A two-thirds vote is necessary for election to membership.

3. Newly-elected Avengers shall serve a probationary period of not less than six months.

a. During the probationary period, a special committee consisting of one primary team member, one reserve substitute, and two members of the Avengers support crews shall investigate the candidate's public record for any violations, breaches of trust, or depredations, legal or moral, which may preclude said candidate from assumption of full active status.

b. While on probation, the new Avenger shall have limited access to Avengers facilities and records.

c. At the end of probation, the new Avenger shall assume full active status, unless objections are raised by any active member, or by the United Nations Security Council.

C. The Avengers shall select new members whenever the Chairbeing or two-thirds of the active membership determines that the ranks are not at optimal strength, or when there is a vacancy in the ranks.

1. It shall be the prerogative of the Chairbeing to limit the number of active members.

D. Active Avengers shall be the designation given to those Avengers who are full-time members.

1. Active Avengers shall be required to log all individual cases into the main computer file, that the entire membership may benefit from the individual's experience.

2. Active Avengers shall be required to attend all regular business meetings. Members who miss more than one meeting per month without submitting an acceptable excuse may face suspension for a period to be determined by a consensus of the other active members. (See Paragraph G)

3. Active Avengers shall be issued an Avengers identification card and an emergency signal device.

The first page of the Avengers' charter. Note section one, subsection B. We wonder if this was amended following the passage of the Superhuman Registration Act? Bob Harras et al., AVENGERS ANNIVERSARY MAGAZINE 1 (Marvel Comics November 1993).

superheroes, especially ones with significant assets, should be concerned with minimizing their personal liability. The fact that the superhero team members haven't themselves thought about how their relationship works will not stop a court from deciding if one team member might be liable for the actions of another. So if, for example, Robin assaults someone, a plaintiff might sue Robin *and* Batman, under the theory that they're partners, or that Robin is Batman's employee. That seems to make a certain amount of sense, given their relationship. But what if the situation was reversed? What if Batman assaults someone, and the plaintiff sues both of them? Does that work? To figure it out, we have to take a look at the various kinds of business relationships and entities.

Sole Proprietorships

The most basic kind of business entity is the sole proprietorship. Very briefly, sole proprietorships occur when a single individual goes into business for himself and doesn't create any kind of formal business entity. When Peter Parker works as a freelance photographer without forming a business entity through filing appropriate documents with the state government, he's effectively operating a sole proprietorship. Sole proprietors are completely and personally liable for all the debts and torts related to their business activity. What this means is that if the business goes under, all of the proprietor's personal assets are exposed to his creditors. Any business income is treated as personal income for tax purposes. As far as superheroes go, pretty much any superhero—or supervillain—that just sets out to save/conquer the world on his own, without there being any discussion or implication of a business entity, would be treated like a sole proprietor in that there would be no distinction between his "business" activities and his personal activities. He would be fully responsible for both tax and tort liability for everything he does. Spider-Man is a good example, except when he's working with the Avengers or the Fantastic Four, but pretty much any solo superhero/supervillain would fit.

Partnerships

Of course, many superheroes work together as part of a team, and that brings us naturally to partnerships. Partnerships come in several flavors, the most basic of which is a general partnership. General partnerships are basically the same as sole proprietorships except that there's at least two people involved. A general partnership is an association of two or more people or entities to carry on a business for profit as co-owners.[3] The association is only a contractual association and can be demonstrated by a written agreement, oral agreement, conduct, or some combination of the three.[4] The parties must also intend to carry on the business as co-owners, which generally requires the parties must intend to share both the profits and control over the business, though this does not require equal sharing.[5] Finally, especially important for superhero teams, the parties must *intend* to make a profit, though the business does not need to actually earn any profits or income so long as it is set up with the intention of being a commercial enterprise.[6] If the parties do not intend to make a profit, such as an unincorporated nonprofit association, they cannot meet the requirements of a general partnership.[7]

---

3. Uniform Partnership Act § 202(a) (1997). Every state except Louisiana has adopted some version of the Uniform Partnership Act.

4. *See, e.g., In re* Brokers, Inc., 363 B.R. 458 (Bankr. M.D.N.C. 2007) ("A partnership may be formed without a written or oral contract. In the absence of an express contract, the existence of a partnership may be established by examining the manner in which the parties conducted business. A partnership may be created by the agreement or conduct of the parties, either express or implied.").

5. Uniform Partnership Act § 401(b) (by default, "Each partner is entitled to an equal share of the partnership profits") and § 401 cmt. 3 (partners may agree to share profits other than equally).

6. *See, e.g.,* Reddington v. Thomas, 45 N.C. App. 236 (1980) ("The word 'profit,' as it is used in the Act relates to the purpose of the business, not to whether the business actually produced a net gain.").

7. Uniform Partnership Act § 202(a), cmt. 2.

A general partnership is the "default" business entity, meaning it is the business organization that results where parties do not make any filings with a state electing an alternative business form.[8] All partners have equal authority to bind the partnership, and all partners—including their personal assets—are on the hook for any contract, debt, or tort related to the business and activities of the partnership.[9] One advantage of a partnership is that it enjoys what is known as "pass-through taxation." That is, the partnership itself does not pay income tax, though it must still file an annual information return. Instead, it "passes through" any profits or losses to its partners, who then pay any required income tax.[10] Some other kinds of business entity, such as C corporations, must pay corporate income tax first in addition to the taxes paid by the employees or shareholders.

For example, the Green Lantern and Green Arrow's association looks a lot like a general partnership, in that they seem to work largely as equals, and neither one of them is really capable of ordering the other around, at least not in terms of their joint activity. Like most superhero teams, however, they aren't trying to make a profit, which means they definitely would not qualify as a partnership. If they wanted to form a business entity they would have to choose something else, and we'll talk about those options later in this chapter.

Then there are limited partnerships. Unlike general partnerships, which are implied by default, limited partnerships are created by filing a certificate with the state government where the partnership wants to be registered.[11] These entities are composed of one or

---

8. *Id.*

9. UNIFORM PARTNERSHIP ACT § 301, -306 (1997).

10. INTERNAL REVENUE SERV., PUBLICATION 541, PARTNERSHIPS, *available at* http://www.irs.gov/pub/irs-pdf/p541.pdf.

11. UNIFORM LIMITED PARTNERSHIP ACT § 201 (2001).

more general partners who are just like partners in a general partnership, and one or more limited partners. Limited partners have an ownership interest in the partnership but no control over its assets or business activities. Unlike general partners, limited partners are not liable for the debts of the partnership beyond their investment. Like general partnerships, limited partnerships must be for-profit. Taxation works the same as in other kinds of partnership. Limited partners can be employees of the partnership, and would be liable for their activities as employees just like any other employee of any other entity, but as long as the limited partners do not exercise too much control over the business, they remain immune from liability for the actions of the general partner and of the partnership as a whole.[12]

Batman and Robin are iconic superhero partners, but they probably aren't a general or even a limited partnership. Batman definitely calls the shots. He owns the Batcave, he supplies all the gear, he pays all the expenses. Robin looks for all the world like some kind of limited partner, but limited partnerships aren't something courts are going to recognize without the proper filings, and Batman and Robin aren't a for-profit organization in any case. Instead, a court would probably recognize some kind of employer-employee relationship between Batman and Robin. Batman would be liable both for his own actions and for those actions Robin takes on his behalf,[13] but Robin wouldn't be liable for what Batman does, because Batman is really the one in charge.

The Fantastic Four, by contrast, are probably one of the few examples of a superhero team that could qualify as a partnership because they each have a more or less equal say in how the team is run and they actually take in money, primarily through Reed Richards's

---

12. Gavin L. Phillips, Annotation, *Liability of Limited Partner Arising From Taking Part in Control of Business Under Uniform Limited Partnership Act*, 79 A.L.R.4th 427 (1990).

13. See discussion of *respondeat superior* later in this chapter.

inventions. A partnership is probably not the ideal business organization for the Fantastic Four (more on that later), but at least it's an option.

There are other kinds of partnerships, such as limited liability partnerships (LLPs). LLPs emerged in the early 1990s in the wake of the real estate bust of the 1980s. Cascading bank failures and cratering asset prices left investors with few other options than to go after the attorneys and accountants who had helped structure the deals that had gone south. This isn't necessarily a bad thing: someone who signs off on a deal that, in hindsight, is obviously flawed, should probably be held accountable. But what about other professionals in the partnership who had nothing to do with the transactions in question? Remember, in a general partnership, which almost all professional firms were at the time, every partner is personally liable for the actions of every other. The prospect of sending thousands of innocent professionals and their families into bankruptcy was sufficiently distasteful to encourage most state legislatures to pass acts permitting the creation of LLPs. In an LLP, there are no general partners, and each partner is only liable for his or her own wrongdoing. Like other partnerships, LLPs enjoy pass-through taxation. That is, the LLP itself does not pay income tax. Instead, the income is only taxed when partners collect it. Like limited partnerships, LLPs aren't something a court is going to read into a liability situation.

There are also more exotic forms of partnership like limited liability limited partnerships (LLLPs), but that's starting to get pretty far into the weeds. We turn instead to the other major kind of business entity: the corporation.

Corporations
Another potential option for our heroes would be a corporation. Corporations are creatures of statute, created by filing papers as required by state incorporation laws. Every state has its own incorporation statute, but the statutes are not uniform. Some states have favorable

incorporation laws and thus attract a lot of filings, historically Delaware, but more recently Nevada and a few others. Delaware has such a head start here that more than 50 percent of publicly traded companies in the U.S. are Delaware corporations.[14] But regardless of where they are created, corporations share some basic common features. First, they all offer limited liability. It is very difficult to hold the owners (i.e., shareholders), directors, officers, or employees of a corporation personally liable for the actions or debts of the corporation. Doing so is known as "piercing the corporate veil" and is very difficult to pull off in the courts.[15] The limited liability protections of limited liability partnership entities are borrowed from this corporate concept.

Many state corporation acts also provide an option for incorporating as a not-for-profit (also sometimes referred to as nonprofit) corporation. Unlike typical corporations, profits from not-for-profit corporations are not distributed to the shareholders, but are instead used by the corporation for its own purposes. The ability to operate as a not-for-profit is extremely useful for many superhero teams, most of which do not seek to earn a profit or even have income, although they may own assets such as a headquarters or vehicles. There are generally two major steps to creating a not-for-profit corporation: first, incorporating under state law and second, applying for exempt status with the Internal Revenue Service.[16]

---

14. *About Agency*, Delaware Department of State, http://corp.delaware.gov/aboutagency .shtml (last visited Mar. 14, 2012).

15. *See, e.g.*, Robert B. Thompson, *Piercing the Corporate Veil: An Empirical Study*, 76 Cornell L. Rev. 1036 (1991). Thompson studied a pool of about 1600 cases, finding that courts pierced the veil in only 40 percent of cases. In no case did a court pierce the corporate veil in a case involving a publicly held corporation. Courts applying Delaware law likewise universally declined to pierce the corporate veil. *Also see* John H. Matheson, *Why Courts Pierce: An Empirical Study of Piercing the Corporate Veil*, 7 Berkeley Bus. L.J. 1 (2010) (finding an overall piercing rate of 31.86%).

16. There may be additional registrations with states and municipalities once a federal tax-exempt application is approved. The requirements vary by state and municipality.

Corporations have two general options for taxation. "C" corporations are taxed "twice": first, at the corporation income tax level and second when the profits are distributed to the shareholders as dividends. "S" corporations, named after subchapter S of the Internal Revenue Code, have "pass through" taxation like partnerships, but there are limits on ownership, including the number of shareholders and their citizenship (no foreign shareholders for S-corps). The vast majority of big publicly traded corporations are C-corps. Not-for-profit corporations, assuming they meet the requirements to qualify as a not-for-profit under federal and state laws, are exempt from federal corporate income tax and, in most states, state corporate income tax as well. Individual states and municipalities may also offer exemptions from other taxes, such as sales tax and property tax, for not-for-profit corporations.

The most frequently encountered not-for-profit corporations qualify for tax-exempt status under §501(c)(3) of the Internal Revenue Code. To qualify as a 501(c)(3) not-for-profit entity, the corporation must be organized and operated exclusively for one of the exempt purposes listed in this section of the code: charitable, religious, educational, scientific, literary, testing for public safety, fostering national or international amateur sports competition, and preventing cruelty to children or animals.[17] "Charitable" is used in its generally accepted legal use and includes "relief of the poor, the distressed, or the underprivileged . . . lessening the burdens of government; lessening neighborhood tensions; eliminating prejudice and discrimination; defending human and civil rights secured by law; and combating community deterioration and juvenile delinquency."[18] Many superhero organizations could qualify under one or more of those provisions, particularly "lessening the burdens of government"

---

17. 26 U.S.C. § 501(c)(3).

18. INTERNAL REVENUE SERV., INTERNAL REVENUE MANUAL § 7.25.3.5 (1999), *available at* http://www.irs.gov/irm/part7/irm_07-025-003.html.

and "defending human and civil rights secured by law; and combating community deterioration and juvenile delinquency."

However, there are important restrictions in the amount of political campaigning and legislative or lobbying activities that a 501(c)(3) not-for-profit corporation can engage in, which may be relevant to a superhero organization that opposes a law such as the Superhuman Registration Act or which opposes an anti-mutant candidate for office. We're afraid that the finer details of nonprofit and campaign finance are beyond the scope of this book, however.

Limited Liability Companies

Regular corporations are not the only kind of corporate form. Limited liability companies are an increasingly popular alternative to regular corporations in many contexts. Like corporations, LLCs are defined by state statutes, and there are variations in the statutes from state to state. LLCs are a rather unique "hybrid entity," in that they have limited personal liability like corporations, but have the option of being taxed like a corporation, a partnership (i.e., pass-through taxation), or, for single-member LLCs, the entity can be disregarded for tax purposes. Through this combination of limited personal liability and partnership taxation, and without the restrictions on membership that S-corporations have, the LLC can provide advantages unavailable to corporations, partnerships, or limited partnerships. LLCs can have a single or multiple members, and most states permit all members to participate in the management and control of the company without the member losing their limited personal liability.[19] As an alternative method of control, many state statutes also allow the LLC to appoint one or more managers to control the business of the company.[20]

---

19. J. WILLIAM CALLISON AND MAUREEN A. SULLIVAN, LIMITED LIABILITY COMPANIES: A STATE-BY-STATE GUIDE TO LAW AND PRACTICE § 1:1 (2011); *Id.* at § 1:3.

20. *Id.* at § 1:3.

LLCs are also comparatively easy to set up in most states and often require fewer corporate formalities or annual filings, which makes them appealing for superheroes who are looking for a corporate structure where they do not need to publicly disclose as much information. The LLC is typically formed by filing articles of organization with the state government.[21] The owners of the company (called "members" of the LLC) can, or in some states must, create a written operating agreement that sets forth the rules governing the business, not unlike the Avengers' charter.[22] Several states have also recently allowed the creation of low-profit or not-for-profit limited liability company statutes, which may be of particular interest to superhero organizations.[23]

The question then becomes which of the above would be best suited for something like the Avengers or the Justice League?

Choosing a Business Organization

As a first order question, we should probably ask whether our organization is going to be part of the private sector at all. Since the *Civil War* event in the Marvel Universe, the Avengers are organized under the auspices of the federal Fifty State Initiative and thus probably don't need to have any kind of corporate entity. But prior to that they were a private group funded by Tony Stark through the Maria Stark Foundation, his personal not-for-profit.[24] The Justice League's origins are a little harder to discuss with any kind of certainty due to the frequent and conflicting retcons DC has had over the past few decades, but it seems plausible that the group could have alternated

---

21. *Id.* at § 3:2.

22. *Id.* at § 3:7; *See, e.g.*, Mo. Rev. Stat. § 347.081(1) (2004) for an example of a state statute requiring the adoption of an operating agreement.

23. *Id.* at § 1:1.

24. As a not-for-profit, the Maria Stark Foundation itself is likely organized as a corporation.

between public and private at various points in its history. The Fantastic Four almost certainly have (or should have) a business organization that leases the Four's headquarters, owns its vehicles and other assets, and takes in income and pays the team members.

Anyhow, what form are we going to choose? The heroes certainly seem to act like they're partners much of the time, but here's the thing: One of the biggest reasons to be a partnership rather than a corporation has to do with taxes, as corporations have a higher income tax rate than individuals. True, multinational companies are infamous for coming up with zero or even *negative* tax liabilities despite record-breaking profits, but you need to generate way more revenue than most of our superheroes ever do, even working together, to achieve that kind of silliness. Those sorts of manipulations involve complicated accounting practices related to expenses, capital depreciation, and shifting revenue to overseas subsidiaries, which just aren't relevant here. Since most superhero teams have no income—and thus would pay no taxes—why not be a regular corporation? The limited liability protection would certainly be nice, right?

Well, for one thing, corporate governance is kind of a pain in the neck, which is the other reason many small businesses are partnerships or LLCs: doing anything as a corporation just involves more paperwork. It's hard to imagine Superman and Wonder Woman sitting down in the boardroom deciding whether they, together, have enough shareholder votes to get the League to do a mission they support or whether they need to bring in someone else, maybe giving him additional control of . . . It's boring just thinking about it! Luckily, comic book writers can happily gloss over those messy details.

Partnerships are significantly less formal. Partners can act independently, and if they don't get along, hey, that's the end of it. Each is more or less capable of taking his ball and going home, particularly when said ball doesn't involve messy, illiquid capital investments such as a headquarters or vehicles. The problem is that most superhero groups aren't profit-seeking organizations, which means they can't organize as a partnership of any kind.

An LLC could suit many superhero organizations quite well. Only a few states require that LLCs be for-profit businesses, and some states even explicitly recognize not-for-profit LLCs. In a state that does not require LLCs to be for-profit, a regular LLC that isn't trying to make a profit simply won't get the tax benefits of being a not-for-profit. LLCs also have the advantage of being easy to set up and easier to run than corporations, but provide the similar liability protections, unlike partnerships. As a result, an LLC is a good choice for most superhero teams, especially smaller ones like the Fantastic Four and the Justice League.

The Avengers, however, are not an informal group. They own bases and vehicles, have a large operating budget, and employ numerous superheroes and regular employees. Rather than a partnership of more or less equals, like the Justice League, the Avengers have a hierarchy organized along traditional company lines. As a result, a regular corporation or LLC likely suits them best.

Superhero Corporations and Liability

Of course, for some superheroes the question of involvement with a corporation is not a hypothetical one. The Fantastic Four, Bruce Wayne, and Tony Stark all have ties to companies, and this naturally raises questions about whether the superheroes' actions could affect their respective businesses—and vice versa!

Superheroes and *Respondeat Superior*

Respondeat superior ("let the master answer") is the legal doctrine by which employers can be held accountable for the torts of their employees under certain circumstances.[25] Specifically, the employee

---

25. In some states, the employer can then seek indemnification from the employee (i.e., sue them). As a practical matter, however, many employees are "judgment proof" and cannot afford to pay the damages, which is one of the justifications for *respondeat superior*.

must be acting within the scope of his or her employment.[26] "An employee acts within the scope of employment when performing work assigned by the employer or engaging in a course of conduct subject to the employer's control. An employee's act is not within the scope of employment when it occurs within an independent course of conduct not intended by the employee to serve any purpose of the employer."[27] This is a very important distinction, as it makes the difference between liability and non-liability for some superheroes.

For example, while Bruce Wayne often uses Wayne Enterprises resources when fighting crime as Batman, such crime fighting isn't work assigned by his employer or subject to his employer's control. In fact, most Wayne Enterprises employees and shareholders are, like the general public, unaware that Bruce Wayne is Batman. And while Batman may sometimes take actions that benefit Wayne Enterprises (e.g., preventing a criminal from stealing from the company), his motivation is to fight crime in general, not to benefit his employer. Thus, Wayne Enterprises is probably not liable for Batman's torts. Which is good, because there are a lot of them.

The situation is very different when one considers DC's recent *Batman Incorporated* title. Batman, Inc. is a recent effort by Batman to adopt a franchise model for Batman, funding various Batmen around the United States and the rest of the world. This presents a significant liability problem because Wayne Enterprises directly and publicly funds and equips these new Batmen, although Bruce Wayne's identity as Batman is still a secret. Since Wayne Enterprises is providing the funding, equipment, and coordination, a court would likely view the Batmen as employees rather than independent contractors.[28]

---

26. *See* RESTATEMENT (THIRD) OF AGENCY §§ 2.04 and 7.07(1) (2006).

27. RESTATEMENT (THIRD) OF AGENCY, §7.07(2) (2006).

28. *Respondeat superior* only applies to the torts of employees, not independent contractors. It is possible to sue someone for the negligent hiring of an independent contractor, but that's harder to do than suing an employer under *respondeat superior*.

As a result, Wayne Enterprises has opened itself up to potentially massive liability. A more prudent approach would have been to create a separate nonprofit organization (not owned or controlled by Wayne Enterprises) that funds the Batmen; the intermediary organization would shield Wayne Enterprises from liability. Our next example actually follows that model.

When Tony Stark works with the Avengers as Iron Man, he isn't there as an employee of Stark Industries,[29] nor does Stark Industries fund the Avengers directly. That's the role of the Maria Stark Foundation, which functions as a liability shield. However, because the Avengers are themselves a corporate entity of some kind, the Avengers organization may be held liable for the torts of the individual Avengers if the torts were committed within the scope of the members' employment. But at least liability would be effectively limited to the assets of the Avengers organization (and possibly the Maria Stark Foundation) rather than potentially bankrupting all of Stark Industries.

The Fantastic Four are, like the Avengers, another example of a superhero team to which *respondeat superior* would likely apply. It's not clear exactly how the Fantastic Four are organized as a business, but it is clear that there is some kind of entity that leases the Fantastic Four headquarters and collects licensing revenue from Reed Richards's patents. When the Fantastic Four act as superheroes, they seem to do so under the auspices of that same organization. As a result, the organization could be liable for any torts they commit while on a mission.

Piercing the Superhero Corporate Veil

What about liability flowing in the other direction? Could Bruce Wayne or Tony Stark be personally liable for the actions of Wayne

---

29. Or Stark International, Stark Enterprises, etc. The name of Stark's company changes almost as often as his armor does.

Batman sets up franchises. Grant Morrison et al., *Resurrector*, in BATMAN INCOPORATED 2 (DC Comics February 2011); Grant Morrison et al., *Scorpion Tango*, in BATMAN INCORPORATED 3 (DC Comics March 2011); Grant Morrison et al., *Nyktomorph*, in BATMAN INCORPORATED 6 (DC Comics June 2011).

Enterprises or Stark Industries? Although most of their wealth is probably tied up in shares of stock in their companies, both of them are independently wealthy and would make very attractive targets in a lawsuit. We noted that "piercing the corporate veil" to sue the managers or shareholders of a corporation, the partners of a limited liability partnership, or the members of an LLC is very difficult. But it's not impossible.

There are a few different theories under which a court will pierce the corporate veil. A common one is the "alter ego" theory, under which the corporation is a "mere extension of the individual."[30] Some of the factors that a jury may look to when deciding if a corporation is an alter ego include

> if the individual controls the corporation and conducts its business affairs without due regard for the separate corporate nature of the business; or that such separate corporate nature ceased to exist; or if the corporate assets are dealt with by the individual as if owned by the individual; or if corporate formalities are not adhered to by the corporation;

---

30. Or a subsidiary corporation, but we're concerned with individuals here, not corporate shell games.

or if the individual is using the corporate entity as a sham to perpetrate fraud or to avoid personal liability.[31]

Luckily for our heroes, this doesn't come up much. Both Wayne Enterprises and Stark Industries are massive, well-run conglomerates with boards of directors (and in the case of Wayne Enterprises a professional CEO). Both companies are generally good "corporate citizens" that follow the law. As a result, it would be highly unlikely for either Wayne or Stark to be personally liable for anything their respective companies did.

The situation with the Fantastic Four is a little closer cut. The company seems to consist of the Four themselves, without a lot of other employees or directors providing oversight. They also live in the company's headquarters. As a result, the Fantastic Four will have to be careful to maintain a separate corporate existence (e.g., maintaining separate corporate accounts, signing letters and documents as corporate officers rather than individuals, properly maintaining corporate minute books).

Superpowers and the Americans with Disabilities Act

In chapter 1, we discussed how superpowered individuals, specifically mutants, could be protected by the Constitution. But there's more to civil rights than the Constitution. Congress and the state legislatures have also passed laws that go beyond the constitutional minimums, and many of these laws primarily regulate businesses rather than individual behavior. One of the most important of these is the Americans with Disabilities Act.[32] The ADA is particularly

---

31. Castleberry v. Branscum, 721 S.W.2d 270, 275–76 (Tex. 1986).

32. 42 U.S.C. § 12101 *et seq.*

important because people with disabilities are not a protected class under the Constitution, so their legal protections must come from the legislature.[33] Could mutants and other people with superpowers be covered by the ADA?

The Scope of the ADA

The ADA defines a disability as "a physical or mental impairment that substantially limits one or more major life activities."[34] Perhaps equally importantly, a disability can also simply consist of "being regarded as having such an impairment."[35] In other words, even if you aren't actually impaired, it's sufficient that you are discriminated against in violation of the ADA because you are regarded as being so impaired. Both of these definitions depend heavily on the meaning of phrases like "major life activity." Luckily, the statute goes on to define those terms as well:

> [M]ajor life activities include, but are not limited to, caring for oneself, performing manual tasks, seeing, hearing, eating, sleeping, walking, standing, lifting, bending, speaking, breathing, learning, reading, concentrating, thinking, communicating, and working. . . . [A] major life activity also includes the operation of a major bodily function. . . .[36]

Furthermore, Congress intended for all of these terms to be construed broadly:

> The definition of disability in this chapter shall be construed in favor of broad coverage of individuals under this chapter,

---

33. *See* Cleburne v. Cleburne Living Center, 473 U.S. 432 (1985).

34. 42 U.S.C. § 12102(1)(A).

35. 42 U.S.C. § 12102(1)(C).

36. 42 U.S.C. § 12102(2)(A-B).

to the maximum extent permitted by the terms of this chapter. . . . An impairment that substantially limits one major life activity need not limit other major life activities in order to be considered a disability. . . . An impairment that is episodic or in remission is a disability if it would substantially limit a major life activity when active. . . . The determination of whether an impairment substantially limits a major life activity shall be made without regard to the ameliorative effects of mitigating measures. . . .[37]

Armed with a sense of the scope of the ADA, let's analyze whether it might apply to superpowers.

What Superpowers Qualify?

Right off the bat, we can see that, in general, voluntarily controlled superpowers generally will not qualify as disabilities. It's pretty hard for, say, the ability to fly to substantially limit a major life activity, especially if you can simply choose not to use it. But not all superpowers are voluntary, and whether the power is continuous (like Rogue's involuntary life-draining power) or only poorly controlled (like Bruce Banner's transformation into the Hulk) doesn't matter because an episodic impairment still counts.

Before her power evolved, Rogue's involuntary, lethal ability to drain the life out of others simply by touching them would have qualified because touching others seems like a major life activity. Certainly it is a common part of communication and many jobs (e.g., handshakes, receiving money from customers and returning change). Bruce Banner's power definitely qualifies as it also frequently interferes with work and communication ("Hulk smash!"). Cyclops's power may also qualify. A slightly less serious example along the same lines is Moist from Joss Whedon's *Dr. Horrible's Sing-Along*

---

37. 42 U.S.C. § 12102(4)(A,C-D) and (E)(i).

Ready for that shower now? Zack Whedon et al., DR. HORRIBLE AND OTHER HORRIBLE STORIES (Dark Horse September 2010).

Blog, whose "power" consists of the uncontrollable production of pro-digious amounts of sweat.

Although Hank McCoy's (Beast) and Kurt Wagner's (Night-crawler) physical appearances might not be considered outright dis-abilities, they may be discriminated against because they are *perceived* as being impaired, which fits 12102(C).

The Protections of the ADA

The ADA offers many legal protections to disabled individuals. In general, discrimination on the basis of disability is prohibited in employment, provision of public services, and in public accommoda-tions and services provided by private entities. For the purposes of this chapter we will focus on employment discrimination.

The general rule against employment discrimination is this:

No [employer] shall discriminate against a qualified indi-vidual on the basis of disability in regard to job application procedures, the hiring, advancement, or discharge of employees, employee compensation, job training, and other terms, conditions, and privileges of employment.[38]

Seems straightforward and complete, right? However, there are important defenses to charges of discrimination, such as when discrimination is "job-related and consistent with business necessity, and such performance cannot be accomplished by reasonable accommodation" and when a qualification standard includes "a requirement that an individual shall not pose a direct threat to the health or safety of other individuals in the workplace."[39] Reasonable accommodation is a broad term, but it's basically anything that isn't an undue hardship ("an action requiring significant difficulty or expense").

Since there are defenses, the natural question is, what can employers get away with?

Reasonable Accommodation and Undue Hardship

Two examples of powers that can almost certainly be reasonably accommodated are Rogue's power and Cyclops's power. For most jobs, Rogue could simply be allowed to wear gloves and other appropriate clothing. There are very few jobs for which Rogue could not be reasonably accommodated. Similarly, Cyclops could be allowed to wear his blast-taming glasses or other appropriate headgear. He probably couldn't be reasonably accommodated as an actor in a commercial for eyedrops or the like, but that's about it.

Other cases are less clear. Bruce Banner would probably not be so well protected. His power would definitely raise the issue of "a direct threat to the health or safety of other individuals in the workplace." Any work environment that involved close interaction with

---

38. 42 U.S.C. § 12112(a).

39. 42 U.S.C. § 12113(a, b). We're looking at you, Mr. Banner.

other employees, customers, or other sources of stress would pose a significant challenge. In many cases there simply may be no reasonable accommodation for someone who turns into an "enormous green rage monster" at the drop of a hat.

Although most superpowers are not impairments, many superpowered individuals (particularly mutants in the Marvel Universe) face discrimination despite the fact that they are not actually impaired. In addition, there are some superpowers that do impair their possessors. As a result, the ADA would protect many superpowered individuals from discrimination in several important areas of life.

Supervillains and Business Law

Sometimes even supervillains can find themselves dealing with business law, at least on the wrong end of a lawsuit. This example from *Manhunter* touches on labor laws, employee class actions, and bankruptcy.

In the story, a multinational pharmaceutical/biotech/medical device company called Vesetech runs a plant in El Paso, Texas, where it employs many Mexican women who live in Ciudad Juárez across the border. While investigating the disappearances of a large number of women in the area, Kate Spencer (a.k.a. Manhunter) discovers that Vesetech was kidnapping the women and using them in unethical medical experiments. After busting up the supervillain-led research team, Spencer, who is also an attorney, announces at a press conference that she is leading a class action lawsuit against the company on behalf of the former employees.

Federal Labor Laws

Kate says that Vesetech pays the women "pennies," suggesting a violation of minimum wage laws. For violations of the federal minimum wage (the same as the state minimum wage in Texas), employees

Kate Spencer announces her class action suit against Vesetech on national news. A good trial lawyer knows how to make good use of publicity. Marc Andreyko et al., *Forgotten, Part Six: Full Circle*, in MANHUNTER (VOL. 3) 36 (DC Comics January 2009).

can sue for both back wages and an equal amount as liquidated damages.[40] However, violations of the federal minimum wage law are frequently enforced by the Department of Labor's Wage and Hour division, which is empowered to sue on the employee's behalf.[41] If the Department of Labor steps in, then that terminates the employee's right to sue on her own behalf.[42] So there's a very good chance that part of the suit could be dismissed. But there would still be the injuries suffered by the women who were experimented on.

Class Actions and Federal Jurisdiction

Kate also announces that she will represent the women in a class action lawsuit, but things aren't that simple. A judge must first certify the class, and the plaintiffs in this case may not meet the re-

40. 29 U.S.C. § 216(b).

41. 29 U.S.C. § 217.

42. 29 U.S.C. § 216(b).

quirements. For simplicity we'll assume that the case would be brought in federal court. Bringing a case in federal court requires (among other things) that the court have subject matter jurisdiction. That is, since the federal courts are courts of limited jurisdiction, it must be the kind of case that the federal courts can address.

In brief, federal courts can get subject matter jurisdiction three ways: the "Arising Under" clause,[43] diversity of citizenship,[44] and supplemental jurisdiction.[45] The Arising Under clause grants jurisdiction in cases involving a question of federal law. Diversity of citizenship applies when no plaintiff is a citizen of the same state as any defendant and the amount in controversy is at least $75,000. Supplemental jurisdiction allows state law issues to tag along when they are related to another claim or controversy that the court had jurisdiction over.

In this case, federal jurisdiction seems likely since the plaintiffs are all Mexican citizens, whereas the defendant is a US corporation, giving a federal court jurisdiction under diversity of citizenship.[46] There may also be federal question jurisdiction (e.g., if the women sue for wages and the Department of Labor doesn't step in).

In any case, federal class actions are governed by Federal Rule of Civil Procedure 23. There are several requirements,[47] but the biggest issue in this case is probably commonality: Are there "questions of

---

43. U.S. Const., Art III § 2, cl. 1.

44. 28 U.S.C. § 1332.

45. 28 U.S.C. § 1367.

46. Legal pedantry note: It is broadly assumed that this is so, but the Supreme Court has indicated in dictum that a foreign plaintiff may not claim federal jurisdiction under diversity of citizenship. Verlinden BV v. Central Bank of Nigeria, 461 U.S. 480, 492 (1983). It is not completely clear what the answer is in a case like this, with foreign plaintiffs and a US defendant.

47. These requirements are usually referred to as *numerosity* ("the class is so numerous that joinder of all members is impracticable"), *commonality* ("there are questions of law or fact common to the class"), *typicality* ("the claims or defenses of the representative parties are typical of the claims or defenses of the class"), and *adequacy of repre-*

law or fact common to the class?" The problem is that there are at least two groups of plaintiffs: women who were paid below minimum wage and the women who were experimented on (or at least the deceased women's estates). Admittedly, members of the latter group may also be members of the former group, but the questions of law and fact are very different between the two groups. It is possible that a federal court would consolidate the cases, but they would probably best be brought as two separate suits.

But even that may not be enough. Unless the women were subjected to at least broadly similar mistreatment at the hands of Vesetech's "scientists" then a class action may not be the best way to resolve their claims. A court could decide that the women's injuries are too unique to be treated as a class.

The Measure of Damages

During the press conference Kate explains that data gleaned from Vesetech's human experiments may have been used to develop a range of highly profitable and widely used products. Kate says that this is "fruit of the poisonous tree" (a rather terrible misuse of a legal phrase; read Chapter 4 on criminal procedure to learn why). Anyway, it is implied that this has something to do with the women's case. Ordinarily the women's damages would be what it took to compensate them (or their estates) for their injuries, plus likely punitive damages of up to ten times the compensatory damages.[48] The women would ordinarily not be entitled to any share of the ill-gotten gains derived from their suffering.

However, the equitable remedy of restitution may allow the women to recover some of those ill-gotten gains. But as an equitable

---

sentation ("the representative parties will fairly and adequately protect the interests of the class").

48. *See* State Farm Mut. Auto. Ins. Co. v. Campbell, 538 U.S. 408 (2003) (holding that Due Process generally requires punitive damages be less than ten times the compensatory damages).

remedy, restitution is discretionary, so a court may or may not impose it.

Tort Claimants and Bankruptcy

The real bad news is that Vesetech is almost certainly going to be bankrupt in short order: All of its facilities around the world were raided, virtually every aspect of its business is suspect, and it is looking at massive criminal penalties. What's more, tort claims are general unsecured claims, a.k.a. "the back of the line" in bankruptcy. So even if the women's case is successful, they may ultimately receive nothing as secured creditors and the government take everything the corporation owns in liquidation. Sad, but that's the law for you.

CHAPTER 8

Administrative Law

In a classic Silver Age comic, Superman finds himself facing that most dreaded of foes: the IRS agent.[1] The IRS figures out that Superman has been receiving a fortune in reward money, squeezing coal into diamonds, and digging up buried treasure, all without paying taxes on it. In typical Silver Age style, Superman tries a variety of crazy schemes to earn money to pay the billion dollars in back taxes he is assessed, but in the end everything is resolved with a simple loophole: Since Superman routinely saves the entire planet, he can claim everyone on Earth as a dependent, thus zeroing out his tax bill. Although the story is lighthearted (and that tax dodge almost certainly wouldn't work), it's one of many examples of the ways administrative agencies like the IRS can affect superheroes.

Administrative agencies touch on almost every aspect of life and business. There are over 160,000 pages of federal regulations alone! It's not surprising, then, that there are many regulations that impact superheroes, from flying machines to weapons to experimental med-

---

1. Robert Bernstein et al., *Superman Owes a Billion Dollars!*, in SUPERMAN (VOL. 1) 148 (DC Comics October 1961).

Two things are certain in life, even for Superman: death and taxes. Robert Bernstein et al., *Superman Owes a Billion Dollars!*, in SUPERMAN (VOL. 1) 148 (DC Comics October 1961).

ical procedures. And, as that Superman story showed, the IRS catches up to everyone eventually. But the wide reach of administrative agencies is a relatively new development.

Beginning in the middle of the twentieth century, right when superheroes took off, the American legal system was transformed by what amounts to the introduction of an entirely new *kind* of law. Legislation has existed basically forever, case law has been part of common law systems for centuries, and written constitutions became a touchstone of American jurisprudence in the late eighteenth century. But the introduction of administrative law in the New Deal period and its formalization after World War II was something new and different.

The New Deal saw the creation of a wide variety of federal agencies the likes of which had never before been seen, e.g., the Federal Deposit Insurance Corporation (FDIC), the Federal Housing Administration (FHA), the Civil Works Administration, the National Labor Relations Board, the Social Security Administration, the Tennessee Valley Authority, etc. A significant number of current federal agencies can trace their origins to some part of the New Deal.

The function of these agencies was not merely to implement congressional legislation—the executive branch had been doing that for a century at that point—but to essentially create *new* laws governing their particular area of competency, i.e., whatever the agency was in charge of regulating. So rather than following specific directions to do particular things, the agencies were given a significant deal of freedom to operate.

Congress was not entirely sanguine about this. The creation of these agencies shifted power from the legislative branch to the executive, and legislators are never really happy about that. But the circumstances of the Great Depression that led to the New Deal were dire, and WWII immediately followed, so Congress was unwilling to do all that much to rein in these agencies, many of which acted with almost zero oversight.[2] But once World War II was over, Congress wasted little time in reasserting its authority as the king of the hill in Washington.

This it did by passing the Administrative Procedure Act of 1946 (APA).[3] The APA, as it is known, sets forth a unified set of procedures by which all federal agencies must operate. The details of the law are the subject of an entire law school course, and there is insufficient space to do the topic justice here, but suffice it to say that since the 1940s, administrative law has played a bigger and bigger role in the lives and businesses of Americans.

Administrative Agencies v. Military Operations

Given the reach of administrative law, it is unsurprising that superheroes might run into issues. But there is one distinction that needs to be teased out before we launch into administrative agencies proper: Civilian administrative agencies are different from military operations.

2. This is particularly true of some of the agencies Roosevelt set up to manage various aspects of the war effort, e.g., the Office of Scientific Research and Development, which was run more or less as the personal fiefdom of Vannevar Bush.

3. Pub. L. No. 79-404, 60 Stat. 237 (codified at 5 U.S.C. § 500 *et seq.*).

This is significant because civilian agencies are subject to the APA and must be created and funded directly by Congress. Any rules they promulgate must go through the Notice and Comment procedure,[4] and the agency's funding is authorized by Congress. But military organizations such as the National Security Agency (NSA) and Central Intelligence Agency (CIA) are divisions of the Department of Defense, and their powers are far less circumscribed by civilian law than agencies like the Federal Communications Commission (FCC) and the Environmental Protection Agency (EPA). Budgets for these sorts of military agencies are frequently "black," or classified, and for quite some time the NSA was jokingly referred to as "No Such Agency," because it did not officially exist.[5]

Further, whereas civilian agencies require the passage of an "organic statute," i.e., a statute that creates and funds the agency, military organizations can be created by an Executive Order that does not require congressional involvement. Congress's ability to control defense spending is more limited than its ability to control other kinds of spending, because it shares war powers with the presidency. Once funding has been authorized for the Defense Department, the President and the Secretary of Defense have a significant amount of freedom to spend that money as they see fit, without necessarily telling Congress what's going on.

This is a very rough overview of the differences between military and civilian agencies. The relationship of the military and Congress has been fraught with controversy for almost the entire period since World War II, and though many military agencies do have or-

---

4. Essentially, before a rule becomes effective, the agency proposing it must give public notice of the proposed rule and respond to comments by the public on that rule. This is where a lot of lobbying happens.

5. On a more technical note, the CIA and other military agencies are not specifically exempted from the requirements of the APA, and they would seem to count as an "administrative agency" under 5 U.S.C. § 701. Regardless, as a matter of practice, the CIA does not comply with most of the requirements of the APA. The same goes for most other intelligence agencies and Department of Defense projects.

ganic statutes (e.g., the National Security Act of 1947, which authorized the National Security Agency), many of these statutes simply provided congressional authorization for organizations that already existed. Whether or not the President is *allowed* to create these agencies on his own authority has never really been established, but the fact is that it happens. The 9/11 attacks have not lessened the tension between Congress and the President caused by their shared War Powers, and this area of law continues to evolve.

As a result, the public does not have much information about what these sorts of agencies do, and their ability to engage in operations is presumably significantly broader than that of traditional law enforcement or other civilian agencies. So if a comic book character runs into a fictional agency that appears to be related to the military, there's a fair chance that whatever legal problems may be involved aren't strictly administrative law problems.[6]

Politics and Agency Administrators

Let's take a look directly at civilian agencies then. The Marvel *Civil War* event ran during 2006–2007 and tells the story of the passage of the Superhuman Registration Act and its aftermath. The gist of the story is that the American populace had been growing increasingly uncomfortable with the thought of unlicensed and unknown individuals with superhuman abilities just sort of running loose across the country, but these fears were, until then, balanced out by the efforts of some of these superhumans to protect and serve. This calculus changed when an irresponsible group of young mutants wound up involved in the destruction of an elementary school in Stamford, Connecticut, on live television. The SHRA was passed due to the huge public outcry.

---

6. For example, see the discussion of the draft in chapter 1.

The constitutionality and other aspects of the law are discussed in chapter 1. Here, we are interested in the implementation. What the law seems to have done is to follow Congress's typical pattern when it wishes to regulate something. For example, rather than set specific environmental targets by statute, Congress created the EPA to do the work of figuring out what those targets should be and giving the EPA the authority to enforce those regulations. Likewise, rather than coming up with a plan detailing exactly how superheroes are to be registered and what happens to them once they do (or if they refuse), Congress created a new federal agency that it empowered to take care of things.[7] Tony Stark, whose identity as Iron Man was public knowledge by this point, is initially chosen as the head of the new agency, which given his business experience and political connections makes a certain amount of sense. CEO types are frequently appointed heads of federal agencies.[8]

In this case, though, things end badly. Stark has never really been known for being a humble, cooperative type. On the contrary, he's pretty egotistical and arrogant, and once he's convinced he's right, he tends not to pull any punches. This persuades Captain America to lead a resistance movement, kicking off the eponymous civil war among superheroes. In addition to the main civil rights issue (see chapter 1), many of the resisters did not trust Stark or his agency to adequately care for registered heroes' privacy or protect them from the resulting danger.

---

7. Well, sort of anyway. The specifics of the law are never really worked out all that well, and S.H.I.E.L.D., the fictional Office of National Emergency, and the real-life Department of Homeland Security are inconsistently depicted as having responsibility for varying aspects of the law's implementation. It seems likely that the editors never sat everyone down and decided how this was going to work, which would explain a lot of consistency problems in the event.

8. Which is actually a pretty controversial political issue and has led to a perceived "revolving door" between government and industry. The issue is that putting former industry executives in charge of regulating their own industries does little to allay suspicions of sweetheart deals and even outright corruption.

But in a *What If?* issue published towards the end of the event, the authors took a look at what might have happened if Steve Rogers rather than Tony Stark had been appointed head of the agency. The suggestion is that things would have turned out quite differently, as Rogers is widely trusted by just about the entire superhero community and his leadership would have allayed many of the resisters' fears.

What's so interesting about this is that administrators really can have a huge impact on the conduct and mission of federal agencies. This is one of the main reasons why winning a presidential election is such a big deal. In addition to the ability to sign or veto laws passed by Congress, the President has the opportunity to appoint the heads of almost every federal agency out there.[9] This is *hugely* important, as administrative agencies have a wide range of discretion in the regulations they pursue and enforce.

Take the recent issue of "net neutrality," i.e., how the Internet is or is not to be regulated. President George W. Bush was generally of the opinion that the federal government should basically leave this alone, and the chairman of the FCC, at his direction, focused his energies elsewhere. But President Obama has made this a priority, and under its new chairman, the FCC has spent a decent amount of Obama's term trying to develop net neutrality rules. Similarly, Bush's EPA administrator significantly backed off environmental regulations and enforcement, but Obama's has strengthened its enforcement activities and started the process of regulating carbon dioxide, something never attempted before. Picking a different agency head has a huge impact on how that agency works. So it is entirely realistic to believe that if Captain America had been in charge of the registration effort rather than Iron Man, the conflict in *Civil War* might have been almost entirely avoided.

---

9. Some agencies, like the Federal Reserve, are "independent," meaning they do not answer directly to . . . well anyone really. But these are the minority among agencies.

Air Traffic Control and the FAA

But hypothetical registration acts are not the only places where our heroes might find themselves running into administrative law problems. For example, many comic book characters fly, either via superpowers or awesome vehicles of their own design. Some do both. Many comic book stories tend to take place near major urban areas too, mostly New York City, Metropolis, and Gotham, but occasionally other cities as well.[10]

This is a problem, because all domestic airspace is regulated by the Federal Aviation Administration (FAA) and airspace around major urban areas is pretty tightly controlled. Granted, commercial airline and freight traffic is far more tightly regulated both in terms of inspection requirements and flight-plan filings than private and amateur flights, but unidentified aircraft detected over, say, Washington, DC, tend to result in the scrambling of fighters. Since September 11, 2001, such forces have been on constant standby, and there have been several instances in which wayward private aircraft have found themselves with military escorts, though no one has actually been shot down yet. Suffice it to say that the Fantasticar showing up on radar at the control towers at JFK International Airport and LaGuardia Airport without any kind of prior warning could cause a fairly major incident. It seems likely that a law-abiding superhero who planned on using a homebrew aircraft with any regularity would probably need to establish a working relationship with the FAA, and that would entail compliance with at least some FAA regulations, at the very least those regarding interfacing and communicating with air traffic control.

Superheroes who can fly under their own power, however, are

---

10. For example, see Marvel's various Fifty State Initiative stories to see superheroes at work in Philadelphia, Chicago, and Detroit, among other cities.

probably exempt from current FAA regulations. The FAA's regulations apply to "aircraft," which are defined by statute as "any contrivance invented, used, or designed to navigate, or fly in, the air."[11] The word "contrivance" is also used in the US Code to define vehicles and vessels, and so the implication is clear that a "contrivance" is limited to an artificial device of some kind rather than an innate ability.[12] As a result, Superman and other self-propelled superheroes are out of bounds for the FAA, whereas heroes like Batman, Iron Man, and arguably even the Green Lantern would have to deal with FAA regulations.

Pharmaceuticals, Medicine, and the FDA

Then there's the issue of medical and pharmaceutical regulation. The Food and Drug Administration (FDA) and the Drug Enforcement Administration (DEA) regulate the pharmaceutical market pretty tightly. But interesting drugs and other medical procedures are staples of comic book stories, from the military experiments that gave Wolverine his adamantium skeleton and Deadpool his healing factor, the mind-control drugs of Professor Pyg, or the Extremis virus. All of these are problematic, because under federal law, no medical procedure, device, or drug may be used on a human subject without the involvement and approval of the FDA (and DEA where appropriate).

For supervillains, this isn't all that much of an issue, as if one is planning to destroy all of New York City, an additional charge of violating FDA regulations is the least of one's worries. But for someone like Tony Stark, who maintains a highly public persona as the head of a generally law-abiding multibillion-dollar corporation, this is not the sort of thing one messes with.

One of the reasons that these plot devices are so compelling—

---

11. 49 U.S.C. 40102(a)(6).

12. 1 U.S.C. 3–4 (defining "vessel" and "vehicle").

particularly of the *Weapon X* sort—is that the US and other governments *did* engage in widespread secret medical experimentation throughout the Cold War. The CIA's Project Bluebird involved experiments with mind-control devices, psychedelic drugs hoped to have applications as truth serums, hypnosis, sleep deprivation, and basically everything short of brain surgery in an attempt to develop espionage and counterespionage techniques. What other governments did—especially China—was rumored to be so horrifying that movies like *The Manchurian Candidate* took on an aura of eerie verisimilitude. In essence, what a lot of comic book stories seem to do is to assume that some of these experiments actually *worked*. So while private individuals conducting bizarre medical experiments in secret labs is pretty implausible given the reach and power of the FDA, stories involving off-book military experiments and rogue operatives are distressingly believable.

The FDA Approval Process

Not all comic book medicine is the work of supervillains, however. Reed Richards has tried for years to reverse Ben Grimm's transformation into the Thing, Bruce Banner has sought to cure himself, and many mutants have wished for a way to reverse their mutations, as in *X-Men: The Last Stand*. What would the process look like if these researchers followed the proper protocol for developing a new drug or vaccine?

Once a potential drug has been identified, the next step is usually animal testing. Without a convincing body of research showing that the new treatment was safe and effective in animals, the FDA is unlikely to allow human testing. Animal testing is itself subject to laws and regulations, particularly if the researchers or the institution receives federal funding.[13]

---

13. The Animal Welfare Act requires that federally funded animal research be reviewed by an Institutional Animal Care and Use Committee, which reports to the National Institutes of Health Office of Laboratory Animal Welfare.

Wait . . . Are you even a real doctor? And you want me to do what now? Stan Lee, Jack Kirby et al., *The Hulk vs. the Thing*, in FANTASTIC FOUR (VOL. 1) 25 (Marvel Comics April 1964).

After animal testing has been done, the researchers submit an Investigational New Drug (IND) application to the FDA. If the FDA approves, then Phase I clinical trials can begin. These trials are done with a small number of human subjects, and the purpose is typically to determine safety rather than efficacy. If the drug appears to be safe, then Phase II trials are conducted, which use a larger group of patients and determine both safety and efficacy. Finally, Phase III trials are large, long-term studies that compare the new drug with existing treatments.

Each of these trials are typically required to be overseen by an institutional review board, which ensures that the research is conducted in an ethical manner. If there is a problem with the study or if it is clear that the drug is unsafe or ineffective, then the FDA can stop the testing at each step of this process. If all of the results are promising, however, then the researchers can submit a New Drug Application (NDA). Once the FDA approves the NDA, then the drug can be sold on the market.

In emergency situations, the FDA can waive some of these procedural requirements. It is unlikely, though, that the FDA would ever allow a doctor to repeatedly experiment on a single patient (such as the Thing) without oversight, even if the patient consented.

In the real world this process often takes years and a large number of patients, so it's no surprise that comic books usually omit these details, especially when dealing with a unique disease. *X-Men: The Last Stand* probably comes closest to the reality of drug development: a long, expensive process conducted with significant oversight.

Superman and Taxes

The federal agency that we all butt into eventually is the IRS, and superheroes aren't immune to the long arm of tax law. For example, in *Superman III* Superman crushes coal into a diamond and gives it to Lana Lang. This iconic gift has become closely associated with the Superman character, but because we are attorneys we have to ask: Does someone have to pay tax on that? It might seem strange to think that the IRS would bother trying to come after Superman, but as mentioned earlier in this chapter, it's happened before. And speaking of which, just what about Superman's plan to claim the whole world as his dependent? First, we'll talk about the diamonds, which are also mentioned by the IRS agent in *Superman* #148.

There are actually two different questions in this case: (1) are the diamonds taxable income for Superman (or Clark Kent) and (2) are they taxable income for a recipient such as Lana Lang?

The answer to the first question is "probably not." A traditional, almost fundamental principle of income tax is that a gain in value must be realized before it can be taxed, although the definition of "realized" has expanded over the years, somewhat eroding the principle. The Internal Revenue Code provides that one example of income is "gains derived from dealings in property."[14] "Dealings" are not defined in the statute, but 26 U.S.C. § 1001 (a) defines the com-

---

14. 26 U.S.C. § 61(a)(3).

putation of "the gain from the sale or other disposition of property." It seems clear that improving the value of the carbon by turning it from coal to a diamond is not such a taxable event, since there is neither a sale nor disposition of the property. An analogy might be made to painting a picture or one that appreciates in value; the increase in value is not taxed until the painting is sold or otherwise transferred to someone else.

The answer to the second question is very different. If the diamond is given to Lana Lang, that is a gift, which has its own set of special rules. In the United States, gifts are generally not taxable income for the recipient.[15] But there is a gift tax that is ordinarily paid by the giver.[16] However, there is a significant exclusion for gifts that currently stands at thirteen thousand dollars per recipient per year, as well as a unified lifetime credit.[17] This credit may not solve the problem, however. Superman may have made other gifts that already used up the credit; he has certainly been around long enough to have done so! Presuming the diamond was given as a gift today and the lifetime credit was not available, would they exceed the exclusion?

Obviously this depends on the size and quality of the diamond and the state of the diamond market, but for example the diamond given to Lana Lang in *Superman III* appears to be about 3.5–4 carats and of very good quality. A similar diamond would cost somewhere between $150,000 and $400,000, depending on the particulars, which is far beyond the gift exclusion. So how much would Superman be on the hook for? The answer is "a lot." For example, if the ring were valued between $150,000 and $250,000, then the gift tax would be $38,800 plus 32 percent of the excess beyond $150,000, so potentially as much as $70,800.

---

15. 26 U.S.C. § 102(a).

16. 26 U.S.C. § 2501(a)(1) and 26 U.S.C. § 2502(c).

17. 26 U.S.C. § 2503 and 26 U.S.C. § 2505. The unified lifetime credit counts against the estate tax credit of 26 U.S.C. § 2010.

But is the fair market value of the diamond simply that of an ordinary diamond of like size and quality? The general rule for computing the value of gift of property is given in 26 C.F.R. § 25.2512-1: "The value of the property is the price at which such property would change hands between a willing buyer and a willing seller, neither being under any compulsion to buy or to sell, and both having reasonable knowledge of relevant facts." The unusual origin of the diamond is almost certainly a relevant fact, and if diamonds created by Superman are rare, which seems to be the case, then this particular diamond would command a significant premium, and the tax would be correspondingly higher.

This is a problem, since Clark Kent probably doesn't make enough money to pay the tax, and Superman probably doesn't want to get tangled up with the IRS. It is possible to perform a "net gift" for which the recipient pays the tax, but it is unlikely that Lana has the money for that either. She could sell the ring to pay the tax, of course, but that would defeat the purpose of the gift. Alternatively, Superman could give her several diamonds with the intention that she keep one as a ring and sell the others to pay the taxes on all of the diamonds. As complicated as that would be, it might be the only way to keep things aboveboard.

There is a way for Superman to avoid the gift tax, however. Unlike gifts of property, gratuitous services are not taxed (on the other hand, neither are they tax deductible if performed for a charity). Instead of giving Lana a diamond, Superman could crush a piece of coal that she owned, transforming it into a diamond. There are few ways in the real world to transform essentially worthless material into something extremely valuable with relatively little effort—celebrity autographs are one example—so the tax code doesn't bother trying to tax gratuitous services. In short, this is a tax loophole for Superman!

What if Lana doesn't have a lump of charcoal handy for Superman to transform into a diamond? Couldn't he give her a lump of coal (a low-value gift) and then perform the gratuitous service? Alas, the courts and the IRS would look past the form of the transaction to its substance.[18] In this case, the substance of the transaction would be that Superman is really giving Lana a diamond rather than improving the value of a piece of property that she already had.

And speaking of Superman and tax loopholes, could he really claim everyone in the world as a dependent? We think not. The law allows two kinds of dependents, qualifying children and qualifying relatives, and most of the world is neither from Superman's point of view.[19] Among other requirements, a qualifying child must be a son, daughter, stepchild, foster child, or a descendant of any of them (e.g., a grandchild) or brother, sister, half brother, half sister, stepbrother, stepsister, or a descendant of any of them (e.g., a niece or nephew). Most versions of Superman have few or no such close relatives, so we don't even need to consider the other requirements for a qualifying child (age, residency, support, and the joint return test).

Similarly, there are several requirements for being a qualifying relative, but the killer is that the person must either live with you year-round or be related to you in one of several specified ways, none of which apply in Superman's case.[20] Alas, it looks like this particular tax dodge won't work.

---

18. *Gregory v. Helvering*, 293 U.S. 465 (1935).

19. 26 U.S.C. § 152.

20. These include children, stepchildren, foster children, or a descendant of any of them; siblings, half siblings, and stepsiblings; parents, grandparents, or other direct ancestors but not foster parents; stepparents; sons and daughters of a sibling or half sibling; aunts and uncles; and siblings-in-law, parents-in-law, and children-in-law. 26 U.S.C. § 152(d)(2).

CHAPTER 9

Intellectual Property

Intellectual property issues come up in comic books more often than one might think, sometimes explicitly and sometimes implicitly. As an area of law, intellectual property includes patents, copyrights, and trademarks. Each of these protects different subject matter, and comic books provide examples of all of them.

Patents

Broadly speaking, patents protect inventions.[1] Numerous superheroes and supervillains rely on gadgets, doomsday weapons, and other advanced technologies, so it makes sense that they would be interested in patent protection. In fact, Reed Richards (a.k.a. Mr. Fantastic) finances the Fantastic Four in part through licensing his patents. Both Wayne Enterprises and Stark Industries are multinational conglomerates that almost certainly rely on patents. A little further out

---

1. More specifically they protect new, useful, and nonobvious processes, machines, articles of manufacture, compositions of matter, and improvements thereof. 35 U.S.C. §§ 101, 103.

on the fringes are issues like whether the movie version of Spider-Man (who was bitten by a genetically modified spider) might infringe a gene patent simply by developing superpowers.

Congress is empowered to grant patents by the Constitution's Patent and Copyright Clause: "Congress shall have power to promote the Progress of Science and useful Arts, by securing for limited Times to Authors and Inventors the exclusive Right to their respective Writings and Discoveries."[2] Combined with the Supremacy Clause[3] and the doctrine of preemption, this means that states cannot enact their own patent or patent-like laws.[4] This is important because the same patent laws apply all over the country, including in Gotham—and thus to Wayne Enterprises—no matter which state Gotham is actually located in.

Batman and Patents

Batman's use of gadgets developed by Wayne Enterprises poses an intellectual property strategy problem for the company. Specifically, Batman's public use of the inventions may actually prevent Wayne Enterprises from obtaining patent protection. Luckily, there's a solution, albeit one that requires a little help from Bruce Wayne's friends in the Department of Defense.

Batman's gadgets are often based on advanced technology unavailable on the open market. Sometimes these gadgets are explained

---

2. U.S. CONST. art. I, § 8, cl. 8. Perhaps counterintuitively, patents apply to the "useful Arts" ("art" is used here in the sense of "artifice" or "artificial"). Splitting the parallel sentence makes this clearer: "To promote the Progress of useful Arts, by securing for limited Times to Inventors the exclusive Right to their respective Discoveries."

3. "This Constitution, and the Laws of the United States which shall be made in Pursuance thereof . . . shall be the supreme Law of the Land; . . . any Thing in the Constitution or Laws of any state to the Contrary notwithstanding." U.S. CONST. art. VI, cl. 2.

4. See Bonito Boats, Inc. v. Thunder Craft Boats, Inc., 489 U.S. 141 (1989) (holding a state law prohibiting the copying of boat hull designs preempted).

Reed Richards funds the Fantastic Four in part through patent licenses and sales but not always under the best circumstances. Selling the patents to the government is actually a reasonable thing to do. The federal government can own patents—in fact, it owns quite a few—and although the government cannot be enjoined from infringing a patent, it must pay reasonable compensation for any unlicensed use of a patented technology. 28 U.S.C. § 1498(a). Thus, the government might be interested in buying Reed's patents either in order to license the patents itself or to avoid having to pay Reed royalties. Mark Waid, Mike Wieringo et al., *Hereafter Part 1*, in FANTASTIC FOUR (VOL. 1) 509 (Marvel Comics March 2004).

as the product of Bruce Wayne's own considerable intellect. In other cases the gadgets (as in the recent movies) have their origin with Wayne Enterprises R & D, perhaps with some modifications for Batman's purposes.

Of course, Batman must always be ahead of the curve, so over time his gadgets have advanced to keep pace with technology. The flip side is that over time gadgets and advanced technologies that were once exclusive to Batman fall into common use, perhaps sold by Wayne Enterprises.

And therein lies the problem, at least for gadgets that come out of Wayne Enterprises R & D. Like many businesses, presumably Wayne Enterprises would seek to patent its inventions. But Batman's own use of the inventions in public may prevent Wayne Enterprises from obtaining a patent. In the United States, one cannot obtain a patent on something that was "patented, described in a printed publication, or in public use, on sale, or otherwise available to the public before the effective filing date of the claimed invention."[5] If Batman starts using a new Wayne Enterprises technology prior to the filing of the patent application, then he may have ruined the company's chance at a patent.[6]

Of course, Wayne Enterprises could always file for a patent before Batman starts using it, but that would mean disclosing the technology to the public eighteen months later when the patent application is published by the Patent and Trademark Office.[7] At most, Batman

---

5. 35 U.S.C. § 102(a)(1). This section was changed by the recently enacted America Invents Act ("AIA"). Historically, there was a one-year grace period during which an invention could be used in public without barring the inventor from filing for a patent. The AIA allows a grace period only if the public disclosure was made by the inventor or someone who obtained the invention from the inventor. 35 U.S.C. § 102(b)(1)(A). Arguably, Bruce obtained the invention from the inventor, but that still only buys Wayne Enterprises a year, and taking advantage of the grace period would effectively require admitting that Bruce Wayne and Batman are the same person.

6. Or if he uses it more than a year before the application date, per the previous footnote.

7. 35 U.S.C. § 122(b)(1)(A).

would have eighteen months in which to use the technology before supervillains could look it up online and start copying it (presumably supervillains are not concerned with patent infringement suits). Perhaps more important, it also means that supervillains could discover any weaknesses or limitations in the technology.

As Bruce Wayne, Batman could also keep the Wayne Enterprises technology to himself: using it in public—and thus destroying patentability—but also ordering Wayne Enterprises R & D to keep the technology on the shelf. In the end Wayne Enterprises still loses, whether because competitors can copy the unpatentable technology or because the company is prevented from selling the technology in order to keep it secret.

So Batman's use of Wayne Enterprise technology puts Bruce Wayne between a rock and a hard place: either harm the company that indirectly finances his heroics by using the technology in public or concede a round of the technological arms race by allowing the technology to be disclosed in a patent.

You might be thinking that all this talk of "public use" is a bit silly. After all, Batman isn't exactly walking around giving public demonstrations of his latest gadgets, much less explaining how they work. The patent laws, however, take a broad view of what constitutes public use. It was long ago established that it is enough that a single instance of the invention was used by a single person in public, even if the device itself and its method of operation were not visible (e.g., a hidden piece of armor beneath Batman's costume).[8] The purpose of this broad definition of public use is to induce inventors to disclose their inventions early; if the invention works well enough to use it in public, then it works well enough to be patented.

There is an exception to this rule for experimentation, but it is a narrow one, and it may not be practical in this case. In general, the

---

8. Egbert v. Lippman, 104 U.S. 333, 336 (1881) (holding that a hidden corset worn in public by a single person was a public use).

exception requires that the experimentation be done by or at the direction of the inventor as part of the development and testing of the invention.[9] Although Batman often uses gadgets that are not yet fully developed, it is doubtful that Wayne Enterprises would call Batman to the stand to testify that he was using a new gadget at the behest of a Wayne Enterprises scientist in order to test its performance under real-world conditions.

Furthermore, the experimental use exception also requires that the testing necessarily be in public, such as in the case of a new pavement material.[10] But most if not all of Batman's gadgets could be tested in a lab or other testing facility. It's hard to argue that it's necessary to test them on actual supervillains and criminals.

But now you might be saying: if Batman keeps his use of the gadget secret, and the criminals he catches don't understand or even notice the new technology, how will this ever be a problem in practice? Who's going to snitch? There are two major possibilities. First, Batman doesn't always have the luxury of operating in the shadows. Sometimes he works in public, and cameras and bystanders may observe new technology in use and equipment such as Batarangs may be left behind.[11] But the second and more serious problem is that Bruce Wayne himself and possibly other Wayne Enterprises employees (e.g., Lucius Fox) know of Batman's use of the technology. Would Bruce Wayne really be willing to break the law by perjuring himself in order for Wayne Enterprises to make more money? Even if he would, could he convince Lucius to go along? The version of Lucius in *The Dark Knight* might well not. We think he would probably choose for the company to forgo a patent in order to keep crime-fighting technology secret a while longer.

---

9. City of Elizabeth v. Pavement Co., 97 U.S. 126, 134 (1877).

10. *Id.*

11. Indeed, this is precisely what happened in the *Gotham Central* storyline "Motive": a neighborhood teen wound up getting hold of a Batarang left behind when Batman fought a villain in a high school.

There is hope for a work-around, however. Patent applications that include classified information are not published until either a set time period has expired or the secrecy order has been lifted.[12] But neither do such applications mature into patents; effectively they are held in limbo while they remain classified. So if Bruce Wayne could persuade, say, the Department of Defense to classify a given technology, then Wayne Enterprises could apply for a patent early on, Batman could use the technology, and once the time was right the classification could be lifted, the patent could issue, and Wayne Enterprises could make a lot of money. Given that Wayne Enterprises does a lot of work for the US military and given that Bruce Wayne is a very well-connected man, this is a plausible solution to the problem, though the Pentagon might make him share his toys.

Spider-Man and Gene Patents

In the 2002 *Spider-Man* film, Peter Parker became Spider-Man after being bitten by a genetically engineered spider, which apparently transmitted the modified genes to Parker.[13] Assuming the spiders were covered by one or more patents, could Spider-Man infringe those patents simply by developing superpowers? After all, patent infringement is a strict liability tort: it does not have to be intentional, and there is no "innocent infringer" defense.[14]

First, we have to decide what, exactly, we mean when we talk

---

12. 35 U.S.C. § 122(b)(2)(ii); 35 U.S.C. § 181; MPEP 120.

13. This is also how Parker got his powers in the *Ultimate Spider-Man* Universe. In the mainstream continuity, it was a radioactive spider, as depicted in Stan Lee, Steve Ditko et al., *Spider-Man!*, in AMAZING FANTASY (VOL. 1) 15 (Marvel Comics August 1962). We're looking at the genetically modified version here because of the way patent law works with biological entities.

14. *In re* Seagate Tech., LLC, 497 F.3d 1360, 1368 (Fed. Cir. 2007) ("patent infringement is a strict liability offense"); Hilton Davis Co. v. Warner-Jenkinson Co., Inc., 62 F.3d 1512, 1523 (Fed. Cir. 1995) (*en banc*) ("Accidental or 'innocent' infringement is still infringement"), *rev'd on other grounds*, 520 U.S. 17 (1997).

about spiders being covered by patents. People often talk about "gene patents," but what are they? In the United States there are two main kinds of claims in gene patents: claims to genetically modified organisms and claims to DNA or proteins produced by DNA.

There have been two recent developments regarding gene patents. First, the Federal Circuit, the appellate court that hears all patent-related appeals, recently affirmed the patentability of DNA sequences, including human DNA sequences.[15] Second, the America Invents Act of 2011[16] amended the Patent Act to prohibit patents "directed to or encompassing a human organism." This change would likely stop a patent infringement suit against Parker. There are other defenses, however.

The validity of claims to genetically modified organisms was first recognized in the landmark case *Diamond v. Chakrabarty.*[17] Although the *Chakrabarty* case involved a genetically modified bacterium, the Patent Office and the courts have subsequently recognized the validity of patents claiming multicellular organisms, including animals. So a genetically modified spider could be patented. But giving a human these same modifications would not be an infringement of the spider patent, because humans aren't spiders. The patent claim is not for the specific genetic modification as such, but for the genetically modified organism as a whole.

But what about claims to the DNA itself? Claims to DNA generally take the form of "purified and isolated DNA, wherein the DNA molecule has a nucleotide sequence as set forth in Fig. 1" or "a purified and isolated protein, as an expression product of a transformed host cell containing a DNA molecule coding for the protein, the

---

15. Ass'n for Molecular Pathology v. Myriad Genetics, Inc., No. 2010-1406 (Fed. Cir. July 29, 2011). Note that this case is likely to be reheard by the Federal Circuit or taken up by the Supreme Court, as it is seemingly contradicted by the AIA.

16. Pub. L. No. 112-29 (Sept. 16, 2011).

17. 447 U.S. 303 (1980).

DNA molecule having a nucleotide sequence as set forth in Fig. 1."
As you can see, these kinds of claims require a purified, isolated
form of DNA, which is not the natural state for DNA in the body, and
so Spider-Man wouldn't infringe such a claim.

Even the second example, a purified and isolated protein (such as
the proteins that make up spider silk), wouldn't apply because spider
silk is made up of several proteins. But one could imagine a patent
claiming spider silk produced by a genetically modified organism
having a particular DNA sequence. In fact, a patent application
claiming a genetically modified silkworm that produces spider silk
was filed in 2010.[18] So could a patent like that spell trouble for Spider-
Man?

We think not. The patent would likely have to claim a genetically modified spider or another specific organism (e.g., a silkworm),
which of course would not apply to a human. A patent that tried to
claim a broad class of organisms (e.g., mammals) modified to produce spider silk would be invalid for lack of "enablement" unless
the patent

> "contain[ed] a written description of the invention, and of
> the manner and process of making and using it, in such full,
> clear, concise, and exact terms as to enable any person skilled
> in the art to which it pertains, or with which it is most nearly
> connected, to make and use the same."[19]

Since genetic engineering is a fairly complex and difficult process, it is unlikely that a patent could describe a general process for
modifying organisms to produce spider silk.

The only way Spider-Man could infringe the patent, then, is if it
specifically claimed and described a genetically modified human

---

18. U.S. Pat. Appl. No. 12/842,269.

19. 35 U.S.C. § 112.

that produced spider silk. However, as discussed, the law now expressly prohibits such patents. Even without that prohibition it is likely that the Fifth and Fourteenth Amendments would forbid claims that covered genetically modified humans. For starters, a patent could not grant someone the right to exclude another human from reproducing (which of course means passing on DNA) because the Constitution protects "personal decisions relating to . . . procreation."[20] Another problem would be the unavoidability of infringement. Although patent infringement is a strict liability tort (i.e., there is no requirement that the infringement be intentional, knowing, or even negligent), there must still be an act of infringement. Simply existing is not an act, and penalizing Spider-Man for it would likely run afoul of the Constitution.[21]

Copyright

Like patents, copyrights are created by federal law and copyright issues have come up in comic books. We'll consider copyright and alternate universes, a copyright claim by the Joker, how copyright affects Peter Parker and Clark Kent, and how superheroes can use copyright to control the use of their image.

Copyright and Alternate Universes

In *New Excalibur*, Nocturne (a.k.a. Talia Wagner, the daughter of Nightcrawler from alternate universe Earth-2182) is transported to Marvel's mainstream continuity (Earth-616) by the Timebroker to "repair" a number of damaged timelines. She happens to have an iPod with a copy of the Beatles fortieth anniversary album on it. In

---

20. Planned Parenthood of Southeastern Pa. v. Casey, 505 U.S. 833, 851 (1992).

21. *See, e.g.*, Robinson v. California, 370 U.S. 660 (1962) (holding unconstitutional a law criminalizing being addicted to narcotics).

A Beatles album from an alternate universe might be the only Beatles music it's legal to copy. Chris Claremont et al., *Old Times Now are Not Forgotten!*, in NEW EXCALIBUR 4 (Marvel Comics April 2006).

her universe the Beatles never broke up, John Lennon wasn't killed, and they went on to create new music for years. Could anyone on Earth-616 (e.g., the "real" Beatles) lay claim to a copyright on this music or otherwise prevent its distribution?

To answer this question we first have to consider how copyright works. Following the Copyright Act of 1976, copyright in the United States "subsists . . . in original works of authorship fixed in any tangible medium of expression, now known or later developed, from which they can be perceived, reproduced, or otherwise communicated."[22] This means that copyright in a work exists the moment that the work is fixed in a tangible medium.[23] The practical upshot is that there is no copyright in the Beatles album unless there was copyright protection when it was created on Earth-2182.[24] Now we must consider the circumstances under which the United States recognizes the copyright of a work created in a foreign jurisdiction. For that we turn to the Berne Convention.[25]

The Berne Convention is an international treaty with 164 signatories—most of the countries in the world. The Convention works to harmonize several key aspects of copyright law, including copyright protection without formal registration and international recognition of copyright. Each signatory nation must treat works created in other signatory nations the same as works created domestically. The flip side is that signatories are not required to recognize a copyright in works created in non-signatory nations. However, because none of the countries on Earth-2182 are signatories to the Earth-616 Berne Convention, it is likely that the Beatles album has no copyright protection at all on Earth-616.

Even if the copyright were recognized, however, the remaining Earth-616 Beatles would not have a claim. They didn't create the tracks, and even if the album incorporated music that was substantially similar—or even identical—to Earth-616 Beatles music, the

---

22. 17 U.S.C. § 102(a).

23. Although registration is not required in order for copyright protection to exist, registration does have several benefits, including proof of ownership and the date of creation. Registration is also required before a copyright owner can sue for copyright infringement. 17 U.S.C. § 411(a).

24. Talia herself can't claim a copyright in the album because she was not the author.

25. The full title is the Berne Convention for the Protection of Literary and Artistic Works. Although it has been around since 1886, the United States only became a party to the Convention in 1989.

defense of independent creation absolves the Earth-2182 Beatles (and thus Talia) of any civil liability for infringement because the Earth-2182 Beatles created their music without ever knowing about the Earth-616 Beatles.[26] Indeed, coming up with the same music in an alternate universe is about as independent as independent creation can get. And independent creation is something the Earth-616 Beatles should be very familiar with.[27]

Just because the Earth-616 Beatles don't have a copyright claim does not mean they might not be able to prevent distribution of the album, however. Trademark law (discussed later in this chapter) and the right of publicity (discussed in chapter 5) provide alternative routes to accomplishing the same goal. Specifically, the Earth-616 Beatles could sue to prevent Talia and others from misrepresenting the music as "Beatles music." They could seek an injunction requiring people distributing the music to describe it as coming from an alternate universe with no connection to the Earth-616 Beatles. This would create a contrast to their own genuine Earth-616 Beatles creations.

Another possible complication comes from the possibility of criminal copyright infringement. While we may assume that Talia properly purchased her copy on Earth-2182, anyone else making copies might run afoul of the criminal copyright infringement statute.[28] If the United States government recognized a copyright in the

---

26. *See, e.g.,* Mazer v. Stein, 347 U.S. 201, 218 (1954). As the Court explained, "[A] copyrighted directory is not infringed by a similar directory which is the product of independent work. The copyright protects originality rather than novelty or invention—conferring only the sole right of multiplying copies. Absent copying there can be no infringement of copyright."

27. *See* Bright Tunes Music Corp. v. Harrisongs Music, Ltd., 420 F. Supp. 177 (S.D.N.Y. 1976). In that case Bright Tunes alleged that former Beatle George Harrison copied the melody of The Chiffons' "He's So Fine" when he wrote "My Sweet Lord." Harrison claimed the defense of independent creation, but the judge held that, while Harrison did not deliberately copy "He's So Fine," he did copy it subconsciously.

28. 17 U.S.C. § 506, which provides for significant fines and even prison sentences.

album, it could prosecute distributors of the work even though the copyright holders couldn't possibly benefit, since they're in an alternate universe.

The Joker's Copyright Claim

In *Detective Comics* #475, the Joker causes all of the fish in Gotham Harbor to take on a twisted, Joker-like expression. He then goes to the Gotham City division of the Copyright Commission[29] and demands to register a copyright on the fish. Why? Well, Batman says in this very comic: "The Joker's mind is clouded in madness! His motives make sense to him alone!" In other words, who knows? In any case, the clerk refuses, saying that fish are a natural resource and cannot be copyrighted. Was he right, or did the Joker have a legitimate copyright claim?

We think the copyright clerk was right. First, living organisms and genetically modified DNA are not copyrightable, although several commentators have proposed it, going back to the early 1980s.[30] Patents can be used to protect genetically engineered organisms,[31] and special plant patents can protect certain kinds of plants.[32] But so far, at least, copyright is right out.

Even if the fish could be copyrighted, there are other defenses which make the Joker's plan problematic. First of all, no one is copying the fish. They reproduce naturally, on their own, so the fact that

---

29. In reality, the Copyright Office (not Commission) is located in the Library of Congress's James Madison Building in Washington, DC, and doesn't have branch offices.

30. *See, e.g.,* Christopher M. Holman, *Copyright for Engineered DNA: An Idea Whose Time Has Come?*, 113 W. VA. L. REV. 699, 704–05 (2011); James G. Silva, *Copyright Protection of Biotechnology Works: Into the Dustbin of History?*, 2000 B.C. INTELL. PROP. & TECH. F. 12801 (2000); Irving Kayton, *Copyright in Living Genetically Engineered Works*, 50 GEO. WASH. L. REV. 191 (1982).

31. Diamond v. Chakrabarty, 447 U.S. 303 (1980).

32. 7 U.S.C. § 2402 (extending plant variety protection to new, distinct, uniform, and stable sexually reproduced or tuber propagated plant varieties other than fungi or bacteria).

The Joker's copyright scheme was, appropriately, as crazy as he is. Steve Engelhart et al., *The Laughing Fish*, in DETECTIVE COMICS (VOL. 1) 475 (DC Comics February 1978), reprinted in SHADOW OF THE BATMAN (VOL. 1) 4 (DC Comics March 1986).

there are an increasing number of them does not constitute an act of infringement by anyone in particular, and we don't think that even the Joker is crazy enough to sue the *fish*. And even if he were that crazy, the courts aren't. But that aside, the fact is that copyright owners lose some of their rights when they sell copies of their copyrighted work.[33] This is called the "first sale doctrine," which states that some of a copyright holder's rights in a *particular copy* of a work are extinguished when the copy is sold or transferred to a new

33. Specifically the rights to reproduce the work, prepare derivative works, distribute the work, and display the work publicly. 17 U.S.C. § 106.

owner.[34] So, for example, when you buy a new CD, you aren't allowed to make and distribute new copies of the CD—the copyright holder retains those rights—but you can decide to sell it or give it away. This is why used bookstores exist. It also means that fishermen, sellers, and consumers of the fish have legal title to the individual fish that they catch, process, and eat. The Joker cannot claim copyright infringement against them for those activities, because his control over the individual fish was lost as soon as the fish were released into the water. By abandoning the fish in the harbor and allowing a legal transfer of ownership, the Joker exhausted most of the rights in the fish that he apparently wants to enforce. The Joker wouldn't lose his alleged copyright as such, just his right to control what happens to particular fish. "Ownership of a copyright, or of any of the exclusive rights under a copyright, is distinct from ownership of any material object in which the work is embodied."[35]

Finally, there is also an argument that Gotham's fishermen and sellers and consumers of fish products have an implied license to use the fish, since they simply used the modified fish as they found them. A license may be implied by a copyright holder's conduct.[36] The Joker left the fish in the wild to be caught, so he can hardly complain if people make use of them in the usual way.

---

34. *See, e.g.,* Quality King Distributors, Inc. v. L'anza Research Int'l, Inc., 523 U.S. 135, 152 (1998) ("The whole point of the first sale doctrine is that once the copyright owner places a copyrighted item in the stream of commerce by selling it, he has exhausted his exclusive statutory right to control its distribution.").

35. Note, by the way, that the Joker wouldn't lose his alleged copyright, just his right to control what happens to the particular fish. "Ownership of a copyright, or of any of the exclusive rights under a copyright, is distinct from ownership of any material object in which the work is embodied." 17 U.S.C. § 202.

36. Effects Associates, Inc. v. Cohen, 908 F.2d 555, 55859 (9th Cir. 1990).

A Tale of Two Superhero Journalists

Peter Parker (a.k.a. Spider-Man) and Clark Kent (a.k.a. Superman)[37] are both journalists: Parker is a freelance photographer who primarily sells his work to the *Daily Bugle* and Kent is a reporter for the *Daily Planet*. In order to publish their photographs and stories, the newspapers must either own the copyright to the photo or story or have a license. As it turns out, the law treats Parker and Kent differently because of the different relationship each journalist has with their respective newspapers.

In general, copyright belongs to the author of a new work by default.[38] This means that when Peter Parker snaps a picture of Spider-Man, Parker owns the copyright in the work. When Parker sells a photo to the *Bugle* he either also sells the copyright or at least grants the *Bugle* a license to use the photo. This gives Parker leverage to potentially sell the same photo to multiple newspapers or to charge the *Bugle* a premium for an exclusive, at least if he can talk J. Jonah Jameson into it.

The situation is different for Clark Kent. Works that Kent, as an employee of the *Daily Planet*, prepares within the scope of his employment (i.e., stories he writes as part of his job as a reporter) are "works made for hire."[39] The employer owns the copyright in a work for hire unless explicitly agreed otherwise.[40] This means that Kent has no rights in the stories he writes; he can't sell them to another paper or reprint them on a blog, for example.

So how do the courts decide if someone is an employee for copy-

---

37. Apologies for the spoilers!

38. "Copyright in a work protected under this title vests initially in the author or authors of the work." 17 U.S.C. § 201(a).

39. 17 U.S.C. § 101.

40. 17 U.S.C. § 201(b).

right purposes? The Supreme Court has held that the courts should use a long list of factors derived from the common law of agency, including who provides the tools for the work; the duration of the relationship between the parties; whether the hiring party has the right to assign additional projects to the hired party; and the extent of the hired party's discretion over when and how long to work.[41] Unsurprisingly, these factors show that Parker is an independent contractor while Kent is clearly an employee.

Copyright and Superhero Merchandising

In the real world, comic books themselves are plainly subject to copyright protection, but within the comic book world the characters are real people, so their own physical appearance isn't copyrightable (though it is protected by the rights of privacy and publicity discussed in chapter 5). So what could a character copyright? Copyrightable subject matter is defined in 17 U.S.C. § 102, and our best bet is probably the "pictorial, graphic, and sculptural works" category.[42] Could this include costumes and vehicles?

Costumes

Historically the law has not favored intellectual property protection for fashion designs.[43] But, in a classic example of legal hairsplitting, there is a distinction between the design of an article of clothing (i.e., its cut and shape) and the design of the fabric from which it is made

---

41. Community for Creative Non-Violence v. Reid, 490 U.S. 730, 751–52 (1989) (the Court listed several additional factors).

42. As a "musical work" a superhero theme song could be copyrighted too, but those usually don't exist within the comic book universe.

43. See, e.g., Cheney Bros. v. Doris Silk Corp., 35 F.2d 279 (2d Cir. 1929); Whimsicality, Inc. v. Rubie's Costume Co., Inc., 891 F.2d 452 (2d Cir. 1989) ("We have long held that clothes, as useful articles, are not copyrightable.").

(i.e., the print or pattern). "[F]abric designs . . . are considered 'writings' for purposes of copyright law and are accordingly protectible [*sic*]."[44]

So this suggests, for example, that no superhero (or supervillain) can lay claim to the classic cape-and-tights combo, but a costume with an original fabric pattern could be protected. Good examples would be the web pattern on Spider-Man's costume and the golden fish-scale pattern on Aquaman's costume. There's a bit of a gray area when it comes to logos and symbols (e.g., Batman's stylized bat, Superman's *S* shield, Flash's lightning bolt). Some superhero logos are too simplistic to be protected under copyright (e.g., the Fantastic Four logo) as they are basically "basic geometric shapes [that] have long been in the public domain."[45] More likely though, they could count as trademarks and thus fall into a different category of intellectual property law with its own protections. Generally speaking, a work can be eligible for either copyright or trademark protection but only rarely will a particular work be eligible for both. Trademarks are discussed in more detail later in this chapter.

Vehicles

Like articles of clothing, vehicles are useful articles, and as such aren't ordinarily subject to copyright, but just like fabric patterns, the nonfunctional design aspects of a car might be copyrighted. For example, the web pattern on the (short-lived) Spider-Mobile may be protected, but the design of the vehicle itself (e.g., the giant wings on the *Batman Forever* Batmobile) is not likely to be protected. Design patents[46] provide better protection for ornamental design features

---

44. Knitwaves, Inc. v. Lollytogs Ltd., 71 F.3d 996 (2d Cir. 1995).

45. Tompkins Graphics, Inc. v. Zipatone, Inc., 222 U.S.P.Q. (BNA) 49 (E.D. Pa. 1983).

46. In contrast to regular (aka "utility") patents, design patents cover the ornamental design of a functional article. They are commonly used to protect car designs, among many other things. In fact, at least three Batmobiles have been the subject of design pat-

of useful articles like vehicles, but they must be applied for, cost money, and last for only fourteen years, unlike copyright, which is virtually eternal.

Why Worry About Copyright Protection?

So why should superheroes care if they have copyright protection in their costume or vehicle? One major reason is to control merchandising rights. Many superheroes either work for a living (e.g., Spider-Man), seem driven by fame and fortune (e.g., Booster Gold), or could always use another revenue stream to fund their work (e.g., Iron Man), so getting a cut of the merchandising rights would be very useful. Others might not care about money but simply want to ensure that their image isn't used inappropriately (e.g., Superman).

Many superheroes may also be concerned about copycats and impersonators, whether because of ego, image maintenance, or a concern that a non-superpowered impersonator might get themselves hurt.

Of course, supervillains might care too. More or less sane villains might want to prevent the sale of toys and other merchandise that portray them as bad guys ("every villain is the hero of his own story," as the saying goes). Or a villain like the Joker might want to have a hand in the production of Joker toys as part of an evil plot. And the villains might be able to do it too, even from behind bars. While a criminal's assets are often subject to forfeiture, the law usually focuses on tangible assets, particularly those that are themselves contraband (e.g., illegal drugs), proceeds from illegal activities, or that were used to commit crimes.[47] Intellectual property assets like copyrights and patents are intangible, and they don't fall into any of those three categories, so it might be difficult for the government to seize them.

---

ents, including the Batmobiles from the Adam West TV series (U.S. Pat. No. D205998), *Batman Forever* (U.S. Pat. No. D375704), and *Batman & Robin* (D396662).

47. *See* Bennis v. Michigan, 516 U.S. 442, 459 (1996) (Stevens, J., dissenting).

Superheroes and supervillains might use trademarks to control the use of their iconic symbols for many of the same reasons.

Trademarks

Unlike copyright, which is exclusively federal, there are both federal and state trademark laws in the United States. However, as commerce has become less and less localized, the importance of state trademarks has diminished somewhat, so we will focus on the federal scheme.

Federal trademark law is primarily governed by the Lanham Act.[48] Individuals and corporations seeking federal trademark protection must register their marks with the United States Patent and Trademark Office. Unlike applying for a patent, applying for and maintaining a trademark is usually fairly straightforward, though there are some minor pitfalls and one big catch that we'll discuss later.

All kinds of things may be trademarked: words, graphic designs, shapes (e.g., a Coca-Cola bottle), sounds (e.g., the NBC chimes), and even colors (e.g., green and gold dry cleaning pads).[49] Of these, words and graphic design marks are the most common, and they're likely the most applicable for superheroes and supervillains. There are some exceptions to what may be trademarked, and these are given in 15 U.S.C. § 1052.

Most importantly, § 1052(e)(5) prohibits trademarking anything that "comprises any matter that, as a whole, is functional." Functional things are pretty much the exclusive province of patent protection. You can't copyright them, nor can you trademark them. So, for

---

48. Pub. L. No. 79–489, 60 Stat. 427 (July 6, 1946) (codified as amended at 15 U.S.C. § 1051 *et seq.*).

49. *See* Qualitex Co. v. Jacobson Prods. Co., 514 U.S. 159 (1995).

example, trademarking a Batarang would be difficult because the shape of the device is arguably functional. Another example would be the arc reactor in the Iron Man suits. Images of that have been used as logos for the films in the real world, but in the Marvel Universe, trying to use an image of the arc reactor as a logo is going to be subject to challenge on § 1052(e)(5) grounds unless the image is sufficiently stylized. The same probably goes for Thor's hammer: it's an obviously functional thing, so using it as a logo is going to be a tough sell unless you stylize it pretty heavily.

But what about something like Captain America's shield? Although the shield itself is functional, the image on it isn't functional at all, just a painted logo. Tough paint, to be sure, but ultimately just that: not essential to the functioning of the shield. So the logo on Captain America's shield is probably trademarkable, but the shield itself is probably not. Captain America could go after anyone for using his logo on anything. As an historical side note, Marvel swapped Captain America's original triangular shield for the round one allegedly due to the complaint of a rival publisher that it looked too much like its own character, an example of real world law affecting comic book stories.

And while we're on the subject of Captain America, what about § 1052(b)? That prohibits trademarking anything that "consists of or comprises the flag or coat of arms or other insignia of the United States, or of any State or municipality, or of any foreign nation, or any simulation thereof." This shouldn't be a problem for Captain America because his logo is far enough removed from any official government insignia to be okay while remaining decidedly patriotic. Some versions of Captain Britain's costume might not be so clear cut, however.

The Minor Pitfalls

Other than those exceptions, there are three pitfalls to watch out for here. First, trademarks cannot be generic terms for the marked good or service (e.g., you can't trademark "Soft Drink brand carbonated beverages"). Second, if the mark is merely descriptive of the good or service, then you can't trademark it unless you can show that the mark has acquired "secondary meaning," that is, consumers now associate the mark with a particular source of goods or services rather than considering it a mere description. For example, the marks "Holiday Inn," "All Bran," and "General Motors" are all basically descriptive of the products they deliver, but they have acquired such a strong association with a single product or company that they are still entitled to protection. Third, the mark must be used in commerce or the applicant must have a good faith intention to use it in commerce (and they have to carry through with that intention at some point). That means a superhero or villain can't just register the mark defensively as a way to prevent others from using it. Some kind of merchandising has to be going on and "Superman brand superhero services" may not be enough, unless Superman is actively marketing his services.

In most cases, though, these aren't going to be significant issues for superheroes and supervillains. Their names and logos tend to be arbitrary or fanciful rather than generic or merely descriptive (this shouldn't be surprising, since most of them are also trademarks in the real world). And they're probably all happy to slap their name and logo on merchandise, even if they'd prefer the proceeds go to charity.

The Big Catch

Unlike rights of privacy and publicity and copyright, trademarks carry with them a unique burden. A trademark owner must both continually use the mark in commerce and enforce his or her rights to exclusivity (i.e., must "police the mark") or risk losing it. This is because the real purpose of trademark is to protect the buying public by ensuring that a good or service bearing a mark only comes from the owner of the mark. If there are multiple, unrelated sources using the mark (or if nobody is using the mark), then there is no public benefit. Without enforcement, a trademark loses its strength, and it may eventually become a generic term or even be considered abandoned outright. Speaking in the closely related trade dress context, the Sixth Circuit held:

> Although it appears unlikely that failure to prosecute, by itself, can establish that trade dress has been abandoned, it is possible that, in extreme circumstances, failure to prosecute may cause trade dress rights to be extinguished by causing a mark to lose its significance as an indication of source.[50]

Beyond the general threat of loss of protection, failure to sue individual infringers in a timely fashion can give rise to a defense of laches if the trademark owner does eventually decide to sue.[51]

---

50. Herman Miller Inc. v. Palazzetti Imports and Exports, 270 F.3d 298, 317 (6th.Cir. 2001).

51. "Laches" is an equitable defense (i.e., based on fairness and judicial discretion rather than legal rules) that prevents a party from bringing a claim. More specifically, laches is "the neglect or delay in bringing suit to remedy an alleged wrong, which taken together with lapse of time and other circumstances, causes prejudice to the adverse party and operates as an equitable bar." AC Aukerman Co. v. RL Chaides Const. Co., 960 F.2d 1020, 1028–29 (Fed. Cir. 1992) (en banc).

CHAPTER 10

Travel and Immigration

Superheroes and supervillains tend to be a rather peripatetic lot, and one of the coolest parts about many comic book stories are inventive ways of getting around. The Fantastic Four have the Fantasticar. Batman has the Batmobile, Batcopter, and Batwing. Superman, the Flash, and Nightcrawler don't even need to bother with such pedestrian things, as they can go basically anywhere they want under their own power.

All of which is well and good, but as any traveler knows, especially in this post-9/11 world, crossing international borders is kind of a big deal. But even absent security checkpoints, customs and immigration are real legal issues and have been for centuries. Going from Metropolis to Ohio isn't a problem, as travel within the United States can be done almost entirely without government authorization, particularly if you aren't using a commercial airline. But in addition to massive violations of airspace (see chapter 8), simply showing up in another country without going through customs is illegal. In this chapter, we take a look at some of the implications of this area of the law for comic book stories.

International Travel and Arms Control Regulations

Wolverine deciding to leave Professor Xavier's mansion to go to Alberta to discover his origins is all well and good, but he's going to have to cross the border *somewhere*, and that means either showing a passport or jumping the border. In essence, a law-abiding superhero is going to need official documents, and as discussed in chapter 12, that has its own problems.

But that's just the beginning. Another potential wrinkle is the issue of teleporters. Does it matter that while Superman does need to actually cross a border at some point, Nightcrawler can disappear on one side and reappear on the other without ever actually traveling in between? Probably not. The law is written in such a way that it isn't just crossing the border without authorization that's illegal, but rather simply *being* in a given country without permission. Said permission is usually obtained at the border, but it needn't be, and the fact is that teleporting across the US border would probably annoy US Customs and Border Protection quite a bit.

But there's another issue, aside from the mere fact of travel, which is likely to be an issue for a certain category of superhero, namely those whose "powers" are based on technology, like Iron Man or Batman. The issue is that the federal government, like most other national governments, takes a pretty dim view of people transporting weapons across its borders without permission.

Here we run into the International Traffic in Arms Regulations (ITAR)[1] and specifically the United States Munitions List (USML).[2] This is where the federal government lays out in great detail the restrictions placed on the export of weapons and related technologies.

1. 22 C.F.R. parts 120–130.

2. 22 C.F.R. part 121.

So, for example, it is illegal to export a gas turbine specifically designed for use in a ground vehicle. The regulation probably has in mind things like the M1 Abrams tank, but as the Batmobile is (in some versions anyway) powered by a gas turbine, it would be subject to the regulations too. Just about everything in one of Iron Man's suits is going to find its way on the list somewhere, from the armor itself down to the micro-controllers in the servo motors. Almost everything specifically designed for a military application, and even some things that aren't, is on the export list. The ITAR even apply to civilian-developed software encryption, so they could easily apply to something as kickass as the arc reactor.

So what about S.H.I.E.L.D.? If the story goes that S.H.I.E.L.D. is under the control of the United Nations, it would clearly be a "non-US person" under the terms of the USML, making it illegal for any US person to share restricted tech with it without government authorization. But if the Department of Defense doesn't have access to S.H.I.E.L.D. gadgetry, it seems unlikely that the Department of State would authorize such a transaction. It gets worse. It is a violation of federal law[3] to export any item on the USML without a license, and "export" is defined as "sending or taking a defense article out of the United States in any manner, except by mere travel outside of the United States by a person whose personal knowledge includes technical data."[4] Even assuming that Bruce Wayne or Tony Stark invents his weaponry completely using his own funding and resources, the ITAR do not limit themselves to weapons developed with federal money: they apply to everything that fits into one of the categories on the USML. So Iron Man's little jaunt to Afghanistan in his first movie and Batman's little extradition trip to Hong Kong in *The Dark Knight* almost certainly constituted a violation of federal arms control laws, but Iron Man's *invitation* by the US military to assist in

---

3. 22 CFR § 127.1(a)(1).

4. 22 CFR § 120.17.

fighting the Mandarin in Southeast Asia on a few occasions in the 1960s was probably okay.

Here we actually run into some difficulty trying to make the legal system in the real world sync up with the legal system in the comic book world. It is highly unlikely that the federal government would either (1) decide to scale back arms-control laws when faced with gadget-based superheroes or (2) decide to give those superheroes a pass, especially if they wouldn't share their toys. So the question becomes, why doesn't the US Attorney attempt to prosecute Tony Stark for this violation of federal law? More to the point, why is Congress messing around with hearings when they can simply send Stark to jail?

Well, probably because having Tony Stark do ten years for arms control violations[5] would be a pretty boring story, and because fining Tony Stark the $1 million penalty wouldn't really make him think twice. Ultimately, this may just be one of those places where we have to remember that if we're okay with a world where guys can shoot laser beams out of their eyes or turn into metal, arms control regulations may be the least of our worries.

Immigration and Citizenship

Kurt Wagner (a.k.a. Nightcrawler) is a German national. Piotr Rasputin (a.k.a. Colossus) is Russian. Superman isn't even *human*, for crying out loud. If it's so difficult for regular old humans to establish residency in a country of which they are not a citizen, shouldn't this be an issue in comic books from time to time?

There have been a few times when the writers have picked up on this. For instance, in one alternate reality, Superman ran for President after his secret identity was revealed. In the story, the United States Supreme Court ruled that Superman was actually a natural-

---

5. As provided for in 22 U.S.C. § 2778(c).

You can tell this story is from the 1990s because the decision was unanimous.
Roger Stern et al., *Executive Action*, in ACTION COMICS ANNUAL 3 (DC Comics 1991).

born citizen and thus eligible to run for President. Did they get it right? To answer that question we look to immigration law.

Immigration law is a purely federal matter and is codified in Title 8 of the United States Code, particularly Chapter 12. Regulations on the subject—the practical implementation of statutes—are found in Title 8 of the Code of Federal Regulations, especially Chapter 5. There are enough different situations created by various superhero characters that we can really put these laws through their paces.

Birthright Citizenship

Let's start with how a character might get US citizenship in the first place. The easiest ways are to be born to at least one American parent (aka *jus sanguinis*) or to be born inside US territory (aka "birthright" citizenship or *jus soli*). The latter method is how Superman was able to run for President. The Supreme Court ruled that Superman was a natural-born US citizen, as he wasn't technically "born" until he was extracted from the Kryptonian "birthing matrix" in Kansas.[6] Clearly the Supreme Court justices in this alternate universe are not constitutional originalists!

But in most versions of the Superman mythology, Ma and Pa Kent stumble across little Clark after he's been "born." What then? Well, in that case, we turn to the Foundling Statute:

> The following shall be nationals and citizens of the United States at birth . . . (f) a person of unknown parentage found in the United States while under the age of five years, until shown, prior to his attaining the age of twenty-one years, not to have been born in the United States.[7]

Superman is definitely of unknown parentage, was found in the US, and appeared to be under the age of five when found, so he's looking good so far. The last criterion, i.e., no showing of having been born outside the US before he turns twenty-one, is a little stickier, because the Kents presumably know that Clark was born elsewhere, or at least has his origins somewhere else. But if neither they nor anyone else come forward to expose him, Clark Kent will probably be eligible for citizenship under the Foundling Statute.[8] If Superman obtained his citizenship this way, then he would likely qualify as a natural-born citizen and be eligible for the presidency because citizenship under the Foundling Statute implies citizenship from birth.

---

6. Interestingly, this implies that Superman has the same legal rights as a human being, despite being a non-human alien. For more on that issue, see chapter 13.

7. 8 U.S.C. § 1401(f).

8. Or, at least, he would be today. The predecessor to the current statute, the Nationality Act of 1940, also covered foundlings, but Superman had been around for quite some time before that.

This may solve his immigration problems, but where is he going to keep those 193 passports? He doesn't even have pockets! Otto Binder et al., *The Story of Superman's Life*, in SUPERMAN (VOL. 1) 146 (DC Comics July 1961).

Private Acts of Congress

There's another way that someone can become a citizen without going through the immigration process: a "private act" of Congress, i.e., a law targeting a specific person and declaring him or her to be a citizen.[9] Although unusual today, private acts have a long history in the United States.[10] Members of Congress regularly put forward names of constituents to be granted citizenship or residency, and though most of the time nothing comes of it, it is certainly within Congress's power to take such action. As a matter of fact, in at least one story, Superman is granted citizenship by every country in the world, presumably by their respective versions of a private act of Congress. This method would not, however, result in someone being a natural-born citizen, which is necessary for running for President.

---

9. *See, e.g.*, Private Law 104-4, Oct. 19, 1996, which made a man named Nguyen Quy An eligible to be naturalized as a citizen despite not having permanent residency. These bills are not very common, nor are they usually passed, but it happens.

10. In fact, for decades after the founding of the country, private acts by state legislatures were the only way for a legitimate (i.e., non-annullable) marriage to be dissolved. Similarly, prior to the passage of general incorporation statutes, which create the procedures by which corporations may be chartered with state-level secretaries of state, creating a corporate entity required an act of the state legislature.

For other immigrant superheroes, however, Section 1181 of Title 8 provides that with certain exceptions:

> [N]o immigrant shall be admitted into the United States unless at the time of application for admission he
>
> 1. has a valid unexpired immigrant visa or was born subsequent to the issuance of such visa of the accompanying parent, and
> 2. presents a valid unexpired passport or other suitable travel document, or document of identity and nationality, if such document is required under the regulations issued by the Attorney General.

This creates immediate problems for Superman. He's not going to have any documentation, as he never went through customs and thus never had an opportunity to acquire the appropriate documentation. The basic story is that Superman (nee Kal-El) is born on the planet Krypton just before it was destroyed by . . . something. Depends who you ask. Anyway, Kal-El's parents put him on a starship escape pod that crash-lands in rural Kansas, where Jonathan Kent finds him and takes him home, raising him as Clark Kent, and only learning later about his superpowers.

The actual history of Superman comics is of note here, as *Action Comics* #1 was published in 1938, just after the country, still reeling from the lingering effects of the Great Depression, was smacked by the Recession of 1937. Unemployment was well north of 15 percent. The Dust Bowl was recent history. So the idea that a motorist in Kansas would discover an abandoned baby on the side of the road was depressingly plausible. In an age when immigration laws were far more lax than they are today,[11] no one was going to

---

11. At least for white immigrants; for nonwhites the story was very different. *See, e.g.,* United States v. Wong Kim Ark, 168 U.S. 649 (1898); United States v. Thind, 261 U.S. 204 (1923).

ask any questions about the origin of such a child or his lack of a birth certificate.

Granted, this storyline means Kal-El would have crashed to Earth sometime earlier in the twentieth century, but it seems plausible that the environment in which the comic was actually published would have a lot to do with the way original readers interpreted things.

Of course, recent rewrites do not necessarily enjoy the benefits of those earlier legal environments. Adopting a random infant is actually a lot harder to do these days, as state laws about that sort of thing create many hoops for potential parents to jump through. The upshot is that some kind of documentation would be needed for an infant who basically appears out of thin air. That would require clever forgeries at the very least,[12] and the *Man of Steel* suggestion that Jonathan and Martha were snowed in for six months doesn't really ring as true in the 1980s as it might have in the 1920s.[13]

Employment Visas and Green Cards

But that's just for characters that seem to have been born in the United States. How can a superhero that isn't born here get his immigration status worked out?[14] In short, the same long, hard, and often expensive way that everyone else does. Section 1151(d) provides for employment-based visas, and § 1153(b)(1)(a) and (b)(2) give aliens[15] with "extraordinary abilities" preferential treatment. Anyone likely to be of interest to the leader of a superhero organization would probably be deemed to have "extraordinary abilities" almost automatically. Sure, having a Ph.D. or being an excellent manager

---

12. This is how the 2001 television series *Smallville* handled it.

13. *See* John Byrne et al., *From Out of the Green Dawn*, in THE MAN OF STEEL (VOL. 1) (DC Comics October 1986).

14. Characters who are highly placed in foreign governments are another issue, which we discuss in Chapter 11.

15. That is, "people without U.S. citizenship," though extraterrestrials certainly qualify.

is impressive and all, but being able to, say, *turn one's body to organic metal* is just a whole different level of awesome. So Professor Xavier could probably sponsor Kurt Wagner and Piotr Rasputin for employment-based visas and expect to get that sorted pretty quickly. Generally speaking, any superhero connected to some kind of organization that works for the public good, whether it is a public or private organization, e.g., the X-Men, the Avengers, the Justice League of America, etc., will probably be able to get this done pretty easily, as they've got an employer willing to put their extraordinary abilities to immediate use for the benefit of the country. But a character without a sponsor might have a hard time of it.

Still, the process is not immediate. These types of visas may be issued on a priority basis, but getting a green card—i.e., permission to reside and work in the US permanently—can take a year or two, and actual citizenship can take another seven years.[16]

Renouncing Citizenship

Recent comics have raised another potential immigration wrinkle. In *Action Comics* #900, Superman actually deals with the other side of the coin and says he's going to *renounce* his US citizenship.[17] It turns out that you can, in fact, renounce your citizenship. Section 1481 of Title 8 governs the voluntary renunciation of citizenship through a variety of ways, e.g., taking up arms with a foreign government or committing treason, but also by simply making a statement to that effect to an appropriate diplomatic officer. In some ways it's surprisingly easy; the hardest part is traveling outside the country to do it.[18] The State Department has actually formalized the Oath of Renunciation:

---

16. And even this is a best-case scenario.

17. The story was actually a one-off written for the 900th issue, and it's probably not canon. David S. Goyer et al., *The Incident*, in ACTION COMICS (VOL. 1) 900 (DC Comics June 2011).

18. The renunciation has to occur outside the United States because otherwise the renouncer would immediately become an illegal alien and have to be deported. Requiring the would-be renouncer to leave the country first avoids this problem.

Although he never actually went through with it, this announcement was one of the most controversial things Superman has ever done, drawing ire from several real politicians and pundits. David S. Goyer et al., *The Incident*, in ACTION COMICS (VOL. 1) 900 (DC Comics June 2011).

I desire and hereby make a formal renunciation of my US nationality, as provided by section 349 (a)(5) of the Immigration and Nationality Act of 1952, as amended, and pursuant thereto, I hereby absolutely and entirely renounce my United States nationality together with all rights and privileges and all duties and allegiance and fidelity thereunto pertaining. I make this renunciation intentionally, voluntarily, and of my own free will, free of any duress or undue influence.

So if Superman, or anyone else for that matter, wants to rid himself of his US citizenship, he need merely appear before a consular officer outside the United States and make the above oath. It might not necessarily be that easy, however, as the Secretary of State could refuse to accept his renunciation. Renunciations are refused in some

A summary of Superman's many taxable assets. The solid gold key alone would be worth hundreds of millions of dollars. Geoff Johns et al., ACTION COMICS ANNUAL 10 (DC Comics April 2007).

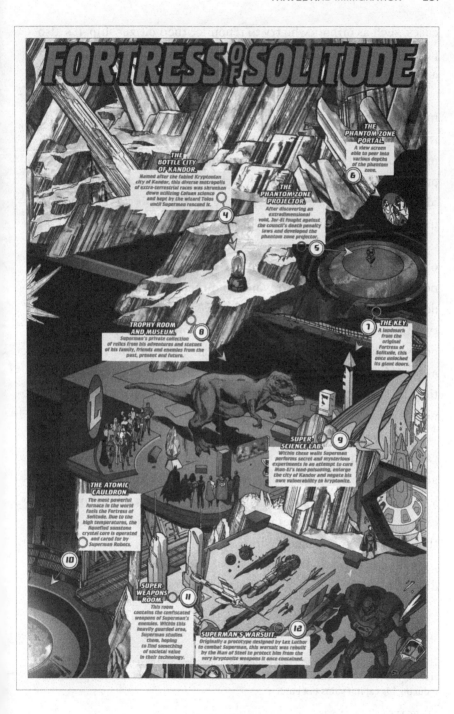

FORTRESS OF SOLITUDE

THE PHANTOM ZONE PORTAL.
A view screen able to peer into various depths of the phantom zone.
6

THE BOTTLE CITY OF KANDOR.
Named after the fabled Kryptonian city of Kandor, this diverse metropolis of extra-terrestrial races was shrunken down utilizing Coluan science and kept by the wizard Tolos until Superman rescued it.
4

THE PHANTOM ZONE PROJECTOR.
After discovering an extradimensional void, Jor-El fought against the council's death penalty laws and developed the phantom zone projector.
5

TROPHY ROOM AND MUSEUM.
Superman's private collection of relics from his adventures and statues of his family, friends and enemies from the past, present and future.
8

THE KEY.
A landmark from the original Fortress of Solitude, this once unlocked its giant doors.
7

SUPER-SCIENCE LAB.
Within these walls Superman performs secret and mysterious experiments in an attempt to cure Man-El's lead-poisoning, enlarge the city of Kandor and negate his own vulnerability to kryptonite.
9

THE ATOMIC CAULDRON.
The most powerful furnace in the world fuels the Fortress of Solitude. Due to the high temperatures, the liquefied sunstone crystal core is operated and cared for by Superman Robots.
10

SUPER-WEAPONS ROOM.
This room contains the confiscated weapons of Superman's enemies. Within this heavily guarded area, Superman studies them, hoping to find something of societal value in their technology.
11

SUPERMAN'S WARSUIT.
Originally a prototype designed by Lex Luthor to combat Superman, this warsuit was rebuilt by the Man of Steel to protect him from the very kryptonite weapons it once contained.
12

cases, such as minors who try to renounce their citizenship. It's also possible that Congress could impose US citizenship on Superman via a private act, but this is an untested legal theory as far as we know.

Of course, renouncing one's citizenship has consequences. The most obvious is that a person who renounces his citizenship is an illegal immigrant *everywhere* unless he can work out some arrangement with a state willing to take him. Statelessness is actually a pretty awful thing. It's so bad that the Supreme Court has held that "denationalization," as a punishment for crime, is a cruel and unusual punishment in violation of the Eighth Amendment.[19]

That aside, renouncing one's citizenship *doesn't* affect certain obligations. The most important one is taxes. The IRS assumes, and not without reason, that anyone who renounces his citizenship is doing so to avoid taxes.[20] Therefore, if your net worth is in excess of two million dollars on the date of your renunciation, the IRS imposes an "expatriation tax." Basically, your entire net worth is treated as taxable income in the year of your expatriation.[21] Ouch. In addition, an expatriate will still owe taxes on any income earned for the next *ten years*, regardless of where they live.

This is a problem for Superman in particular, as he has significant assets in the Fortress of Solitude, including priceless historical artifacts and alien technology, not to mention a giant key made of solid gold. Whether or not he actually has enough cash to cover the expatriation tax on those assets is an open question. Either way, that's a lot of coal to squeeze into diamonds!

Renouncing one's citizenship also does *not* excuse one from the draft. Even illegal aliens are subject to the draft, and lack of citizen-

---

19. Trop v. Dulles, 356 U.S. 86 (1958).

20. This is allegedly why Facebook cofounder Eduardo Saverin renounced his US citizenship shortly before the company announced its initial public offering, potentially reducing his capital gains tax burden.

21. 26 U.S.C. §§ 877–877A.

ship is no excuse. For more about the draft, see chapter 1. Finally, renouncing citizenship is essentially irrevocable. Apart from a private act of Congress, it would be virtually impossible for Superman to become a US citizen again.

Citizenship and Parallel Universes

Parallel and alternate universes are a frequent feature of comic books. For example, in *She-Hulk* #21, a company made a business out of transporting normal people from "Earth A" to "Earth B," where they became superpowered heroes and villains.[22] An interesting question is what legal rights, if any, a visitor from Earth A would have in Earth B. We think such visitors would have a pretty difficult time of it, actually. Since "America A" doesn't seem to have an immigration treaty with "America B," they would likely find it very difficult to be legally present in America B, or any other Earth B country for that matter. The fact that the two versions of the United States may be essentially identical probably wouldn't matter: they're still distinct, sovereign nations.[23] Luckily, all of the illegal immigrants could be sent back to Earth A; if deportation were impossible, they might be able to claim asylum somewhere.

---

22. Dan Slott et al., *Another Me, Another U*, in SHE-HULK (VOL. 2) 21 (Marvel Comics October 2007).

23. Note that a time traveler from the past to the future would not have the same problem. As long as his or her home country still existed in the future, his or her citizenship should still be valid, just as if he or she had simply lived a long time (proof might be a bit tricky, though!). This argument does not necessarily cut the other direction, however, because the past is fixed but the future is not. In other words, the past version of a country will not necessarily become the future version that a time-traveler came from.

CHAPTER 11

International Law

S.H.I.E.L.D. is one of the most significant entities in the Marvel Universe. First introduced in *Strange Tales* #135 in August 1965, the organization, usually led by Nick Fury, is sometimes presented as a branch of the US military and others as an arm of the UN. Either way, the organization routinely engages in missions both on and off US soil, and is a good reminder of the implications of international law on comic book stories. In this chapter, we'll start by looking at some of the more unusual countries in comic book worlds, the treatment of foreign dignitaries and diplomatic missions, then at the status of organizations like S.H.I.E.L.D.

International Law, Generally

The important thing to remember about international law, particularly in the context of the law of nations,[1] is that international law

---

1. The laws for private parties contracting across international borders is actually pretty well settled and mostly comes down to "choice of laws," i.e., the parties deciding

is a matter of custom and practice as much as it is anything else. This is true of domestic law as well, and is really the reason the common law exists: a "law" is, essentially, a custom or tradition that is enforced by a government. In the case of common law that tradition is built up by the decisions of courts. But while governments have pretty effective tools for coercing their citizens to obey the laws, coercing other governments to play ball is a lot harder. A whole lot depends on various countries, more or less voluntarily, abiding by treaties and generally accepted standards. Reneging on a treaty can lead to war or economic sanctions, but short of that, the most significant consequence is that the breaching nation takes a hit to its reputation. If country A breaks its treaty with country B, *every* country is going to wonder whether this means that country A is going to ignore other treaty obligations.

In addition, international law is significantly a sort of collaborative dance between the countries of the world. Countries violate certain aspects of international law *all the time*, but for various reasons are permitted to get away with it. For example, Chinese companies often infringe the intellectual property rights of foreign companies, and they are generally permitted to do this without consequence, because everyone wants access to Chinese manufactured goods. Similarly, the US has engaged in all sorts of questionable military operations since World War II, but the combination of being the world's largest economy and having an overwhelmingly powerful military has led to very few reprisals there. On the other hand there are rogue states like Iran, which routinely flouts the international community simply because, unless the rest of the world decided to invade, there is precious little that can be done about it. All diplomatic options have essentially been exhausted, and there aren't really any further trade sanctions available once an embargo has been imposed.

---

which nation's law they're going to use. Once that choice is made, the remaining issues can be settled by that country's domestic legal system.

So as we consider the "legality" of various international law situations, it is important to remember that the question of practicality is at least as important as the technical legality of a given situation. If a particular situation is legal, but the international community would never permit it, that's a problem. On the other hand, some stories have events and actions which are blatantly illegal, but which the international community would probably either ignore or even approve.

Unusual Sovereignties

Comic book stories frequently make up fictional countries as locations for our heroes to do their heroing overseas without referencing any place that could embarrass any potential readers or require the writers to do actual research. Many of these are sort of one-off countries that are never mentioned again, but some wind up becoming part of the canon. Some of these are pretty unremarkable, legally speaking. Latveria, ruled by Dr. Doom, is a fictional nation in the Marvel Universe carved out of Romania, Hungary, and Serbia. During Dr. Doom's rule it was a dictatorship or absolute monarchy, a form of government, which while increasingly unfashionable today, does still exist. Latveria, for all intents and purposes, is just another small nation unfriendly to US interests. It stands with half a dozen or so other nations in that respect, including some of the former Soviet republics, depending on how the winds are blowing. But Latveria is presumably officially recognized by the United States and other modern governments, and given its inclusion in the Marvel graphic novel *1602*, it's been around as an otherwise normal sovereign state for at least four centuries. So far, there isn't much to say here. Latveria does not present any legal issues the State Department doesn't already handle every day. The whole mad-dictator-using-supernatural-powers thing is a bit unusual, but it isn't a strictly *legal* problem. This also probably goes for the dozen or so fictional African nations in various Marvel continuities: they may as well be a real country for all the difference it makes.

But what about Wakanda, the fictional, technologically advanced African nation ruled by T'Challa, aka the Black Panther? Wakanda is also called "The Hidden Land," and it is largely closed off from the rest of the world. The fact that the country has existed for thousands of years without regular contact with the outside world is problematic because recognition is a big part of what makes a state sovereign.

If Wakanda exists inside the putative borders of at least one other country, then there is a potential for conflict with those nations, possibly even war, if Wakanda's existence becomes known to the wider world. Not that the other countries are likely to be able to win that war, but states don't readily let go of territory where possible, and antagonistic neighbors are inconvenient even if they aren't a military threat. Even the weakest of countries can make things diplomatically and logistically difficult for their neighbors.[2]

Alternatively, Wakanda might exist outside the borders of other countries, though that supposes some extraordinary method of concealment to avoid the hole–in–the–map problem. That's especially hard in the era of satellite mapping. But if Wakanda reveals itself under those circumstances, then unless some powerful countries promptly recognize Wakanda's sovereignty, there might be a land grab by neighboring countries fighting over the new territory and its rich natural resources (e.g., vibranium, the nigh-indestructible material of which Captain America's shield is made).

Things are different still with underwater nations. Aquaman and Namor occupy their respective universes' versions of Atlantis, which somehow survived its submersion thousands of years ago. In

---

2. See, for example, the nuisance that the Somalians have made of themselves off the Horn of Africa.

addition to the problems facing hidden states in general, these pose the additional problems of not actually being on dry land. International waters are a rather fraught issue in international diplomacy, as they represent among other things access to the world's shipping lanes, an invaluable economic and military resource. "Territorial waters," i.e., waters where states exert the full force of their sovereignty, are pretty universally recognized to extend twelve miles from the low-tide mark, though some countries claim more than that.[3] "Contiguous zones," where states may exert some limited authority mostly related to border protection and customs activities, extend twelve miles beyond territorial waters. The "exclusive economic zone" goes all the way out to two hundred miles from shore, and in that range a state may exert exclusive control over economic activities like drilling, fishing, etc., but it may not prohibit or interfere with transit or just hanging around.

But all of these definitions are based on the low-tide mark. What are the territorial waters of Atlantis, which has no low-tide mark because it is completely underwater? Even if one were to simply grant the same sorts of rights as land-based nations, where do the borders of Atlantis start and stop? The edge of the city? Some distance beyond? There isn't exactly a natural feature—on the surface anyway— where one could draw an obvious line, nor are there going to be other countries with which to define a border. Even if a ship was trying to respect the borders, without GPS or a *really* good navigator, it would be almost impossible to tell when you were trespassing.

It's possible that other nations might not recognize that Atlantis has territorial waters at all, as it would be pretty inconvenient to do so. States are accustomed to having pretty much free rein in the

---

3. The definitions of territorial waters, contiguous zones, and exclusive economic zones come from the 1982 United Nations Convention on the Law of the Sea, which has been ratified by most of the countries in the world. Before the Convention was created, different countries claimed different territorial waters, ranging from two to six nautical miles.

Atlantic, so a huge hole in the map defined solely by law created to respect Atlantean territorial claims might not be of much interest to other states. One could always make the argument that Atlantis is free to do whatever it likes on the ocean floor provided it does not interfere with surface traffic, but even then (1) why would Atlantis agree to that, and (2) what about submarine traffic? And given that Atlantis would probably need to be willing to go to war to get what it wants, would it? Could it? Namor has certainly launched an attack on more than one occasion,[4] but that never seems to go very well. It would probably be best for all involved if the undersea kingdoms kept to themselves and did not advance any territorial claims to the ocean itself. International disputes like this one have historically been solved with armies. Or, navies, as the case may be.

Interplanetary Law

So we've got some basic grasp about what to do about the various terrestrial fictional countries. But what about the Inhumans, the villains first introduced in the *Fantastic Four*?[5] Attilan, their city, *really* gets around, having been found in the North Atlantic, the Andes, the Himalayas, and . . . the Moon. To what extent do Earth's laws reach the Moon? Or just places outside the Earth's atmosphere in general?

Earthbound legal systems don't normally extend beyond the Earth's atmosphere.[6] Indeed, individual nations' legal systems don't

---

4. *See, e.g.,* Stan Lee, Jack Kirby et al., FANTASTIC FOUR ANNUAL 1 (Marvel Comics September 1963), in which Namor unsuccessfully invades New York City as a reprisal against the destruction of the original site of Atlantis by nuclear testing.

5. Stan Lee, Jack Kirby et al., *Beware the Hidden Land!,* in FANTASTIC FOUR 47 (Marvel Comics February 1966).

6. With the exception of spaceships launched from a terrestrial country, which are under the jurisdiction of the country that launched them, much like a ship at sea.

The Blue Area of the Moon, secret home of the Inhumans. Brian Michael Bendis et al., *New Avengers: Disassembled (Part 4)*, in NEW AVENGERS (VOL. 1) 24 (Marvel Comics November 2006).

extend much beyond their borders, but we've already got a terrestrial example: the high seas.

Oceans outside the territorial claims of any particular country are all but lawless. The UN Convention on the Law of the Sea has been ratified or at least signed by almost every country, but apart from addressing piracy it is mostly concerned with mundane issues like establishing territorial boundaries and exclusive economic zones. Admiralty law is a little more detailed (and one of the oldest continuously operating bodies of law in the world) but even that has mostly to do with the conduct of vessels and salvage rights.

But even there, national courts are widely held to be able to exert jurisdiction over persons for actions they commit while at sea once the person is brought to shore. One of the most famous cases in every law student's criminal law class is *R. v. Dudley & Stephens*,[7] about some shipwrecked sailors who cannibalize the cabin boy. The defendants were brought to trial and convicted once they returned to their native country, and jurisdiction was not one of the real issues. But if they had been rescued by, say, an American ship, it's possible they could have been brought to trial in an American court. Crimes committed on the high seas can generally be tried everywhere, e.g., Somalian pirates being tried in New York City. The theory is that crimes committed outside national boundaries are, in a sense, crimes against civilization, and thus may be tried anywhere.[8]

There is a limit here: the acts in question need to be obviously criminal by anyone's standards. Murder is a pretty easy example. So is piracy. But what about things that are only illegal by statute, like gambling? A ferry that runs between Maine and Nova Scotia passes through international waters, and the on-board casino is only open when outside both the US's and Canada's territorial waters. There really hasn't been all that much law here, but it's unlikely that any given nation would be able to enforce its particular regulatory regime on the high seas over anything but a ship registered under that nation's flag.

Outer space is quite similar. There is, in fact, a statute[9] that extends federal jurisdiction to spacecraft flying the US flag and that also discusses maritime jurisdiction with similar results. State laws do not apply, but federal laws do. But again, note that enforcement would require bringing a defendant back to US soil for trial, just as it would for crime on the high seas.

The same statute, specifically subsection 7, also grants US juris-

---

7. 12 Q.B.D. 273 (1884).

8. The controversial doctrine of universal jurisdiction has some of its origins in this concept.

9. 18 U.S.C. § 7(6).

diction over "any place outside the jurisdiction of any nation with respect to an offense by or against a national of the United States." This is kind of a catchall clause. If no one else has jurisdiction and a US national is either the defendant or the victim, then the US has jurisdiction. So if a supervillain commits a federal crime against an American superhero on, say, Mars, then assuming the supervillain can be brought back to Earth, he can be charged in federal court.

Turning back to the Inhumans specifically, Attilan would probably be treated mostly like a foreign country, despite its extraplanetary location. The Inhumans certainly seem to talk as if they should be treated as a foreign country. Black Bolt, the king of the Inhumans, has imposed what amounts to a universal ban on Earthlings hanging around the Moon, which seems to amount to a territorial claim. While the US might not be all that happy about this—the whole Moon? Really?—there doesn't seem to be all that much that anyone can do about it, nor ultimately all that much incentive to either. The Inhumans don't exactly have representation at the UN or any other international bodies, don't seem to spend all that much time on Earth, and the US doesn't have any ongoing presence on the Moon, even in Earth-616. So really, Inhuman/US relations seem analogous to any other nation with which the US does not have formal relations. The fact that it takes a spacecraft to get there doesn't change things too much.

Foreign Dignitaries and Diplomats

Let's lower our sights now and consider the legal implications of comic book characters that have some kind of formal status with a foreign government. As part of Marvel's 2006 *Civil War* event, the Black Panther, as King T'Challa of Wakanda, marries Ororo Munroe (Storm of the X-Men), in what is described as *the* wedding of the decade. Which is sweet and all, but winds up having some pretty weird international law implications as the story unfolds. The *Civil War* story touches pretty heavily on the issue of diplomatic missions and the effect of US laws on foreign citizens.

As in the real world, the United States in Earth-616 is watched fairly closely by other countries as something of a weather vane for world events. So when the federal government passed the Superhuman Registration Act (SHRA), all eyes were keenly fixed on the US to see how that was going to play out, not only in the superhuman community, but by foreign governments. Things get really interesting where the two overlap, such as with Dr. Doom and T'Challa.

The writers seem to recognize the fact that the SHRA's effect outside of the US is pretty limited. When Ben Grimm realizes that he can't support either side of the conflict in good conscience, he relocates to Paris under the correct assumption that it will be difficult for federal agents to make him do much of anything if he's in France. A number of other characters discuss fleeing to Canada. But it should be noted that Grimm did register with the government before he moved, whereas a superhuman who did not could theoretically be in violation of the SHRA in the same way that a draft dodger might escape punishment but still be in violation of the law. So Grimm's registration and subsequent self-imposed exile does not necessarily violate the law (unless participation in The Initiative is mandatory, which some stories suggest may be the case).

Beyond that, the writers raise the question of whether a superhuman temporary visitor (who wasn't a head of state or otherwise qualified to diplomatic immunity) would be required to register. This is never resolved in the comics, but it would stand to reason that this would work in much the same way as similar laws interact with immigration status. In general, when the government requires people to register for something, be it for Selective Service or whatever, that duty only attaches when permanent residence (or employment of some kind) is established. So a vacationer or exchange student or a visiting Canadian superhero team like Alpha Flight would probably not be required to register, but someone seeking refugee status, permanent residency (a "green card") or citizenship (naturalization) would. Requiring temporary visitors to register would not only be an absolute hassle, but would probably piss off other nations by imposing arguably unnecessary and burdensome obligations on their citizens. Even given the anti-super fervor that swept the country, one can imagine Congress taking a measured approach here. You don't want Alpha Flight's Sasquatch taking his grievances to Capitol Hill.

Finally, there is also the issue, as mentioned, that certain characters are both superhuman and highly placed in foreign governments. Victor von Doom is the head of state of Latveria. T'Challa is the king of Wakanda. There's also the Atlanteans, who in at least one case are diplomatic envoys (though their spies probably don't count, as spies can be detained). All of these will be entitled to diplomatic immunity, and attempting to abrogate that—as War Machine does in *Civil War*—would constitute an act of war, which should probably have caused a far bigger international incident than it seems to have. Even more, a foreign head of state actively taking sides with an insurrection, as T'Challa does with the Anti-Registration forces, is just completely out of bounds. This would be on the same level as France assisting the American colonies during the American Revolution,[10] or Britain coming in on the side of the Confederacy in the American Civil War,[11] i.e., it would immediately lead to a state of warfare between the US and the offending foreign power. The fact that T'Challa is a former Avenger is given far more weight to the resolution of this situation than seems appropriate, and why the US and Wakanda aren't completely at each other's throats is never adequately explored.

---

10. Britain declared war on France about a month and a half after France and the American colonies formalized their alliance.

11. The Union actually threatened to declare war against Great Britain if the latter entered the war on the side of the Confederacy, and the historical record suggests that this threat was not an idle one.

Then we come to Storm, aka Ororo Munroe, aka T'Challa's wife and the reigning Queen of Wakanda, who happens to be a US citizen—in theory, anyway. It seems unlikely that she would be permitted to retain her citizenship after taking up her office in the Wakandan government, even though her official status is never worked out in any great detail. But as the Wakandan monarchy appears hereditary, it would seem that marrying T'Challa would invest her with at least some official political authority. So when federal troops attempt to arrest her when she returns to the US as part of their honeymoon political tour . . . it's not entirely clear that (1) she is still subject to the SHRA given her questionable citizenship, or (2) why her status in the Wakandan government does not grant her diplomatic immunity. T'Challa certainly seems to take a dim view of the attempt.

Why the US should care about this is significantly less a question of law than *Realpolitik*. If the US is seen to be flouting international law by attempting to arrest foreign dignitaries, the State Department is going to have one hell of a time trying to explain to other countries why the government decided that any domestic political issue trumped long-established international law, and why it isn't going to happen again.

Embassies

The climactic battle of the *Civil War* event takes place in New York City, and in the carnage, the Wakandan embassy is essentially leveled, to the point that Black Panther and Storm need to find another place to stay in the US. Embassies are generally subject to a limited form of extraterritoriality under the Vienna Convention on Diplomatic Relations, of which the US is a member. Essentially, while still technically the sovereign territory of the host nation, embassies remain under the *jurisdiction* of the represented nation, and the host nation may not enter without permission. This is why so many intelligence operations are centered around embassies: The host nation cannot come and go as it pleases.

So if simply setting foot in an embassy without permission is a big deal—and it is—how much more is completely leveling one? Wakanda seems to basically shrug this off, and T'Challa decides not to make a big deal out of it. But this is far from the end of the matter. It's actually quite remarkable that no other countries said anything about the incident. We're talking about the destruction of a foreign embassy on US soil, which the government does not seem to have been able to prevent. That's not going to give the international community warm and fuzzy feelings, and it's entirely possible that other governments could use this incident as a pretense to beef up security at their own embassies in the US without the State Department being able to object as much as they otherwise might.

And they would certainly want to object. Embassies, being essentially enclaves of sovereign power on foreign soil, are incredible assets in intelligence gathering and espionage. This is one of those areas in which official practice and actual practice differ pretty significantly. Officially, it is against international law to use embassies for espionage or intelligence purposes. Unofficially, *every country in the world does this*. Everybody knows this, but the countries of the world have collectively decided, without officially saying so, that the risk posed by other countries engaging in espionage via their embassies is at least balanced out by the value of being able to do that right back. But part of this game is that the intelligence gathering activities need to be discreet. The gentlemen's agreement is basically "Look, we all know we're doing this, but we can't turn a blind eye if you make too much noise, so keep it on the down low."

So when the US "permits" the destruction of a foreign embassy on its soil, other countries would be able to put additional assets in play, bolstering their own security—and intelligence!—activities, and the US would lack any plausible way of objecting. As such, the US government would probably have wanted to take additional steps towards preventing the destruction of the embassy and certainly would have thrown the book at anyone involved in its destruction.

International Organizations

Lastly, comic books frequently include organizations that operate across national borders. We're going to focus on S.H.I.E.L.D. here, as it's the most prominent, superhero-related international organization out there that has some kind of official government status.[12] The exact nature of the organization is somewhat in doubt, as various writers have inconsistently depicted it as being either a US or a UN entity, but the current consensus appears to be that it is an agency of the latter.[13] Actually, the confusion is somewhat justified by the nature of international organizations in the real world. For example, the International Monetary Fund and the World Bank, while technically international organizations, are widely perceived to be subservient to American and European interests, as both organizations are headquartered in Washington, DC, and no non-American, non-European has ever been the head of either agency. So the fact that the head of S.H.I.E.L.D. has always been an American would tend to blur this line somewhat.[14]

But assuming that S.H.I.E.L.D. is a truly international organization under the UN, this poses some interesting problems, because

12. The various incarnations of DC's Justice League seem mostly to be more or less informal groups of superheroes who decide to work together, but are not generally organized by any government or governmental agency, and tend not to have any kind of official status.

13. Then again, 2012's *The Avengers* and the Marvel Cinematic Universe generally really starts to make it look like a domestic military organization again. S.H.I.E.L.D. is an inter-story and inter-*medium* ambiguity.

14. But it still doesn't excuse the fact that the writers took a few decades to make up their minds as to what was actually going on.

the UN does not actually possess any jurisdiction of its own. Rather than existing on its own or as the expression of the political will of its citizenry, the UN exists at the behest and pleasure of its member states and cannot take any action without their authorization. The UN does not have an army of its own and is not capable of raising one. UN peacekeepers are, in fact, soldiers on loan from member nations. They operate under the flag of the UN but remain part of their own nation's chain of command. The ability of UN peacekeepers to act on their own initiative, outside the generally narrow rules of engagement with which they are authorized, is severely limited. For example, UNAMIR, the peacekeeping force in Rwanda, largely stood aside during the Rwandan genocide of 1994. The force is thought to have been *capable* of putting a stop to the violence, but it lacked the legal authority to do so, leading to the deaths of an estimated 850,000 people.

What, then, are we to make of S.H.I.E.L.D.? The basic idea is that the organization was chartered to deal with the threat posed by either the terrorist group HYDRA or superhuman/supernatural threats more generally. This is plausible enough, except for the fact that the UN really hasn't proved all that effective a means for dealing with purely human threats. The Korean War is the last and only time when the UN has unambiguously authorized full-scale military action of any sort, and that only because the USSR stormed out in protest (which, in retrospect, was a really silly mistake that they never repeated). The current "wars" in which the US is engaged are not precisely authorized by the UN, despite a more or less broad spectrum of support from a variety of US allies. The idea that a technologically advanced, militarily powerful, standing international strike force could be authorized by the UN beggars belief. Such an agency could, in fact, exist, but every single deployment would require the authorization of the member states, so the potential scope of authority in each engagement is likely to be very limited.

No, S.H.I.E.L.D. seems to represent what the UN might or even arguably *should* be, but it doesn't really represent the way the UN actually is today.

But what about the possibility that S.H.I.E.L.D. is actually just a top-secret US military force? That clears up a lot of problems, like the question of why it can exist in the first place, and it doesn't necessarily introduce any new problems that aren't already in play in the real world. A top-secret military agency running missions of high-level importance that never make it to the public eye and to which other governments don't object? There are, what, half a dozen of those? More? We don't even know. Sometimes other governments don't object because the State Department throws its weight around. Sometimes it's because they've formally or informally invited the US in to do the job. Other times they don't even know about it. Is any of this legal? Not technically. Running military operations inside the borders of another country is generally considered to be *casus belli*.[15]

But if one side decides not to make an issue out of it, which as discussed they might not for a variety of reasons, that's more or less the end of it. There isn't really anything like an international court to which nations can bring their disputes (outside of narrow areas like trade disputes brought before the WTO). No one and nothing has jurisdiction over sovereign states as such, and forcing a national government to do something involves either diplomacy or war. If one of the nations is positioned like the US, which, for good or ill, holds most of the cards in many situations, there isn't much the other state can do about actions they don't like other than complain: good economic relations with the US are too important, and few countries could even begin to mount a military response. Now that wouldn't be true for countries like China, Russia, or even some of our more prominent allies like the UK. But pretty much anywhere in South America or Africa and a good chunk of Asia is more or less fair game, as evidenced by the fact that the US has conducted military opera-

---

15. A Latin phrase that means, roughly, "justification for acts of war."

tions throughout those regions with relative impunity for most of the past sixty years.

So positing a S.H.I.E.L.D., which is really just a branch of the Pentagon responsible for intervening in supernatural/paranormal situations all over the world, would involve the US violating international law in quite significant ways. But the US does this kind of thing all the time. So while it isn't the optimal way of setting up something like S.H.I.E.L.D., it's certainly a plausible one.

Extradition

Extradition is an area of law that comes up surprisingly infrequently in comics, given that supervillains often commit crimes all across the world before retreating to a base of operations in another country. In fact, one of the best examples of comic book extradition comes not from the trial of a supervillain but rather the trial of a superhero: Bucky Barnes, sidekick (and sometimes replacement) for Captain America.

Barnes was put on trial in the United States after it was revealed that he had been brainwashed by the Soviets and employed as an assassin, a job that included killing Americans. Although Barnes had a solid defense, he ultimately changed his plea to guilty, but the judge sentenced him to time served. Any relief is short-lived, however, as the Russian ambassador to the United States announces that he has extradition orders to bring Bucky to Russia, where he has already been convicted in absentia of crimes against the state. And sure enough, he is hauled away to Russian prison, although he later escapes.

There's just one little problem here: The United States doesn't have an extradition treaty with Russia.[16] Extradition is not a judicial

---

16. *See* list attached to 18 U.S.C. § 3181, *available at* http://www.state.gov/documents/organization/71600.pdf.

Russia is not at the top of the list of places to which it's fun to be extradited. Ed Brubaker et al., *The Trial of Captain America, Part 5*, in CAPTAIN AMERICA (VOL. 1) 615 (Marvel Comics April 2011).

function but rather a function of the President's power to conduct foreign policy.[17] As such, without an extradition treaty, Bucky can't be extradited. Of course, that's here in the real world. It's entirely possible that Russia and the United States have an extradition treaty on Earth-616. Let's assume there is one; is that enough?

One might think that being convicted in absentia is a problem. What about due process, after all? Unfortunately for Bucky, it is not clear that trying someone in absentia is even prohibited by the United States Constitution, and there is case law supporting the extradition of defendants convicted in absentia in a foreign country.[18]

In fact, because extradition is an executive function, the role of the courts in an extradition proceeding is a minimal gatekeeping function. Basically the only question for the court is "are the terms of the extradition treaty being complied with?" This is called the doctrine of non-inquiry, which "precludes extradition magistrates from assessing the investigative, judicial, and penal systems of foreign nations when reviewing an extradition request."[19] As the Supreme Court explained:

> When an American citizen commits a crime in a foreign country, he cannot complain if required to submit to such modes of trial and to such punishment as the laws of that country may prescribe for its own people, unless a different mode be provided for by treaty stipulations between that country and the United States.[20]

---

17. *See, e.g.*, Martin v. Warden, 993 F.2d 824, 828 (11th Cir. 1993).

18. Crosby v. United States, 506 U.S. 255 (1993) (holding that Fed. R. Crim. P. 43 permits trials in absentia in at least some cases, declining to address constitutional issue); Gallina v. Fraser, 278 F.2d 77 (1960) (permitting extradition of a defendant convicted in absentia in Italy).

19. *Martin*, 993 F.2d at 829.

20. Neely v. Henkel, 180 U.S. 109, 123 (1901).

So Bucky probably couldn't complain to a court, but luckily that's not the last stop in the process. Here's an explanation of the process from a federal circuit court case:

The [extradition] statute establishes a two-step procedure which divides responsibility for extradition between a judicial officer and the Secretary of State. In brief, the judicial officer, upon complaint, issues an arrest warrant for an individual sought for extradition, provided that there is an extradition treaty between the United States and the relevant foreign government and that the crime charged is covered by the treaty. If a warrant issues, the judicial officer then conducts a hearing to determine if "he deems the evidence sufficient to sustain the charge under the provisions of the proper treaty." If the judicial officer makes such a determination, he "shall certify" to the Secretary of State that a warrant for the surrender of the relator "may issue." It is then within the Secretary of State's sole discretion to determine whether or not the relator should actually be extradited.[21]

Thus, Bucky (perhaps via his friends in high places) could petition the Secretary of State not to extradite him to Russia. If Russia doesn't like the decision, its only recourse is diplomatic because extradition treaties generally don't have enforcement provisions.

So as long as we're willing to assume (1) that Russia and the US have an extradition treaty on Earth-616 and (2) that Bucky exhausted his political capital already, then it's entirely possible for Bucky to be extradited under the circumstances presented in the comic.

---

21. United States v. Kin-Hong, 110 F.3d 103, 109 (1st Cir. 1997).

CHAPTER 12

Immortality, Alter Egos, and Resurrection

Hob Gadling was drinking in an English tavern in AD 1389 when he made the comment that "Death is a mug's game."[1] Dream and Death, of the Endless, happened to hear Gadling's comment, and at Dream's request, Death agreed to let Gadling live until he wanted to die. Dream approached Gadling for a drink and the two arranged to meet at the same bar at the same time on the same day—a hundred years in the future. Gadling thought it was a joke, but a hundred years later, there he was.

Gadling is a recurring character in Neil Gaiman's epic *Sandman* run, and one of the characters that most directly addresses one of the problems with immortality: How can one retain one's fortune over the years without people figuring out that one is immortal? There are a number of reasons one might wish to keep such a thing secret—pitchforks, torches, etc.—but completely reinventing one's self every few decades defeats one of the obvious advantages of immortality,

---

1. Neil Gaiman et al., *Men of Good Fortune*, in SANDMAN (VOL. 2) 13 (DC Comics February 1990).

That, my friend, is how you do it. Neil Gaiman et al., *Men of Good Fortune*, in SANDMAN (VOL. 2) 13 (DC Comics February 1990).

i.e., the ability to accumulate wealth over a much, much longer period of time than we mere mortals.

In this chapter, we take a look at some of the legal issues surrounding death and dying. First, whether there are any inherent problems with abnormally long life spans. Second, the problems associated with creating and maintaining successive cover identities. Finally, we'll examine the implications of resurrection on inheritance and property law.

Successive Identities

"The days of our years are threescore years and ten; and if by reason of strength may be fourscore years, yet is their strength labour and sorrow; for it is soon cut off, and we fly away."[2] Or, at least, that's been the received wisdom since longer than anyone can remember. And because death after seventy or eighty years is such a fundamental part of the human experience, the difference between living two hundred years and not dying at all is, from the perspective of the legal system, pretty trivial.

Turning back to Gadling, one of the problems he ran into was people starting to get suspicious about his preternatural agelessness. This required him to disappear off to Scotland or the East Indies on a number of occasions, to return as his own long lost "son." This gets at one of the main issues that an immortal who doesn't want his immortality to be widely known will have to face: the creation and maintenance of successive cover identities.

The idea of an alter ego comes with certain legal complications, as has been recognized long before the publication of the first comic book. In Robert Louis Stevenson's *Strange Case of Dr. Jekyll and Mr. Hyde*, first published in 1886, one of the main plot drivers is Jekyll's

---

2. *Psalms* 90:10 (King James).

Hob Gadling explains some of the practical details of amassing wealth and creating new identities as an immortal being. Neil Gaiman et al., *Men of Good Fortune*, in SANDMAN (VOL. 2) 13 (DC Comics February 1990).

pains to ensure that he maintains access to his property when he changes into Hyde.[3] This largely took the form of instructing his servants to pay heed to Hyde and executing a will leaving everything to Hyde should Jekyll disappear.

Legally, there is no reason Jekyll could not do this. A property owner may dispose of his property in any legal way that he sees fit, and giving it to himself, while usually pointless, is not illegal. The problem is not that Jekyll's design was illegal, but that it was *unusual*, to the point that people noticed something was up. Indeed, it was the very attempt to create and maintain this alter ego that led to the discovery of his dual identity. If Jekyll/Hyde had been content to live two entirely different identities with no overlapping property or affairs, i.e., if Hyde had been willing to forego all of Jekyll's advantages, the story could have ended quite differently.

So the problem is not only in the creation of an alter ego, but doing so within the bounds of the law in ways that will maintain the integrity of the illusion. Both of these will cause problems on a number of levels.

The relationship between one's real and cover identities is significant. If one starts life as a mundane person and then acquires a masked identity, e.g., Bruce Wayne becoming Batman, things are fairly straightforward. Wayne doesn't usually run errands as Batman, so his cover identity doesn't really need legal papers or even identification. But creating a new mundane identity to live and work in, as one would need to do if faking one's own death or moving from one mundane identity to another, is more difficult. Governments do this for people on a regular basis for things like witness protection programs, espionage, and undercover operations, but there are two main facts about this that present problems for superheroes. First, government-created identities are obviously created

---

3. In the actual short story, the fact that Jekyll and Hyde are the same person is the twist ending, not known from the start, which really gives the problems of alter egos a pretty thorough going-over.

with government approval, so no laws are being broken. Second, outside of witness protection these identities are rarely intended to be used either for significant transactional purposes or for very long, i.e., they are not intended to fully or permanently replace the original identity.

The basic problem then is that to create a new identity without government authorization requires the commission of a number of federal felonies, potentially including making false immigration statements, identification document fraud, perjury and numerous related offenses under state law.[4] And trying to live in contemporary society without such documents will be very, very difficult. One cannot buy a car, rent an apartment, get a checking account, or engage in a host of transactions essential to the logistics of mundane life without some form of government identification, identification that a superhero wanting to create a new mundane identity would need to forge. Creating successive false identities all but requires one to engage in illegal activities. See, for example, the discussion of immigration law in chapter 10. Hob Gadling actually comments that maintaining these identities has gotten harder with the bureaucratization of society in the twentieth century.

Even if our hero can stomach breaking the law in this way, these sorts of illegalities do tend to attract enough attention to make maintaining a secret identity pretty difficult, particularly if one wishes to maintain some kind of base-level commitment to law and order. Al Capone was eventually brought down not for racketeering or the St. Valentine's Day Massacre, but for simple tax evasion.

Speaking of taxes, transferring large sums of money without a paper trail is difficult to do legally. Money laundering is a federal offense, and suggestions of financial shadiness tend to attract the attention of prosecutors. Jumping through offshore banks is no guarantee of secrecy either, as the discipline of forensic accounting

---

4. 18 U.S.C. §§ 1015, 1028, 1621.

exists almost solely to analyze patterns of financial transactions for irregularities. Even sticking to cash transactions is no solution: (1) one cannot move more than ten thousand dollars in cash across the border without declaring it; (2) banking transactions over ten thousand dollars in cash in a single day must be reported to regulators.[5]

So even though money must technically be "dirty," i.e., the proceeds of or used for some unlawful activity,[6] in order for disguising the origin and ownership of such funds to be a felony, simply the attempt to disguise it is likely to raise red flags all over the place, because most of the people engaged in that sort of activity are doing so for nefarious reasons. If our superhero or an artificial "mundane" persona is going to need to spend any money, this poses problems of the sort that could easily trigger an IRS audit. As the Joker observed, "I'm crazy enough to take on Batman, but the IRS? No, thank you!"[7] So again, it seems that some of our heroes are faced with a difficult choice: maintain their secret identity or live within the bounds of the law. But even breaking the law in this way is no guarantee of success.

So basically, if an immortal wants to disguise his immortality, he's going to have a pretty tough time doing it. Much of what he'll need to do is illegal, and even the technically legal things are often so shady as to attract unwanted attention. This is not to say that it's impossible, but most of the people who have successfully pulled off something like this usually tend to lie low.

---

5. These regulations are part of the Bank Secrecy Act in the US. Many other countries have similar laws.

6. 18 U.S.C. § 1956.

7. From *The New Batman Adventures* episode "Joker's Millions," based on David Vern et al., *The Joker's Millions*, in DETECTIVE COMICS 180 (DC Comics February 1952).

Immortality and the Law

Generally speaking, the legal system is set up to deal with people dying on a regular basis, and even someone living past a hundred does odd things to societies in which inheritance is important.

But when people start living much past that, especially if they aren't aging normally, things can get *really* weird. This is important for comic book stories, because even ignoring the fact that time passes somewhat strangely in comic book universes (i.e., the origin story of various characters has been "time shifted" forward—Tony Stark was once imprisoned in the Vietnam War, then the first Gulf War, and now it's Afghanistan) when compared with how time passes in the "real world," comic book universes are full of characters that live for a long time, potentially forever.[8] Marvel has Wolverine, Apocalypse, Deadpool, and Dr. Strange, and that's not even the whole list of arguably human characters. DC has Ra's al Ghul, Wonder Woman, and quite possibly Superman as well. Is there anything illegal, as such, about being immortal?

Not as such, at least not in the real world or in comic books that aren't *Logan's Run*,[9] and there aren't any laws against reaching any particular birthday either. But there are a few legal doctrines for which immortality could prove quite problematic. The biggest one has to do with property ownership. The way things are now, when a person buys a piece of real estate, he can generally assume that he has what is called a "fee simple," i.e., complete freehold ownership of the land with no termination condition.[10] This is frequently referred

---

8. Some stories make a distinction between "true" immortality and simply living a really long time. While this distinction may be important for various plots, the legal significance is minimal: anyone who lives more than about a hundred years without aging normally is going to run into these issues.

9. Marvel actually did a seven-issue series starting in January 1977.

10. The term "fee" derives from "fief," a feudal landholding. It effectively means "interest in land," but because that's cumbersome, the "fee" terminology has survived.

to as having "clear title," and it's so important that banks will generally not sell a mortgage for a property where clear title is in question.[11]

As it turns out, the legal system is actually pretty invested in making sure this happens, and the device that ensures it is the bane of first-year law students everywhere: the Rule Against Perpetuities, frequently abbreviated as the RAP. To explain the RAP, we're afraid we'll have to turn to a non-comic-book example.

Consider a family dairy farm. Say mom 'n' pop are sentimental about the farm, so they leave it to their son with some conditions, like so: "To our son, we leave the family dairy farm, but if he ever stops using it as a dairy farm, the property will go to our eldest grandson." This means that the son will not have a fee simple to the land,[12] because there is a condition wherein he might lose it. But the *grandson* can do whatever he wants with it: the condition stops with the son's ownership.

But what if they said: "To our son, we leave the family farm, but if he *or any of our descendants* ever stop using it as a dairy farm, the property will go to the next-eldest descendant." That's quite a bit more restrictive, because while the first example would theoretically permit the grandson to turn the farm into a subdivision (or a horse ranch or whatever) because the condition only applied to the son, the latter example does not. This will make it a lot harder to use the property as anything but a dairy farm, *even if the property can't be used that way anymore* (e.g., if zoning regulations prevent it or cows go extinct or something).

The RAP dates back to early-modern England, when it was realized that aristocratic families were doing *exactly* this sort of thing, usually in order to preserve the family fortune. Aristocrats would

---

11. Which is actually one of the big problems with mortgage securitization and the recent financial crisis. Property ownership can get so tangled that it's becoming almost impossible to get good title to some houses. We'll be sorting out that mess for *years*.

12. The technical estate would be a "fee simple subject to an executory limitation," a type of "defeasible fee."

place restrictions on the use of their lands in an effort to keep them from being parceled up and sold off. There were insanely complicated systems of shifting interests that sometimes endured for centuries. So much real estate was so encumbered with conditions on inheritance that it was becoming impossible to transfer good title to vast swaths of the countryside. In response, the courts imposed a rule that no interest was valid unless it could "vest," i.e., become a present interest in a living person, within twenty-one years after the death of some person alive when the interest was created. As a practical matter, this meant that you're allowed to create interests that vest in your kids or their kids, but you can't perpetually encumber your property such that your distant descendants won't have clear title to the property.

Many states have modified or abandoned the RAP, as hereditary land dynasties are no longer fashionable, and simply administering the RAP was a pain in the neck. Law students are still taught it, but as often as not it's a form of hazing, in which professors inflict obsolete doctrines on students because, dammit, *they* had to learn it, so you do too. The RAP comes up rarely in practice.

However, an immortal could, to put things mildly, *completely* screw this up. How? Because the RAP says that you can't create an executory interest that vests more than twenty-one years after the death of someone *currently alive*. Because our immortal isn't ever going to die, he can use *himself* as the "measuring life," and so set up an impossibly complex set of shifting interests, all of which would be permitted by the RAP.

The way this would work would be for an immortal to buy a piece of property, and then sell it to someone else with a condition, which, if violated, would automatically shift ownership to some other person, possibly the immortal himself or herself. Because it is impossible to grant better title to land than that you yourself possess, the condition would not go away if the property were sold to a third party. Ergo, any conditions placed by an immortal would remain on the property *forever*.

This is clearly less than ideal, and though most superheroes would presumably not be unpleasant about this, even a noble superhero who wasn't paying attention[13] could find that he'd inadvertently frozen a community in time by accidentally preventing any change in the land use. Even worse, one can easily imagine a farsighted villain like Ra's al Ghul using this power for evil, if the writers were big enough law geeks. World domination by conquest is admittedly impressive, as is world domination by buying it all over time. But it's far, far more insidious to wind up controlling the whole world because you *used* to own it at some point and nobody ever thought that weird clause in the real estate contract would ever come back to haunt them.

So, in short, while there is no *inherent* problem with being immortal, property law pretty much assumes that everyone is going to die at some point, so the presence of an immortal being could pretty seriously screw things up. It's almost strange that no writer seems to have done much with this yet. . . .

Immortality and Compound Interest

But wait a minute. Why does a character need to rely on property ownership to accumulate wealth? Why can't he just use the magic of compound interest, frequently described as one of the most powerful inventions in human history? It turns out that this isn't nearly as workable a solution in practice as it is on paper. There are two main reasons for this. The first is historical, and the second economic, but together they conspire to make living off your interest a little harder than it sounds.

---

13. And really, if one is acquiring property over a period of centuries, losing track of a few parcels doesn't seem impossible.

The History of Banking

Deposit a thousand dollars in a bank today, make 3 percent a year, and in a hundred years you'll have $19,218.63. Not bad, eh? That's the theory, anyway. But there are a couple of historical problems with trying to do this for really long periods of time. The first is that the oldest currently operating bank is Monte dei Paschi di Siena, founded in Siena, Italy, in 1472. Which is a long time ago, to be sure, but for someone like Apocalypse or Mr. Immortal, that's not actually a very long time. There is one other bank that's been around for that long—also Italian—but the modern banking system really only seems to have gotten started in the seventeenth century. So for characters that live a *really* long time, compound interest on deposit accounts hasn't been available for most of their lifetime.

The other main historical problem is long-term stability. The financial industry is remarkably stable over a period of a few years, and the past few decades—2008 notwithstanding—have shown that they can be pretty stable over the intermediate term, but over the really long term? Much, much rarer. There were only a few periods further back in history that had something like our modern financial system. For example, ancient Roman banks seem to have been pretty sophisticated in historical terms, but they have all, for one reason or another, collapsed. Similarly, during the height of the Umayyad Caliphate, it was possible to write a check in Morocco and cash it in Islamabad, but the Caliphate was overthrown and its successors were not always in charge of the same territory. Since deposit insurance is a creature of the twentieth century, this means that if you are an immortal who lived through the end of a major civilization or even a decent financial panic, there was a good chance that you'd lose everything you'd kept in banks. So if you were depending on your deposits to keep you going, well, that's maybe okay for a few decades, but not on the century timescale, let alone millennia.

To make matters even worse, for a huge chunk of history, the charging of interest was considered ethically problematic. The prohibition against usury still applies in the Muslim world, which is why Islamic banking looks so deeply strange to Western audiences. Western banks used a rather complicated legal arrangement to get around usury prohibitions in the Middle Ages, but the plain fact is that interest-bearing savings accounts the way we think of them really didn't exist until the twentieth century. You could certainly invest your money, but now we're talking about something different from simple compound interest.

Inflation

But even if there was an unbroken continuity of depository institutions that has existed or is likely to exist for more than a few centuries, there's another problem: inflation.

To make a reference outside our normal genre, consider Mr. Darcy of Jane Austen's *Pride and Prejudice*, who is said to have had an income, i.e., money he didn't have to work for, of £10,000 annually. Which even in current terms is not a terrible income, but most Brits with a job make more than that. But when the book was published in 1813, this represented a sum closer to £6.5 million in today's currency, which is substantially cooler. But it also goes to illustrate just how badly individual units of currency have inflated over the years. One observer suggests that the effective inflation rate from 1913 to today is about 3.5 percent a year, something in the neighborhood of 1,929 percent over the whole time period. So someone trying to live purely off interest is going to have one hell of a time keeping up with that. They'd need to make 3.5 percent just to break even, so they'd need to make about 7 percent total just to have something to live on unless they had a massive principal investment to start with.

If you can find a relatively safe investment (i.e., a place you can put money that will give a return without you needing to work at it, that makes 7 percent a year), consistently, for more than a few years in a row, you are, without question, the most brilliant financier in the history of the world. The only way to make more than that is to either (1) own stuff yourself, be it land, a factory, a business, intellectual property, whatever, or (2) get a day job. Rich people choose the former; most people choose the latter, usually out of necessity. But the idea that you can just have a bunch of money, let it essentially sit, and expect to make a decent living for any serious period of time is problematic. Throughout history, the people in the world who have gotten rich have not done so on the basis of interest. Inflation, combined with long-term instability, makes that kind of thing truly implausible.

Don't believe it? Think about the royal houses of Europe. If compound interest works the way it's supposed to under the myth, they should be the richest people in the world. And make no mistake: the royal houses that have managed to survive are pretty well off. But they're far from being the richest people in the world, and a lot of their current wealth comes from marrying people who got wealthy in other ways, e.g., oil barons, shipping magnates, etc. One might realistically ask if they'd be wealthy at all if they'd had to rely solely upon their own fortunes. Others are officially supported by national governments, which is an awesome gig if you can get it, but does tend to preclude the kind of hiding-in-the-shadows, living-a-life-without-obligations thing that Hob Gadling and most other immortal characters tend towards.[14]

One might be tempted to say "ah, but what about the stock market?" Unfortunately, it presents many of the same problems: stock markets haven't been around much longer than banks (the NYSE only goes back to 1817), they suffer the same long-term instability problems, and positive returns on one's investment are impossible to guarantee. Inflation applies to securities exchanges too. Adjusted for inflation, the historic peak of the DJIA was just over 1,000, and in

---

14. Someone like Apocalypse doesn't really "hide in the shadows," but neither does he try to amass legitimate wealth.

the early 1980s would have actually been at a level deep into the plunge of the 1930s! What's more, stock markets and their participants tend to be even more heavily scrutinized than banks these days—complying with SEC regulations is a significant burden on publicly traded corporations and their directors—so in some ways they're an even worse choice for an immortal trying to lay low. You can open a bank account without attracting any regulatory scrutiny, but securities trading is a lot harder to disguise for very long. No, buying stock on public exchanges is no substitute for private ownership, nor is it a plausible way of putting compound interest or something like it to work in the very long term.

Immortality and Social Security

Almost every American old enough to read has at least heard of Social Security, and with good reason: it's been a key part of the United States' social safety net for three quarters of a century. The program is so ubiquitous that Social Security Numbers (SSNs) have become one of the primary ways that United States citizens identify themselves in transactions with the government.

That alone poses a problem for an immortal character trying to lay low, as SSNs are associated with birthdates, and each time an SSN is used in an official transaction, there's the chance that someone will notice a birthdate that's way older than it should be. More than that, though, one's SSN is intimately connected to one's legal identity. It is a unique identifier and without one (or a Taxpayer Identification Number), the federal government isn't necessarily going to be totally sure that you exist, bureaucratically speaking. It's how taxes are tracked, and it's very difficult to engage in even the most routine government transactions without one. If you're curious, the statute that creates them is 42 U.S.C. § 405.

All of which conspires to make the SSN an essential part of constructing an alter ego, as discussed earlier in this chapter. Of course, forging them is a crime, and just running the numbers there's a three percent chance that whatever number you make up is going to be currently in use by someone else (though it's actually even greater than that given the rules for valid SSNs).

The other completely ubiquitous part of Social Security is taxes.[15] Social Security taxes are imposed by the Federal Insurance Contributions Act, better known as FICA, and codified at 26 U.S.C. §§ 3101–3128. At the moment, the Social Security tax rate is 6.2 percent of gross income, plus another 6.2 percent contributed by employers, so really 12.4 percent.[16] The self-employed must pay both halves out of their own pocket, hence self-employment taxes, but the difference is more one of perception than reality.

Either way, if you make money by working, i.e., you earn a wage or salary, the government wants its cut, and the IRS doesn't much care who you are: even Superman can expect a visit from the taxman.[17] If you're earning money, and it's more than a couple of grand a year, the IRS will eventually find out. So unless a character is independently wealthy—which means he'll be paying taxes in other ways, just not FICA—it's going to be very, very hard to evade Social Security taxes for very long.

Then there's the question of benefits. Right now, every American over the age of 67 (lower in some cases) can collect old-age benefits. Fair enough. But the actuarial tables for calculating benefits, taxes, budgets, etc., are predicated on most people dying within a decade of their seventy-fifth (or so) birthday. Wolverine could theoretically have been collecting Social Security—assuming he got his citizenship status worked out—almost since the program was inaugurated!

---

15. Taxes are discussed in more detail in chapter 8.

16. At the time of this writing the employee contribution was reduced by 2 percent, but this reduction is expected to expire eventually.

17. See chapter 8 for the full story.

This is problematic for two reasons. One, when the government is cutting you a check every month, that's one more month where someone might notice that you're still around. A situation in Japan where hundreds of elderly people collecting old-age pensions were discovered to be missing, sometimes for decades, illustrates that while the machinery of bureaucracy does have a lot of inertia, people living beyond their nineties is still quite unusual and does raise red flags.[18] So a character who is either immortal or has a longer than normal lifespan will almost certainly get noticed sooner or later. Whether or not the character minds is dependent upon the facts of their particular story, but this could be problematic for many characters.

But second, Social Security was intended as a sort of last-resort measure to prevent the elderly from becoming destitute. It doesn't really work that way anymore, as those people who have to rely solely upon Social Security pretty much are destitute, and plenty of people who don't need the money at all still collect benefits for decades, but that's still the theory. The discovery of a group of people who aren't going to die at all, or who are going to collect benefits for fifty plus years is likely to encourage Congress to take a long, hard look at establishing some kind of limitation on the ability of people to collect benefits forever. Depending on just how bad the budgetary situation is at that time, this could be as little as a fix to exclude the truly immortal or as draconian as limiting benefits to three decades for everyone. But some kind of congressional action does seem pretty likely, and the existence of immortals among us might just be sufficiently distressing to the American population to give Congress the motivation it needs to actually do something about the government's bleeding balance sheet.

The fact that even in the comics that contain the largest number

---

18. It also may help explain why the Japanese life expectancy is so high; maybe they simply aren't recording the deaths. But that's neither here nor there.

of immortal beings there are perhaps a few hundred in the entire world is not likely to mitigate this fear either. The American media and populace are terrible at issues of scale. This, of course, is just one more reason immortals might want to keep their existence hidden, which means taking pains to conceal their longevity and identity. Simply declining to accept the benefits is probably insufficient to head off congressional action too, since not every immortal is likely to be so charitable.

Resurrection, Return, and Probate

Death is notoriously less than permanent in comic book stories. The basic rule of thumb is that unless we actually *see* a character die, *and* their body afterward, they aren't dead, and even then writers can get creative.[19] But most of the time, the story is that the character wasn't actually *dead*, but was just hiding, or in hibernation, or in a different dimension, or stuck in the pattern buffer, or whatever.

This doesn't present any significant problems for the legal system, which already knows how to deal with people that are presumed to be dead but turn up later. A person who is legally absent, i.e., a person whose whereabouts are unknown for quite some time, will generally be presumed dead after a few years. Five to seven is pretty common, though interestingly for the citizens of Metropolis, New York, gives you only three.[20] It usually takes a court proceeding to get someone officially declared dead in the absence of a body, and in general, the courts will presume that a person is alive until there is clear evidence to the contrary or state statute operates to force presumption.

---

19. For example, Colossus sacrificed himself in Uncanny X-Men #390, his body was cremated, and his ashes were scattered. Nonetheless, he was returned to life three years later in Astonishing X-Men #4.

20. NY CLS EPTL § 2-1.7.

That last bit is actually of interest. Pretty much every state has a statute saying that if one is legally absent for a specified period of time, a court can declare one to be dead. But a few states also have a provision that exposure to a "specific peril of death" can permit a court to rule one dead before the specified period expires.[21] As superheroes are exposed to specific perils of death basically all the time, and would not generally be suspected to be dead in the absence of such a peril, it seems likely that a court, or at least a genre-blind one, would be willing to rule on a superhero's death pretty quickly. Which makes things a bit complicated if they aren't actually dead.

Southern Farm Bureau Life Ins. Co. v. Burney, 590 F. Supp. 1016 (E.D. Ark. 1984) is the big case here. In 1976, John Burney of Helena, Arkansas, ran into financial difficulties. On June 11, he was involved in a traffic accident on a bridge crossing the Mississippi River and managed to clamber over the railing and down the bridge into the river, where he swam to Mississippi instead of back home to Arkansas. He caught a bus and spent the next six years living in Florida as "John Bruce," complete with a new wife and child, neither of whom had any inkling of his former life. He was discovered when he returned to Arkansas in 1982 to visit his father. Unfortunately for him, Burney's wife and business partners had filed claims on various life insurance policies taken out on him and received benefits totaling $470,000. The wife, who may have been annoyed at finding out that her husband had completely abandoned his family and set up another one, contacted the insurer immediately. The insurer *was* annoyed and promptly sued Burney into next Tuesday.

Here's where things get interesting for whack-a-mole-type supers: Burney's wife and business partners, who had no knowledge of Burney's whereabouts and had assumed that he had died in the accident, wound up a total of $470,000 richer. The judge let them keep

---

21. *See, e.g.,* 20 Pa. Cons. Stat. § 5701(c).

that money, theorizing that "the policy of the law is to encourage settlement of litigation and to uphold and enforce contracts of settlement[22] if they are fairly arrived at, not in contravention of law or public policy."[23] Burney wound up being found liable for $470,000 plus interest—whether or not he paid is another matter—but the people who received property as a result of his death were permitted to keep it.

The implication here—and there really isn't much case law beyond this, because most people who are presumed to be dead are actually dead—is that if a person dies or is presumed to be dead, courts are not going to be very eager to disturb the settlement of property distributed via inheritance or devise unless there is a clear statutory reason to do so. Many states have statutes addressing this subject, but they're all over the place.

- Cal. Prob. Code § 12408 specifies that a person who reappears after being presumed dead may recover any of his estate which has not been distributed, but property that has been distributed is only recoverable if it is "equitable under the circumstances," and not at all if five years have passed.
- Va. Code Ann. § 64.1-113 provides that property which has not been distributed and property which is in the hands of someone who received it as a result of the presumption of death shall be returned to the person presumed dead, but bona fide purchasers of estate property are allowed to keep it.
- 20 Pa.C.S. § 5703 requires that if a person is declared dead in whole or in part on the basis of his continued

---

22. The insurer never actually believed that Burney was dead, but chose to settle the claim rather than fight. The judge reasoned that the insurer had figured the likelihood of Burney's actually being alive into the settlement offer.

23. *Id.* at 1022.

absence, no property can be distributed out of his estate without the distributee posting a bond for the value of the property. Clearly, a superhero who fears that he may erroneously be declared dead at some point should consider moving to Philadelphia.

- New York doesn't seem to have a statute on this subject at all, meaning that any property distributed because a person is presumed to have died could be pretty difficult to get back.

So this really becomes a question of the state's law where our supposedly deceased character's will or estate would be probated. A returning or resurrected character could find that they get back most of the property they lost, or they could wind up with nothing. The longer they take to come back, the more likely the second outcome is.

But what if the person really was dead? Like really, honestly, no-foolin', *dead* dead. Like Ben Grimm in *Fantastic Four* #508.[24] While in Latveria in the aftermath of Dr. Doom's exile to hell, Doom started to possess Grimm, and the only way to prevent that was to kill Grimm. Which is what happened. Obviously, Grimm came back from that, but he didn't "get better." Richards didn't clone him back to life. Grimm's soul hadn't been hiding out in a convenient contraption Dr. Doom had left lying around. No, Grimm was dead for reals, to the point that the rest of the Fantastic Four had to *travel to heaven* to try to persuade *God himself* to return Grimm to life.

The rest of the team was, of course, successful in pleading Grimm's case. The question is whether it makes a difference to the legal system whether Grimm was simply presumed dead in error or *actually* dead and then returned to life. The answer is, probably not. This is almost certainly a place where a judge would go with pragmatic

---

24. Mark Waid et al., *Authoritative Action Part 6*, in FANTASTIC FOUR 508 (Marvel Comics February 2004).

analysis. The alternative is to insist that Grimm had actually died and that his resurrection, while restoring him to life, did not restore him to any of the legal positions he had previously occupied. Essentially, the day of his resurrection would be his new "birthday," and he'd have to reestablish his entire legal persona. This would be an enormous pain in the neck for everyone involved, and since there really doesn't seem to be any good reason for going that direction, a judge faced with the question would almost certainly treat Grimm as if he hadn't died in the first place.[25]

Still, resurrection would likely have two important differences from simply being gone for a while. First, if one had never died in the first place, one's legal duties during that time would continue. So if, for example, a character had child support obligations, or owed taxes on interest income, or had a contract duty to fulfill, the character's absence might not exempt them from these obligations. Any exemption would have to come from a case-by-case analysis. But a character that was truly *dead* and subsequently resurrected would probably be entitled to a get-out-of-jail-free card for any obligations during the period in which he was dead.

Second, any time a person dies or is presumed dead, their estate is potentially subject to estate taxes. Estate tax is pretty complicated, and it's the reason there's an estate planning industry. The tax is somewhat controversial, but be that as it may, as of 2011, any estate worth more than five million dollars will pay something like 35 percent of the amount *over* five million dollars to the federal government. This is lower than it has been in years past (in 2001 it was 55 percent of everything over $675,000), but still significant for the very rich, which many superheroes and supervillains are.

---

25. This creates the interesting result that for criminal law purposes, a person could be held to have died and come back, while this would be ignored for estate law purposes. This may seem weird, but there is consistency here: in both cases, the law is being interpreted in the light most favorable to the "deceased." While admittedly a bizarre result, it does seem to be the one most consistent with concepts of equity, which is something courts care about.

So when an estate is probated, estate tax will have to be figured out and, if necessary, paid. The question then becomes whether a person who shows up after taxes have been paid on their estate can get those taxes back. If the person had simply been missing and not actually *died*, the answer may well be yes, though there is not currently case law to support that proposition. The government can be pretty stingy about that stuff. But there is certainly a good argument to be made that if the estate shouldn't have been probated in the first place, taxes shouldn't have been paid, so the person is entitled to a refund. But if the person had really, truly died . . . Like murder, where resurrection does not change the fact that the elements of the crime have been established, the fact that a person is resurrected does not change the fact that they died, which triggers estate tax obligations. Now the IRS could choose to be generous here, but the way the law is written, there is no strictly *legal* reason why a resurrected person whose estate had paid estate taxes would be entitled to a refund. So Ben Grimm would have a whole mess to deal with once he conquered death and returned to the land of the living.

CHAPTER 13

Non-Human Intelligences

One of the most common features of speculative fiction in general is the existence of non-human intelligences. Comic books are no exception. The DC Universe has Superman and various other Kryptonians as well as Gorilla Grodd and other intelligent non-human animals. Marvel has described entire galactic empires, including the Shi'ar and Skrull. Both universes include intelligent machines of various kinds.

Exactly how the law would treat them is a big question, and as there is currently no law on the books that would directly answer this question, finding an answer is going to involve at least as much philosophy and history as it will law, and that's where we begin.

The Evolution of Animal Rights

The American legal system is a common law jurisdiction. This means that it uses precedent, i.e., court decisions, to create law in addition to laws made by the legislature and regulations made by the executive branch. Common law legal systems are based on tradition as much as anything else, and our tradition comes from the English legal system. Most if not all American states incorporate the English common law, at least insofar as it is compatible with the federal and state constitution and laws.[1] This is relevant here because "under the early common law animals were possessed of no inherent right to protection from the brutality or wanton abuse of man."[2] Laws regarding animal cruelty, the protection of endangered species, the prevention of disease and overpopulation, and all other kinds of animal rights are the product of statutes, which mostly have their origin in the twentieth century. Thus, when we discuss the rights of intelligent non-humans, we must start with the assumption that they have no inherent rights under the United States legal system except those explicitly granted by statute. So what rights do they have?

A Brief Overview of Animal Rights Law

There are two major animal rights laws (or categories of law) that might apply to intelligent non-humans: state animal cruelty laws and the federal Endangered Species Act. There are many other laws, both state and federal, but they are either limited to particular species or aren't really the kind of law we're concerned with here.[3] At

---

1. In some states the English common law is incorporated up to the time of the Revolution. *See, e.g.,* N.Y. CONST. § 14 (adopting the common law as it existed in New York up to April 20, 1775). Other states, following a pattern established by Virginia, use the fourth year of the reign of James I (i.e., 1607) as the cutoff. *See, e.g.,* 5 ILL. COMP. STAT. 50/1; MO. REV. STAT. § 1.010. The significance of that year is that it marked the founding of Jamestown, the first successful, permanent English colony in what is now the United States. At that point, the common laws of England and the United States began to diverge. Com. v. Morris, 281 Va. 70, 82 (2011).

2. *See, e.g.,* Regalado v. United States, 572 A.2d 416, 420 n. 7 (D.C. 1990).

3. For examples of the former, see state laws mandating rabies vaccinations for dogs, the federal Marine Mammal Protection Act, and the federal Animal Welfare Act, which is limited to "warm-blooded animal[s] . . . used . . . for research, testing, experimenta-

the state level, animal cruelty laws vary significantly in scope. For example, California's statute encompasses "every dumb creature," which the California courts have held means "all animals except human beings."[4] Some statutes are a little narrower, however. For example, Missouri's only applies to "every living vertebrate except a human being," and some states, such as Arkansas, go one step further and also exempt fish.[5] This means that in some states intelligent non-humans would only qualify for protection if they were vertebrates. This would create problems for some superheroes. It's not known, for instance, whether the Martian Manhunter has a vertebral column and is thus a vertebrate. Likewise, any insectoid alien would run into immediate problems.

And just what counts as cruelty? California's statute is typical. For our purposes, this is the main provision: "[E]very person who maliciously and intentionally maims, mutilates, tortures, or wounds a living animal, or maliciously and intentionally kills an animal, is guilty of an offense."[6] From the standpoint of an intelligent non-human, this is pretty minimal protection, but at least it's something. For example, it would cover Lex Luthor's reckless experimentation on Superman in the rebooted *Action Comics #2*.

So that's the state law situation. Could the Endangered Species Act fill in any gaps? Among other things, the Endangered Species Act prohibits the taking, attempted taking, importation, possession, sale, and transport of a listed species.[7] "Taking" is defined "in the broadest possible manner to include every conceivable way in which

---

tion, or exhibition purposes, or as a pet." 7 U.S.C. § 2132(g). For an example of the latter, see the federal law criminalizing the creation, sale, and possession of depictions of animal cruelty. 18 U.S.C. § 48.

4. People v. Baniqued, 85 Cal. App. 4th 13, 20–21 (Cal. Ct. App. 2000).

5. Mo. Rev. Stat. 578.005; Ark. Code § 5-62-102(2).

6. Cal. Penal Code § 597.

7. *See* 16 U.S.C. § 1538.

Lex Luthor tortures Superman: aggravated assault or animal abuse? Grant Morrison et al., *Superman in Chains*, in ACTION COMICS (VOL. 2) 2 (DC Comics December 2011).

a person can 'take' or attempt to 'take' any fish or wildlife."[8] The Act also empowers the Secretary of the Interior to create specific regulations for the protection of listed species, including the designation of critical habitat.[9] There are five factors that the Secretary may consider when deciding whether to list a species as endangered, two of which are particularly relevant to intelligent non-humans: "the inadequacy of existing regulatory mechanisms" and "other natural or manmade factors affecting its continued existence."[10] As we've already seen, there aren't a lot of existing regulatory mechanisms for intelligent animals or extraterrestrials, and it's likely that their existence could be threatened by natural or manmade factors.

Thus, the Endangered Species Act provides a flexible way for the federal government to grant protection to particular species of intelligent non-humans. It has the benefit of being nationwide and also broader in scope than many state animal cruelty laws. On the other hand, its protections are not automatic, unlike those state laws. But both of these kinds of laws have significant shortcomings. While they provide protection against harm, they do not grant legal personhood. That means no constitutional rights such as free speech and equal protection, no right to own property, and no right to sue for redress.[11] The intelligent non-humans would still be legally dependent upon humans for their protection.

---

8. S. Rep. No. 93-307, at 7 (1973). The Act itself defines "to take" as to "harass, harm, pursue, hunt, shoot, wound, kill, trap, capture, or collect, or to attempt to engage in any such conduct." 16 U.S.C. § 1532(19).

9. *See* 16 U.S.C. § 1533.

10. 16 U.S.C. § 1533(a)(1).

11. Although the courts have held that animals do not have standing to sue, they have held that the Constitution permits Congress to grant them standing, should it choose to exercise that power. Cetacean Community v. Bush, 386 F.3d 1169 (9th Cir. 2004) ("[W]e see no reason why Article III prevents Congress from authorizing a suit in the name of an animal" but "we conclude that the Cetaceans do not have statutory standing to sue.").

So What About Other Rights?

Although granting significant rights to animals is constitutionally permissible, doing so will likely require a clear signal of intent from Congress.[12] And while some of the strongest supports of animal rights have argued that it is within the power of the courts to grant civil rights to animals, most scholars recognize that the Constitution and laws as they presently exist simply do not contemplate including non-human animals—even intelligent ones—within the definition of "person."[13]

Rights and Responsibilities

Rights often, but not necessarily, come with responsibilities. Consider children: they have many rights and legal protections, but they have a reduced potential for criminal and civil liability. Any attempt to grant significant rights to intelligent non-humans also has to consider what legal responsibilities to place on them. In the case of great apes, animal rights supporters do not argue that they should be liable for crimes. But in the case of the hyper-intelligent apes of Gorilla City—including the supervillain Gorilla Grodd—rights would likely come with responsibilities when interacting with human society.

---

12. "[I]f Congress and the President intended to take the extraordinary step of authorizing animals as well as people and legal entities to sue, they could, and should, have said so plainly." Presumably state legislatures are similarly empowered by their own constitutions. *Id.*

13. *See* Steven M. Wise, *The Entitlement of Chimpanzees to the Common Law Writs of Habeas Corpus and De Homine Replegiando*, 37 GOLDEN GATE U. L. REV. 219 (2007) (arguing for common law development of animal rights, at least for chimpanzees and bonobos); Adam Kolber, *Standing Upright: The Moral and Legal Standing of Humans and Other Apes*, 54 STAN. L. REV. 163 (2001) (discussing great ape standing in terms of statutory changes).

Artificial Intelligence

So far we have considered intelligent non-human animals, including aliens. But what about artificial intelligences (AIs) like Brainiac, Awesome Andy, Ultron, or the Vision? The nature of computer programs means that granting rights to AIs poses unique legal challenges, some of which have been addressed by legal scholars.[14] We will note a few challenges of our own: if an AI is a legal person, then is deleting it tantamount to murder? What about simply turning it off? If so, what about unwanted copying? For example, if an AI is copied onto another computer against the computer owner's wishes, is the owner nonetheless required to maintain the computer in perpetuity? What if an AI spreads itself like a virus? Suffice to say that granting AIs rights would open an enormous legal can of worms. But what if artificial intelligences don't have legal rights? What's the status quo?

Right now, both the benefits and liabilities of an artificial intelligence flow to its owner or creator, which may be a human or a corporation. For example, on the benefit side, intellectual property produced by a robot (or a computer program) is the property of the robot's owner.[15] On the liability side, an autonomous robot's owner

---

14. *See* Lawrence B. Solum, *Legal Personhood for Artificial Intelligences*, 70 N.C. L. Rev. 1231 (1992); F. Patrick Hubbard, *"Do Androids Dream?": Personhood and Intelligent Artifacts*, 83 Temp. L. Rev. 405 (2011).

15. See National Commission on New Technological Uses of Copyrighted Works, Final Report 45 (1978) ("Finally, we confront the question of who is the author of a work produced through the use of a computer. The obvious answer is that the author is one who employs the computer. . . . This approach is followed by the Copyright Office today in conducting examinations for determining registrability for copyright of works created with the assistance of computers."). Arthur R. Miller, *Copyright Protection for Computer Programs, Databases, and Computer-Generated Works: Is Anything New Since CONTU?*, 106 Harvard L. Rev. 977 (1993) ("CONTU's conclusion over fourteen years ago that even "computer-generated" works appear to have enough human authorship to qualify for copyright protection continues to be true.").

may be liable for harm caused by the robot, unless the owner can pin the blame on the manufacturer.

At least on the intellectual property side, however, some have argued that non-human creators should be able to own the copyright in their creative works, at least under certain theoretical circumstances.[16] Presumably the same argument would apply to patentable inventions as well. This would allow Ultron, an android that in turn created another android, the Vision, to apply for patents on any technologies it invented in the process.

However, it remains an open question whether allowing a computer to own intellectual property would necessarily endow it with all the other rights that people enjoy. Some scholars have argued that a limited right of intellectual property ownership can be achieved without fundamentally altering the legal landscape.[17] As computers become increasingly sophisticated one thing seems certain: of all of the outlandish legal issues in this book, these are probably the ones most likely to come up in the real world.

---

16. Andrew J. Wu, *From Video Games to Artificial Intelligence: Assigning Copyright Ownership to Works Generated by Increasingly Sophisticated Computer Programs*, 25 AIPLA Q.J. 131 (1997).

17. *See, e.g.*, Dane E. Johnson, *Statute of Anne-imals: Should Copyright Protect Sentient Nonhuman Creators?*, 15 ANIMAL L. 15 (2008) (proposing a limited equitable copyright ownership for animals and discussing copyright ownership by computers).

CLOSING ARGUMENTS

"Comic books aren't just for kids anymore" has been a cliché since at least 1986, when Frank Miller's *The Dark Knight Returns* was published, but it bears repeating. Comic books are an enduring art form with a long history, and we hope that this book is a positive contribution to the scholarship, criticism, and appreciation of that medium. As attorneys, we also believe strongly that "a lawyer should further the public's understanding of and confidence in the rule of law and the justice system because legal institutions in a constitutional democracy depend on popular participation and support to maintain their authority."[1] As a caller on one of our radio interviews put it, "You're giving civics lessons to people that wouldn't get them otherwise."

The Law of Superheroes has been described as an "exploration of the comic book canon" and as "law school seen through the lens of comic book heroes."[2] While we have covered only a small fraction of the more than 160,000 comic books published since 1935[3] and have

---

1. MODEL RULES OF PROF'L CONDUCT Preamble.

2. Jonathan Last, *Invincible Heroes—Except in Court*, WALL ST. J., Nov. 17–18, 2012, at C12; Cory Doctorow, *Law of Superheroes: law-school seen through comic-book heroes' lens*, BOING-BOING, December 20, 2012, http://boingboing .net/2012/12/20/law-of-superheroes-all-of-fir.html.

3. John Jackson Miller, *Things Nobody Knows: How Many Comic Books Have Been Sold, Ever?*, COMICS BUYER'S GUIDE (June 15, 2005), http://www.cbgxtra.com/colum nists/john-jackson-miller-longbox-manifesto/things-nobody-knows-how-many-comic -books-have-been-sold-ever.

only scratched the surface of more than a dozen legal subjects, we hope that this book has nonetheless helped you to think about the complex, weird, and wonderful world of comic books in a new light. Comic books can benefit from the same kind of analysis and criticism as any other work of art or literature. While we specialize in what might be called "legal fact-checking," there is a whole world of comics scholarship out there.[4]

Although complete coverage of each of the legal topics discussed in this book would easily fill a library, our goal was not to provide a legal reference but rather an introduction to the legal system and legal reasoning. The law has a reputation for being an impenetrable maze, impossible to comprehend for anyone who is not a lawyer. We wanted to show our readers that the law is, for the most part, pretty straightforward once you get down to individual issues. While we certainly don't recommend that anyone take this book and walk into a courtroom, we hope that the next time you read about a Supreme Court case you will feel comfortable looking up the case and reading it for yourself. And who knows? You might just find yourself wondering how the decision would affect your favorite superhero.

---

4. *See, e.g.*, Travis Langley, Batman and Psychology: A Dark and Stormy Knight (2012); James Kakalios, The Physics of Superheroes: Spectacular Second Edition (2009); Peter Coogan, Superhero: The Secret Origin of a Genre (2006); Scott McCloud, Understanding Comics: The Invisible Art (1994).

ACKNOWLEDGMENTS

The authors would like to thank Jennifer Beasley, Paul Bender, Maia Elkana, and the users of MetaFilter.com for inspiring *Law and the Multiverse* and encouraging its creation. We are extremely grateful to John Schwartz of *The New York Times* for exposing the blog to a wider audience. We thank Steve Ross, Patrick Mulligan, and the staff at Gotham for their help in turning *Law and the Multiverse* into this book. We also thank our employers and colleagues, particularly F. Scott Kieff, for their understanding and support of our little side project, and our families for putting up with the acquisition of more comic books than strictly necessary. And we thank Sharon Lim for her assistance in ensuring that the citations in the book conformed to the *Bluebook* standard. Last, but most certainly not least, we thank our readers, without whom none of this would have been possible.

INDEX

Printed in the United States
by Baker & Taylor Publisher Services

Printed in the United States
by Baker & Taylor Publisher Services